WINNING RESEARCH SKILLS

Second Edition

WINNING RESEARCH SKILLS

Second Edition

Nancy P. Johnson

Director of the Law Library and Professor of Law
Georgia State University

Robert C. Berring

Director of the Law Library and Professor of Law
University of California, Berkeley

Thomas A. Woxland

Director of the Law Library and Professor of Law
Northern Illinois University

WEST PUBLISHING COMPANY

Minneapolis/St. Paul   *New York*   *Los Angeles*   *San Francisco*

Copyediting: Patricia Lewis
Interior Design: Roslyn Stendahl, Dapper Design
Illustrations: Rolin Graphics
Composition: Parkwood Composition
Production, Prepress, Printing and Binding by West Publishing Company.

• •

 PRINTED ON 10% POST CONSUMER RECYCLED PAPER

ISBN 0-314-02777-7

About the Authors

NANCY JOHNSON has been the Director of the Law Library at Georgia State University since 1986. Previously, she served as a Reference Librarian at Georgia State, the University of Illinois Law Library, and the University of Chicago Law Library. She teaches courses in legal research. She is the co-author of *Legal Research Exercises* and the author of *Sources of Compiled Legislative Histories*. Johnson received her B.A. from Marycrest College, M.L.S. from the University of Illinois, and J.D. from Georgia State.

BOB BERRING has been the Director of the Boalt Hall Law Library since 1982. Previously, he held positions at the University of Washington Law Library, Harvard Law Library, the University of Texas Law Library, and the University of Illinois Law Library. He is the co-author of several legal research texts, including *How to Find the Law*. He teaches courses in legal research, in person and on videotape. Berring is a past president of the American Association of Law Libraries. Berring has a B.A. from Harvard and an M.L.S. and a J.D. from the University of California at Berkeley.

TOM WOXLAND joined the faculty of the Northern Illinois University College of Law in 1989. Prior to that he spent ten years on the staff of the University of Minnesota Law Library, where he was the assistant director for public services. He teaches courses in legal research. He has published several articles on research topics and on the history of legal publishing. He is also the co-author of instructional software used nationally for computer-assisted legal research training. Woxland has a B.A. from St. Olaf College and an M.A.L.S. and a J.D. from the University of Minnesota.

Acknowledgments

The authors thank their staff at the Georgia State University Law Library, the Boalt Hall Law Library, and the Northern Illinois University Law Library. Nancy Johnson specifically thanks Rhonda Rosenberg who helped with the initial phases of the book. A project of this kind is, in a genuine sense, a joint effort; we are grateful to all of the individuals at West Publishing Company who worked on this book. Several persons at West helped with various stages of preparation and completion of this work: Craig Runde, Ann Possis, Sharon Kavanagh, and Kara Johnson, on the first edition; Pamela Brandt, Deborah Lanners, Kathleen Lepp and Stacy Lenzen on the second edition; and Bill Lindberg for his ongoing support of this project. Finally, we thank each other for still being friends.

Contents

INTRODUCTION

L egal research is largely a matter of sex, drugs, and rock 'n' roll. Well, not really, but at least we have caught your attention. The point is, legal research is not the dull, plodding enterprise that it is often made out to be. Unfortunately, many law schools still do not have the resources to teach research well. Some students assume that the research training that is crammed into the first few weeks at those schools represents the full picture of legal research. Nothing could be further from the truth. The structure of how one finds the law is really the *center* of the legal educational enterprise.

This is a book for first-year law students. If you are one, you have probably already heard more than once that one of the main goals of the first year is to teach you how to "think like a lawyer." Most of your first-year courses will be concerned with teaching you methods of analyzing the law and facts in a particular situation. It is this type of *thinking* that is most important. Although the same core courses—Contracts, Torts, and Property—have been taught for over a hundred years, the *content* of these courses is not really as important as the way it is analyzed. In most of these first-year courses, you are being taught to think, question, and analyze. The specific rules of law that you discuss are just part of the process, not the point. This is why you will know very little real "law" at the end of your first year. It is only in the *legal research* enterprise, and the legal writing experience, that you are actually taught how to *do* things. That's why we are here.

A number of books are devoted to the enterprise of legal research. They include large textbooks that explore everything in minute detail and friendly paperbacks that provide a broad overview of the research process and its bibliography. This book falls into neither of those categories. It is an attempt to introduce you to basic research materials and methods, and especially to the products of the nation's leading and most comprehensive law publisher, West Publishing Company. We will devote much attention to one particular product, WESTLAW®, West's computer-assisted legal research (CALR) service. We are not going to make any attempt to argue that WESTLAW (or West books for that matter) are substitutes for all of the other materials, nor would we pretend that using these West products is the only way to do intelligent research. But we do see them as very important parts of the complete research picture. As such, they need to be placed in that context. That is the aim of this book.

West books have been an essential part of any lawyer's library for more than a century. But during the last twenty years, the computer revolution has reached law libraries. A major purpose of this book is to show you how computer-assisted legal research relates to the materials in a traditional law library. One reason we have presented the information in this way is to make clear that the on-line databases are more than simply auxiliary case-finding mechanisms. Lots of people think this, but trust us, they are wrong. Both LEXIS®, and WESTLAW, the two major services, are, in themselves, *law libraries* filled with information.

A generational change is going on in the way people think about legal information. Many lawyers who graduated from law school more than five or ten years ago will always think of law as printed on a page. They may use computers, but in their own minds, they will not *really* be reading law until they see something on the page of a book or in a loose-leaf service. We believe that your generation of law students is riding the crest of what may become a flood tide of change. Information in on-line services is indeed information. A service like WESTLAW contains primary sources, secondary sources, and links between them. With a modem, you can sit at your home personal computer and access much of the world of legal information.

In a way, this book is a hybrid product. It provides a little background on legal information in general and introduces you to relevant ways of using WESTLAW as well as traditional print sources. It is a one-legged enterprise, however, and does not stand alone. It should be used with other tools, as a part of other courses, where it should be a legitimate help for you. WESTLAW offers enormous advantages to users. You should be able to make the most of those advantages. You should also understand the context in which they operate. No one should graduate from law school without understanding what a case reporter is, both in its traditional printed format and in its on-line manifestation. Nor should you leave law school without understanding how statutory materials are organized and why using them on-line might be different or better—or worse. You should know why administrative rules and regulations are important and how you can find them on-line. And you should also be aware of the role secondary sources and indexes play in the real world of legal research.

Of course, a book of this size must necessarily omit a great deal, and, believe it or not, we don't always agree on every point. Our goal, however, is to provide you with something that helps. We recognize that we can only present a tip of the iceberg of legal research materials, and we'll try not to take ourselves too seriously as we present the information. If we were to leave you with only one injunction, it would be to look beyond the four corners of the research enterprise and see that understanding how the tools work, how the pieces fit together, and how the body of research materials function as a whole may be the most important piece of the puzzle.

A Little History

Let's begin with a short history of legal research and go back to the earliest days of the American republic. Finding the law was pretty simple for the small group of American lawyers who practiced two hundred years ago. Legal

research was much easier then. It is only a slight overstatement to say that all you needed to practice law in 1800 was the American edition of Blackstone's *Commentaries on the Laws of England*—the great, multivolume, comprehensive law text of the eighteenth century. With Blackstone, an inkwell, and a desk, you were a lawyer.

By the end of the nineteenth century, both the law and legal research were getting more complicated. Back in 1810, there had been only eighteen volumes of American court reports; a lawyer of the time could literally read *all* the cases. But by 1885, a comprehensive law library had 3,500 volumes of reports, and not even with Evelyn Wood's assistance could you have read all the cases. Speed reading courses might not help, but law book publishers did.

Responding to lawyers' needs, large legal publishing companies developed during the last quarter of the nineteenth century to compile, and provide access to, the explosive growth in legal sources. Many of the commercial legal publishers whose books you will use for the rest of your careers began their work during this period. Among the best known are West Publishing Company; Lawyers Cooperative Publishing, a division of Thomson Legal Publishing Inc.; and the Frank Shepard Company (now Shepard's/McGraw-Hill, Inc.).

Between 1875 and 1900, these publishers introduced many of the now-familiar types of law books, including regional reporters and comprehensive digests from West; citators from Shepard's; and annotated reporters from Lawyers Cooperative. Along with a few other publishers, they also introduced most of the common features of today's legal publications. For example, during this time, publishers developed the basic types of modern supplementation techniques: pocket parts, advance sheets, and—slightly later—loose-leaf services.

In effect, then, in answer to the anguished complaints of lawyers about the outpouring of law from the courts and legislatures, the legal publishers said: "Don't worry. We will publish all of it. And, not only will we publish it, but we will read and organize it for you as well. We will give you indexes and annotations and summaries and digests."

During the second half of the twentieth century, the lawyers' old lament has been heard again. Now there were even more courts and they were deciding ever more cases. To make matters worse, to the steady stream of statutes coming out of the legislatures was added a river of regulations flowing from administrative agencies. *Three million* appellate cases had been published. Federal statutes and regulations filled hundreds of thousands of pages. Fifty states multiplied this torrent by fifty times. The storage capacities of many law libraries were strained. Book budgets were burdened. New and competing publications confused lawyers, not to mention law librarians.

The publishers responded again. This time their answer was high technology. One of the first solutions was to use microfiche for mass storage. A filing cabinet of fiche could replace a whole library of books.

But the computer brought about the biggest change. Computer-assisted legal research systems, principally the WESTLAW service of West Publishing and the LEXIS service from Mead Data Central, were developed in the 1970s and improved in the 1980s. These services contain hundreds of thousands of legal documents, including cases, statutes, regulations, and legal periodical articles, almost all of which can be fully displayed. Together, these documents

contain tens of millions of words, each of which (with the exception of a few very common words) is searchable. The ability to search the "full-text" of documents has made virtually every word in the databases a possible search term and a possible indexing term. In the legal publishing revolution of the nineteenth century, professional editors and indexers read and summarized cases for attorneys. The computer revolution of the twentieth century has added a different type of indexing tool for attorneys to use. The speed and capacity of a service such as WESTLAW provide us all with a new and fantastic level of access to the law's many sources.

The original versions of both WESTLAW and LEXIS were built using a search system called Boolean logic. This method of finding information is based on the theories of George Boole, a nineteenth-century mathematician. Boolean logic involves picking key words (TERMS) and specifying the relationship the terms have to each other by means of CONNECTORS. Choosing the correct terms and understanding how to use connectors efficiently is no simple task. One ends up typing sentences like this:

> government military /p warn*** /p soldier sailor "service member" serviceman military /p radiation

Twenty years ago, Boolean searching was front-page news, and lots of effort was expended in trying to teach people how to use it. It was, and is, a very useful method for some, but its intricacies have kept many people from learning how to do it well.

In 1992 WESTLAW introduced a new system called WIN™ (WESTLAW is Natural™) that can be used as an alternative to Boolean searching. WIN allows the researcher to type in searches in normal language (or at least language as normal as legal research ever gets). Instead of the search above, for example, one could simply type in

> What is the government's obligation to warn military personnel of the dangers of past exposure to radiation?

Using some sophisticated techniques, the WIN system figures out what you want and gives you answers in priority order. Despite what you might think, the WIN system is not based on mystical spells or communicating with UFOs, it's simply the next step in making computers work for you. But for jaded legal researchers, it's pretty amazing. Since you are just beginning this legal research journey, WIN will seem no different than other tools, but trust us, it's really a breakthrough.

Naturally, we will discuss both Boolean (called "Terms and Connectors" in WESTLAW) and WIN searching in this book and in the appendix. We wouldn't want you to miss any of the fun.

The modern law library is a collection of old and new publishing technologies, books and computers, working together. Neither WESTLAW nor LEXIS is the panacea for all of your research needs. For some types of research, the old ways are still the best. For example, searching for broad concepts, such as negligence or proximate causation, is most effectively begun with treatises or digests. For other types of research, the speed, ease, and accu-

racy of computerized legal research should make WESTLAW your starting point.

A Few Helpful Hints

Before we begin looking more specifically at the tools and techniques of legal research, we offer some general hints to remember about legal publications, either paper or electronic: (1) When the same material is published by both a government printer and a commercial publisher, the latter is almost invariably more useful. (2) Different commercial publishers have different publishing philosophies—knowing the "philosophy" helps you understand the scope and content of their publications. (3) You will often find the same legal materials published in both a chronological arrangement and a subject-based arrangement. (4) Finally, the forms of publication for the law of the various states are very similar to the forms of publication of federal law; if you understand the system on the national level, you will understand it on a local level.

Governments—both state and federal—often print the text of the primary sources of their law. They publish the statutes enacted by their legislatures, the decisions handed down by their appellate courts, and the regulations promulgated by their administrative agencies. All of these materials, of course, are in the public domain. Commercial publishers, like West Publishing or Lawyers Cooperative, publish the same statutes, decisions, and regulations as the government printers. These "unofficial" publications are usually more helpful than the "official" government publications for two reasons.

First, the commercial publications are usually more up-to-date than the government publications. Laws change, new decisions appear. Government printers frequently are several years behind in their publications. In contrast, the commercial publishers will publish new cases or statutes in "advance sheet" form within only a few weeks or months of their occurrence.

Secondly, the commercial publishers frequently add other useful information to their publications. For example, the officially published *United States Code* prints only the text of the federal statutes, but the commercially published "annotated" codes also include summaries of judicial cases that have construed or explained those statutes as well as references to other helpful interpretive sources.

Perhaps it seems strange to think of law book publishers as having "philosophies." But it's true. Two of the biggest publishers of law books have very different philosophies, which were enunciated more than a hundred years ago and are still valid. In 1890, John West, the founder of West Publishing, said of his company's publications: "The profession has now the immense advantage of being able to turn to a single set of reports and digests, and be sure of finding *everything* which the courts have said on any given subject." James Briggs, the first president of Lawyers Cooperative, responded: "Much is said by certain contemporaries about 'completeness,' referring simply to the agglomeration of all the opinions of the various jurisdictions of the United States into masses of what are, in fact, largely made up of useless repetitions. . . . [The] work undertaken by my Company . . . is to give that most

valuable in the most elaborate form, and that least valuable in the most condensed." The two companies continue to adhere to their founders' statements. When West and Lawyers Cooperative publish equivalent products—legal encyclopedias or annotated codes are good examples—the West set will invariably be more voluminous. West still provides "completeness," and Lawyers Cooperative still "condenses."

Similar differences in philosophy exist between publishers of computer-assisted legal research services. While both WESTLAW and LEXIS include cases in their databases, WESTLAW adds the traditional West editorial enhancements—the headnotes, key numbers, and other features that we will soon tell you about—to the text of court opinions in its computerized documents. It also applies the same editorial scrutiny to the on-line form that it does to the printed form, assuring accuracy in matters of citations, spelling, and the like. LEXIS, on the other hand, provides the language of the court alone, without the "added value" of any editor's or indexer's work. In addition, largely because WESTLAW was created by a traditional book publisher and LEXIS was not, WESTLAW has emphasized the interconnectedness of books and databases, while LEXIS sees the on-line service as central to the research process.

Our third hint concerns chronological arrangement versus subject arrangement. Most primary sources, whether judicial, legislative, or administrative, are initially published in a chronologically arranged series. As more cases or statutes or regulations appear, another volume or pamphlet is published. If these chronological materials were the only ones available, research would be impossible. How, in three million cases, would you be able to find cases on a certain topic? Publishers have recompiled this material by subject. Case *digests* are subject arrangements of points of law in cases. Statutory and administrative *codes* are topical arrangements of *session laws* and *administrative registers*.

Finally, the forms of legal publication are common throughout different jurisdictions. Federal laws are published chronologically as *session laws* and recompiled as a *statutory code*. Federal regulations appear in a *register* and then in an *administrative code*. Federal cases are published in *reporters* and indexed in *digests*. The same is true, more or less, for each of the fifty state jurisdictions. Therefore, once you've learned the research tools for one jurisdiction, you've learned them for all.

Where to Go for More Help

This book is not going to answer all of your legal research questions. No one book could, and certainly not one as short as this. There are several much more exhaustive (and exhausting) research guides. Two very good and very comprehensive ones are *How to Find the Law* and *Fundamentals of Legal Research*. Both of them will be in your law school library and will also probably be in your law school's bookstore. Every truly compulsive legal researcher will constantly consult those books. Take a look at them. That research maniac who sits next to you in Torts already has.

Furthermore, this book is limited to only *legal* research. As a first-year law student, that is the kind of research you will be doing. But when you become a lawyer, you will quickly discover you will be doing a lot of *nonlegal* research as well. Depending on your practice, you may need business, medical, statistical, or some other kind of information that might help in the representation of a client.

There is a whole world of information that is not found within the books of a law library. A lot of that nonlegal information is now being put into computer databases. The biggest provider of those is DIALOG®, which has an enormous collection of databases. For you, both as a law student and as a lawyer, DIALOG is available through WESTLAW. About the time you get this book, you will probably also receive something called *Beyond Legal Information—Searching DIALOG on WESTLAW: A Guide for Law Students*, by Rosalie M. Sanderson. Look at it; it will open this world of nonlegal information to you.

If you want to know more about the wide range of West's books and services, look at *West's Law Finder.* You have probably already received a complimentary copy. It is handy, helpful, and thin enough to keep in your briefcase.

If you have specific questions about WESTLAW, your best bet is the *WESTLAW Reference Manual.* It is both informative and *well written* (unlike many computer manuals, which appear to have been written by people who scored 800 on the SAT math section and 350 on the SAT verbal). The *Reference Manual* is not only readable and informative, it has a good index. You can find answers in it.

If you have questions that the manual doesn't answer, you can call West Customer Service toll-free at 1-800-WESTLAW. For a really tough question about searching your issue, ask to speak to one of the West Reference Attorneys. Or if you have a really complex technical question—something like "Will WESTMATE be adversely affected if I install it on a turbo PC, running a TSR 'carbon-copy,' that, while using a local modem, will also have a network adaptor card?"—you may be referred to the Technical Specialists (West's "computer jocks"). Don't be afraid to call. The call is free, and these people are paid to answer your questions. Go ahead and make their day.

What Follows

We have tried to keep this book short. You have a lot to read during this year, and while we think that a book on legal research should be at the top of the list, we have known enough law students to realize that it won't be. So we will be as brief as possible.

Chapter 1 will introduce you to the basics of case reporting—how cases are published in hard-copy reporters as well as in the WESTLAW service. Chapter 2 explains how to *find* cases, and Chapter 3 how to *update* cases. Later chapters examine statutory and administrative sources and secondary materials; finally, Chapter 7 reviews the entire research process. Sprinkled liberally along the way are illustrations from both the hard-copy materials and the on-line databases. Even the most careful reader should need only a couple of hours to reach the end.

One last note: Throughout this book are suggestions on how WESTLAW can be used in various research contexts. If you know nothing about the mechanics of full-text searching, you might want to look at the appendix on WESTLAW searching before you begin reading Chapter 1.

1

CASE LAW

Since the ability to find and read cases is fundamental to legal study as well as to legal practice, we will begin with a description of how cases are organized. You will be introduced to the kind of information that is included in the hard-copy case reporters. You will also learn how cases are organized on WESTLAW. The "stuff" of the cases—that is, the words of the judge or justice authoring the opinion—is the same in the hard copy and on WESTLAW, but there are differences in the way the cases are grouped together in the reporters and in WESTLAW databases.

From reading this chapter, you should acquire certain basic skills. You should be able to locate the correct case in a reporter from a legal citation. You should also be able to find parallel citations, a mandatory part of the proper citation form. And you should be able to recognize and understand the various elements of a case in a reporter volume and on WESTLAW.

We will begin by explaining what a court reporter is, how cases are issued and published, and how cases are arranged within the different levels of the court system.

Court Reporters

Reporters or reports are the books that contain the text of court opinions. These are *real* cases, not the edited versions that you find in your casebooks. In fact, you can often learn a great deal about a case in your casebook by reading the "unexpurgated" version in the reporter. Try it. You will notice that the title of the reporter in a citation will be abbreviated. All of the reporters have standard abbreviations. For example, F.Supp. and F.2d are abbreviations for the *Federal Supplement*® and the *Federal Reporter*® second series, respectively. You will memorize these pretty quickly whether you want to or not. You can easily decipher the abbreviation by checking the last pages of *Black's Law Dictionary*® or *The Bluebook:A Uniform System of Citation,* simply known as the *"Bluebook."* A typical F.2d citation, such as 516 F.2d 924 (5th Cir. 1975), includes the following components:

516	F.2d	924	(5th Cir.	1975)
↓	↓	↓	↓	↓
Volume	Reporter	Page	Court	Year

One of the trickiest things about finding the right reporter is making sure you have the correct series. Many of the reporters are published in two or possibly three series. For example, the first series of the *Federal Reporter* goes up to Volume 300, and the second series starts over at Volume 1 and stops at Volume 999. Lots of old series stopped at 300, but no one seems to follow that practice now.

It may come as a surprise to you that the great majority of judicial opinions are not published at all. Most state trial-level cases are not reported. A very high percentage of federal district court opinions is not reported either. In fact, not even all appellate cases are reported. The trend has been to publish considerably fewer opinions on a percentage basis. But since the absolute number of cases being decided continues to skyrocket, plenty are still published. Many are not reported though because the courts deem them to be redundant of previous decisions; others are not reported because they are determined to have no precedential value.

The court rules of each jurisdiction state when publication of an opinion is appropriate. An appellate judge consults with the judges who participated in the opinion on whether it is desirable or necessary to publish the opinion. Occasionally, an editor will recommend that a case not be published, or that an accompanying order not be published.

Many cases that are not selected for publication in print do go into the WESTLAW service, however. Both published and unpublished opinions appear on both WESTLAW and LEXIS.

There is great debate in legal circles as to whether these unpublished opinions, which may only appear on-line, may serve as precedent; that is, whether they can be cited as "law." The argument goes as follows: since all persons, even those represented by attorneys, do not always have access to the computerized services, they could not possibly follow these unpublished rulings. The upshot of the argument is that, in most jurisdictions, unpublished opinions cannot be used as precedent or may be used only under certain guidelines requiring ample notice to the court and the opposing counsel. Even if unpublished opinions may not be useful as precedent, they may be very helpful in determining judicial thinking in similar cases. Think strategically—if you are going before Judge Smith in a products liability case, it may be valuable to know what Judge Smith has done in products liability cases in the past even if you do not use them as precedent. In practice, cases have *many* uses.

The cases that are reported are organized by court, jurisdiction, or geographic proximity. The arrangement of cases is determined by the editors. For example, in a regional reporter the cases from a single state are published together. The arrangement of cases may also be based on a hierarchy of courts within a state. The on-line service WESTLAW organizes its cases into "databases." For example, WESTLAW has state databases, federal databases, and specialized topical databases (Figure 1.1).

The capacities of electronic information storage allow for much more flexibility in the arrangement of materials than the hard-copy reporters do. A database of electronically stored information can be reorganized repeatedly.

Opinions do not appear immediately in bound volumes. Instead, they appear first in official slip opinions issued by the court itself (Figure 1.2).

Figure 1.1 WESTLAW Databases

```
                WELCOME to the WESTLAW DIRECTORY _____P1_____

   GENERAL MATERIAL      TEXT & PERIODICAL        CITATORS        SPECIAL SERVICES
   Federal      P2       Law Reviews,  P404   Insta-Cite,  P446   Dictionaries  P456
   State        P7           Texts & CLEs      Shepard's,         EZ ACCESS     P506
   DIALOG       P184      Restatements P445    Shepard's PreView  Other Services P505
   News & Info. P234      & Unif. Laws          & QuickCite       Customer Info. P507
   ---------------------------- TOPICAL MATERIAL -----------------------------
   Antitrust    P245     Family Law    P295   Labor        P340   Taxation      P388
   Bankruptcy   P248     Finance/Bank. P298   Legal Ser.   P347   Tort Law      P397
   Business     P252     First Amend.  P305   Malpractice  P352   Transport.    P399
   Civil Rights P264     Gov't Benefit P307   Maritime Law P355   Worker Comp.  P401
   Commercial   P268     Gov't Cont.   P310   Military Law P357   SPECIALIZED MAT'L
   Commun. Law  P272     Health Law    P316   Pension      P359   BNA           P450
   Crim. Just.  P274     Immigration   P322   Product Liab P362   Directories   P457
   Education    P278     Insurance     P324   Real Prop.   P365   Gateways      P462
   Energy       P282     Intell. Prop. P328   Sci. & Tech. P368   (e.g. Dow Jones)
   Environment  P287     International P333   Securities   P374   Highlights    P503
                                              Soc. Science P384   Other Pubs.   P480

   If you wish to:
      Select the searchable WESTLAW database list, type IDEN and press ENTER
      Select a known database, type its identifier and press ENTER
      Obtain further information, type HELP and press ENTER
```

Opinions of the U.S. Supreme Court first appear in slim pamphlets published by the U.S. Government Printing Office. Most law libraries do not collect slip opinions from courts other than the U.S. Supreme Court.

Slip opinions and unreported cases generally do not contain editorial enhancements. When West receives slip opinions, it adds them to WESTLAW immediately. Therefore, the fastest way for you to read a new opinion is on-line. In fact, U.S. Supreme Court opinions are in the WESTLAW U.S. Supreme Court database (SCT) within thirty minutes of filing. Slip opinions from the other courts are on-line within different time periods, depending on the court.

The case is then scrutinized by the West manuscript staff who check more than one million citations per year. They also add parallel citations to cases. The statute citations in the case are also checked, and many are corrected. All of the other editorial enhancements, which will be explained in this chapter, are added at this time.

Slip opinions are next gathered into softbound advance sheets (Figure 1.3). Advance sheets allow you to read the decision in the reporter format without having to wait until enough opinions are accumulated to make an entire bound volume. Most of West's advance sheets are published on a weekly schedule. As you have learned in your classes, the rule of *stare decisis* demands access to the latest cases; law publishing has kept pace with this need for current cases either in print or on-line.

At the third stage of publication, the bound case reporter volumes appear (Figure 1.4). The bound volumes contain a large number of decisions arranged in the same sequence as they appeared in the advance sheets. The citation will be identical in the advance sheet and in the bound reporter so you do not have to recheck your citation once the opinion appears in the advance sheet format.

There is a distinction in case reporting between official and unofficial reporters. When a statute or a court order directs the publication of court reports, they are called official reports. The official reports are no more accurate than the unofficial reports; in fact, the unofficial reports came into exis-

Figure 1.2 A Slip Opinion

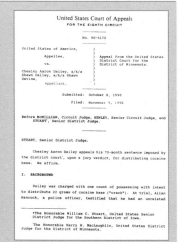

Figure 1.3 An Advance Sheet

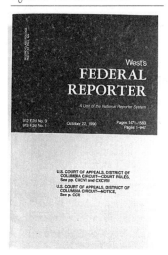

tence because they could be published more quickly than the official reports. Additionally, West editors may contact the court if clarification or corrections are needed, or if it appears that text has been omitted. Many times the corrections are initiated by the court itself.

U.S. Supreme Court and Lower Federal Court Decisions

You will study the jurisdiction of the federal courts during your first year of law school. At the top of the federal judicial pyramid is the Supreme Court of the United States (Figure 1.5). Almost all of its business consists of reviewing the judgments of lower courts. These may be the judgments of state courts of last resort that dealt with questions of federal law, or they may be the decisions of lower federal courts. If a federal question arises in state litigation, that question must be pursued on appeal up through the state court system—to the *state courts of last resort*—before the case is eligible for review by the U.S. Supreme Court. The *lower federal courts* are the federal circuit courts of appeals and the federal district courts. Generally, the Supreme Court hears only cases that have already been appealed through a state appellate court or to one of the thirteen federal circuit courts of appeals.

The Supreme Court could not possibly hear all of the cases that come before it. It disposes of most appeals summarily by denying petitions for a *writ of certiorari*. This is a device used by the Court in choosing the cases it wishes to hear.

The decisions of the U.S. Supreme Court appear in published form in one official reporter and two unofficial reporters. The *United States Reports* (U.S.) is the official reporter for the Supreme Court. It is published by the U.S. Government Printing Office. As with many official publications, the advance sheets and bound volumes of the *United States Reports* appear very slowly. Almost two years pass between the announcement of a decision and its appearance in the advance sheet, and yet another year passes before it is included in a bound volume. The decisions of the U.S. Supreme Court also appear in the *Supreme Court Reporter*® (S.Ct.) published by West and in the *United States Supreme Court Reports, Lawyers' Edition* (L.Ed. and L.Ed.2d) published by Lawyers Cooperative Publishing. The WESTLAW SCT and SCT-OLD databases contain the Supreme Court decisions from the inception of the Court (1790). Although the *Bluebook* requires only the official citation to the *United States Reports,* most citations include all three sources:

Figure 1.4
A Bound Case Reporter

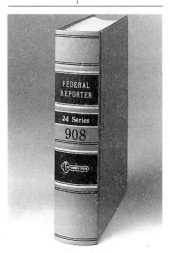

Hustler Magazine v. Falwell, 485 U.S. 46, 108 S.Ct. 876, 99 L. Ed.2d 41 (1988)

Figure 1.5
The Federal Judicial Pyramid

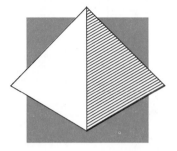

Many law firm libraries and some court libraries have only one of the bound sets available, so parallel citations can be a big help.

Another source for Supreme Court decisions is *United States Law Week®* *(U.S.L.W.)* published on a weekly basis by the Bureau of National Affairs, Inc. *U.S.L.W.* is published in two volumes: One volume contains all of the U.S. Supreme Court decisions as well as other actions taken by the Court. The second volume publishes abstracts of what it considers important lower federal and state court opinions. Other than the on-line services, *U.S.L.W.* is the first place to find the full text of recent Supreme Court decisions in print format. *U.S.L.W.* is also available on WESTLAW.

Below the Supreme Court in the federal system are thirteen federal courts of appeals and numerous federal district courts (Figure 1.6). The jurisdiction of the federal courts of appeals, or circuit courts, is really very simple. It consists of appeals from decisions by district courts, together with appeals from decisions by federal administrative agencies, such as the Federal Communications Commission. The decisions of the federal courts of appeals since 1880 are published in West's® *Federal Reporter* (F., F.2d, and, beginning in late 1993, F.3d). West has also published a collection of earlier cases in a set called *Federal Cases.* Decisions of the courts of appeals, from the beginning of the court, are in the CTA databases on WESTLAW. You can also search in individual courts of appeals databases, for example, CTA8.

The jurisdiction of the district courts is the most complex part of the federal jurisdiction. A case will be tried in district courts if it "arises under" federal law for purposes of federal trial court jurisdiction. In addition to these "arising under" cases, federal courts also have jurisdiction over civil cases involving parties from different states; these are known as diversity cases.

The criminal jurisdiction of the district courts includes all prosecutions for federal crimes. The decisions of the federal district courts since 1924 are published in West's *Federal Supplement* (F.Supp.). Decisions of district courts are in the DCT database in WESTLAW. Since the district courts are the federal trial courts and only a small percentage of their cases are reported in the West reporters, the DCT database on WESTLAW includes both cases that appear in the West reports and those that are unreported.

West's *Federal Rules Decisions®* (F.R.D.), which began in 1940, is a specialized reporter that contains selected opinions of the U.S. district courts on matters related to the Federal Rules of Civil Procedure and Criminal Procedure. In addition to these decisions, the *Federal Rules Decisions* includes articles dealing with federal rules. These articles from the West reporter are in the WESTLAW database Federal Rules Decisions–Articles (FEDRDTP), and the cases themselves appear in the DCT database.

Decisions of Special Courts

A few special federal courts, such as the Tax Court, publish their own decisions. West publishes the *Bankruptcy Reporter®,* which includes cases from the federal bankruptcy courts plus district court bankruptcy cases not reported

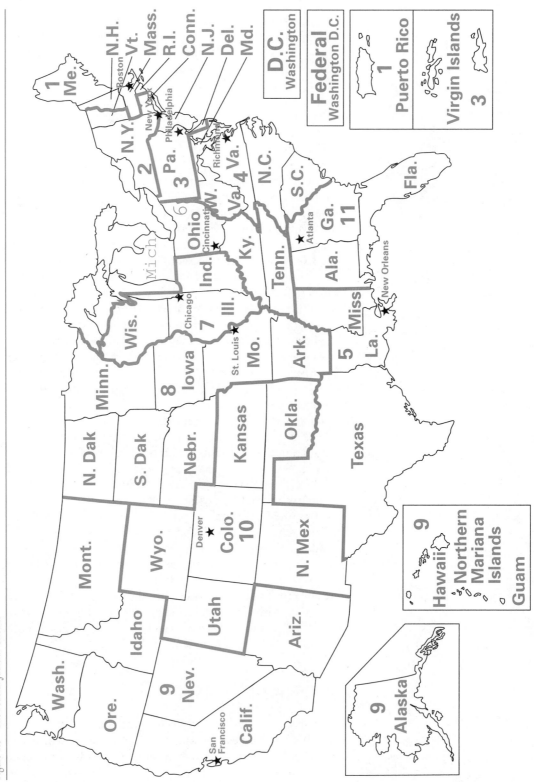

Figure 1.6   The Federal Judicial Circuits

in the *Federal Supplement*. West also publishes reporters compiling federal and state decisions in subject areas, such as the *Education Law Reporter®*. The decisions from these reporters also appear on WESTLAW.

State Court Decisions

It is difficult to generalize about the structure of state courts since each state has a different structure. Suffice it to say that each state has either a triple-layered or a two-tiered hierarchy of courts.

About half the states still publish their own "official" reporters. Many states have ceased publishing their official reports, and attorneys rely on West's National Reporter System® for reporting cases. In some states, the legislature or the courts have designated the West volumes as the official repository of state opinions. In other places, this has been done by default. It is surprising how informal much of this process is. Many states have discontinued their official reports because of long publication delays and untimely publication of new opinions. Even when states publish their own reporters, attorneys often use the West reporters because of the many editorial enhancements—synopses, headnotes, topic and key number indexing—and because the headnotes link the researcher with the key number system, which we will discuss in the next chapter.

West's National Reporter System is a set of reporters that divide the fifty states and the District of Columbia into seven national regions: Atlantic, North Eastern, North Western, Pacific, South Eastern, South Western, and Southern (Figure 1.7). The National Reporter System covers the appellate courts of all the states. The decisions of New York's highest court are reported in the *North Eastern Reporter®* and the *New York Supplement®*. The opinions of New York's lower courts, as well as those of the highest court, are reported in the *New York Supplement*. Similarly, California Supreme Court decisions appear in both the *Pacific Reporter®* and the *California Reporter®*. The opinions of California's lower courts, along with those of the California Supreme Court, are published in the *California Reporter*. The federal reporters published by West are also part of the National Reporter System.

The reporters in West's National Reporter System contain several special features. The advance sheets include a number of tables that later appear in the bound volume. The table that you will use most frequently is the Table of Cases Reported (Figure 1.8). If you are looking for a very recent case, you could search either WESTLAW or the National Reporter System advance sheets. Remember that the Table of Cases Reported in the advance sheets is cumulative for each volume. That means you only have to check the table in the most recent advance sheet for that volume.

Take a few minutes to look at the special tables in the advance sheets in your library. You may one day need to find a listing of all judges sitting on a particular court or a listing of cases that cite the American Bar Association's Standards for Criminal Justice, for example. These tables can be found in the first few pages of each reporter following the Table of Cases Reported.

Figure 1.7 West's National Reporter System

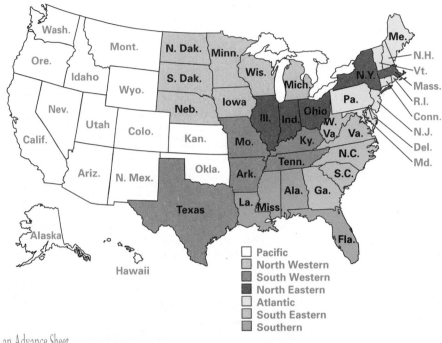

Figure 1.8 A Table of Cases Reported from an Advance Sheet

CASES REPORTED

	Page
Abboud v. Viscomi (Mem.)—N.J.	1286
Abington School Dist.; McCloskey by McCloskey v. (Mem.)—Pa.	329
Abington School Dist. v. Sportmaster (Mem.)—Pa.	329
Aceta; State v.—N.J.Super.A.D.	1317
A Child By Benigno-White, Matter of Adoption of—N.J.Super.Ch.	1345
Acmat Corp.; Gilbane Bldg. Co. v. (Mem.) —N.J.	1293
Adamar of New Jersey, Inc., Petition of—N.J.Super.A.D.	704
Adams v. Leager (Table)—Md.	272
Adderly; State v. (Mem.)—N.J.	1288
A.D.H., State in Interest of (Mem.)—N.J.	1303
Advanced Living, Inc. v. Montgomery County Bd. of Assessment Appeals—Pa.Cmwlth.	948
Advisory Committee on Professional Ethics No. 545, Matter of (Mem.)—N.J.	1274
Advisory Committee on Professional Ethics Opinion No. 562, Matter of (Mem.)—N.J.	1286
American Communication Installations, Ltd. v. Emory (Table)—Del.Supr.	203
AFSCME, Council 4, Locals 196, 318, 355, 478, 538, 562, 610 and 704; State v.—Conn.App.	517
A.N.; M. v.—D.C.App.	579
A.N.; R.N.M. v.—D.C.App.	579
Anam v. W.C.A.B. (Hahneman)—Pa. Cmwlth.	932
Andersen v. W.C.A.B. (Nat. Forge Co.)—Pa.Cmwlth.	971
Andrea W., In re—Me.	596
Anne Arundel County; Chu v.—Md.	250
A.P. Development Corp. v. Band (Mem.) —N.J.	1293
Arlequin; State v. (Mem.)—N.J.	1290
Armen; State v.—Me.	1143
Associated Mountain Top, Inc. v. Greate Bay Hotel and Casino, Inc. (Mem.)—N.J.	1294
Associated Mountain Top, Inc. v. Sands Hotel and Casino (Mem.)—N.J.	1294
Atlantic Home Insulation, Inc. v. James	

Figure 1.9   Regional Databases on WESTLAW

```
____WESTLAW DIRECTORY WELCOME SCREEN_____P1_____
____GENERAL STATE DATABASES:  WEST'S REGIONAL REPORTERS        P22_____

                             CASE LAW
    ATL    Atlantic Reporter (CT DE DC ME MD NH NJ PA RI VT)
    NE     North Eastern Reporter (IL IN MA NY OH)
    NW     North Western Reporter (IA MI MN NE ND SD WI)
    PAC    Pacific Reporter (AK AZ CA CO HI ID KS MT NV NM OK OR UT WA WY)
    SE     South Eastern Reporter (GA NC SC VA WV)
    SO     Southern Reporter (AL FL LA MS)
    SW     South Western Reporter (AR KY MO TN TX)
    Note:  Regional Reporter databases include quick opinions and any unreported
           cases.

    Related Databases:  To see a list of individual state case law databases,
    enter P16


    If you wish to:
       Select a database, type its identifier, e.g., ATL and press ENTER
       View information about a database, type SCOPE followed by its identifier
         and press ENTER
       View the Index to State Databases, type P7 and press ENTER
```

Cases from the regional reporters are also available on WESTLAW in regional databases, such as NE (Figure 1.9). Decisions of every state are also on-line in their own databases. To search in a state court database, you use the state postal abbreviation for that state, followed by –CS (Figure 1.10). The cases databases are retrospective to different dates so you need to check the *WESTLAW Database List* or type SCOPE when you enter a database. The SCOPE command tells you the type of documents available in a database and the scope of coverage for these documents.

Deciphering a Case Citation

If someone hands you the legal citation of a case, you should be able to head to the correct volume and turn to the correct page without checking any indexes or asking for help. Cases that appear in reporters have a citation that consists of the name of the case; the volume of the reporter; the name of the reporter; the page number in the reporter where the case begins; and the year the case was decided:

Halbman v. Lemke,   99   Wis.2d   241,   298   N.W.2d   562   (1980)

| Case name | Volume | Official reporter | Page | Volume | West reporter | Page | Year |

The citation may include a notation of the court deciding the case, or the court may be obvious from the reporter abbreviation, such as Wis.2d. A citation to a particular paragraph or sentence may also include the number of the page of the quotation:

298 N.W.2d   562,   564

| | Page case begins | Page of quotation |

Figure 1.10   A State Court Database on WESTLAW

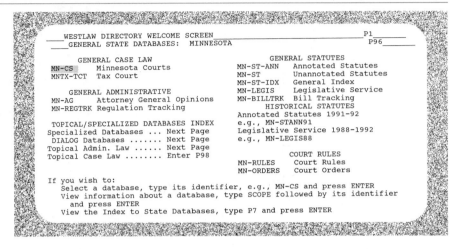

Although books may be your first choice, when the volume that you are looking for is not available, access WESTLAW and use Find. You do not need to access a database identifier, simply type **fi** and your citation; for example, type **fi 298 nw2d 562** to find *Halbman v. Lemke.*

If cases appear only on WESTLAW (a very recent opinion or a case that does not appear in the West reporters), the citations will consist of WEST-LAW Cites™. A WESTLAW cite appears on the screen in the upper left corner of slip opinions and unreported cases. Each WESTLAW cite consists of four parts: the year of the decision, WL (identifying WESTLAW as the place the document is located), a unique document number, and the jurisdiction in which the case was decided. You can use the Find command to retrieve slip opinions and unpublished cases on WESTLAW. Type **fi** followed by the WESTLAW cite (excluding the jurisdiction notation). By typing **fi 1987 WL 9398,** you will retrieve the case shown in Figure 1.11.

Figure 1.11   A WESTLAW Cite of an Unreported Case

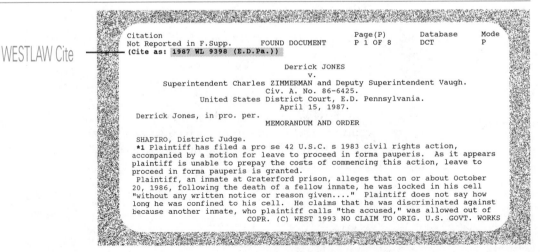

All of the rules for writing and deciphering legal citations appear in the *Bluebook* (Figure 1.12). For instance, if you are formally citing a very recent

Figure 1.12   A Page from *The Bluebook: A Uniform System of Citation*

Cases   10

Basic Citation Forms   10.1

A full case citation includes the name of the case (**rule 10.2**); the published sources in which it may be found, if any (**rule 10.3**); a parenthetical that indicates the court and jurisdiction (**rule 10.4**) and the year or date of decision (**rule 10.5**); and the subsequent history of the case, if any (**rule 10.7**). It may also include additional parenthetical information (**rule 10.6**) and the prior history of the case (**rule 10.7**). Special citation forms for pending and unreported cases (**rule 10.8.1**) and for briefs, records, motions, and memoranda (**rule 10.8.3**) are discussed in **rule 10.8**. **Rule 14.3** provides citation forms for administrative adjudications and arbitrations.

filed but not decided	Charlesworth v. Mack, No. 90-345 (D. Mass. filed Sept. 18, 1990).
unpublished interim order	Charlesworth v. Mack, No. 90-345 (D. Mass. Oct. 25, 1990) (order granting preliminary injunction).
published interim order	Charlesworth v. Mack, 725 F. Supp. 1395 (D. Mass. 1990) (order granting preliminary injunction).
unpublished decision	Charlesworth v. Mack, No. 90-345, slip op. at 6 (D. Mass. Dec. 4, 1990).
decision published in service only	Charlesworth v. Mack, 1990 Fed. Sec. L. Rep. (CCH) ¶ 102,342 (D. Mass. Dec. 4, 1990).
decision published in newspaper only	Charlesworth v. Mack, N.Y. L.J., Dec. 5, 1990, at 1 (D. Mass. Dec. 4, 1990).
decision available in electronic database	Charlesworth v. Mack, No. 90-345, 1990 U.S. Dist. LEXIS 20837, at *6 (D. Mass. Dec. 4, 1990).
published decision	Charlesworth v. Mack, 727 F. Supp. 1407, 1412 (D. Mass. 1990).
appeal docketed	Charlesworth v. Mack, 727 F. Supp. 1407 (D. Mass. 1990), *appeal docketed*, No. 90-567 (1st Cir. Dec. 20, 1990).
brief, record, or appendix	Brief for Appellant at 7, Charlesworth v. Mack, 925 F.2d 314 (1st Cir. 1991) (No. 90-567).
disposition on appeal	Charlesworth v. Mack, 925 F.2d 314, 335 (1st Cir. 1991).
disposition in lower court showing subsequent history	Charlesworth v. Mack, 727 F. Supp. 1407, 1412 (D. Mass. 1990), *aff'd*, 925 F.2d 314 (1st Cir. 1991).
petition for certiorari filed	Charlesworth v. Mack, 925 F.2d 314 (1st Cir. 1991), *petition for cert. filed*, 60 U.S.L.W. 3422 (U.S. Jan. 14, 1992) (No. 92-212).
petition for certiorari granted	Charlesworth v. Mack, 925 F.2d 314 (1st Cir. 1991), *cert. granted*, 60 U.S.L.W. 3562 (U.S. Jan. 21, 1992) (No. 92-212).

opinion available only on WESTLAW, the *Bluebook* provides rules on the correct electronic citation format. The *Bluebook* has many shortcomings, however, and is sometimes more a hindrance than a help. Nevertheless, you will have to use the *Bluebook* during your entire legal career, so you should become acquainted with it now.

Parallel Citations

As we noted earlier, you will often find a string of citations after the case name:

In re Baby M,   109 N.J. 396,   537 A.2d 1227   (1988)

Official reporter   Unofficial reporter

A citation to the same case published in a different reporter is called a *parallel citation*. Parallel citations are different citations to the exact same case and not to different stages of a case.

There are several ways to find a parallel citation if you only know one citation:

1. West's reporters and WESTLAW provide the official citation if it is available (Figure 1.13a). However, since the official reporters are generally slow to be published, the official citation is not usually available at the time the regional reporter is published, unless the West regional reporter is the official reporter. Some of the official state reports not published by West cite to West's reporters. The reporters of the U.S. Supreme Court cases published by West and Lawyers Cooperative both provide citations to the official *United States Reports* and to each other. The *United States Reports* does not supply any parallel citations.

2. If you know the name of the case, check the Table of Cases in the digest that covers the jurisdiction where your case was published, and you will find all of the parallel citations (Figure 1.13b). Digests will be discussed in the next chapter.

3. You can easily find parallel citations by using either *Shepard's*® citators (either in print or on WESTLAW) or Insta-Cite®, which is part of the WESTLAW service (Figure 1.13c). These services will be explained in a later chapter.

4. When you have the official citation and need the West citation, use the *National Reporter Blue Book*, published by West. It will provide you with parallel citations to West's National Reporter System. Just look up your citation, and you will find the West citation (Figure 1.13d).

Figure 1.13   Four Ways of Finding Parallel Citations

(a) A West Reporter

Official Citation ——————————————— 109 N.J. 396

MATTER OF BABY M   N. J. **1227**
Cite as 537 A.2d 1227 (N.J. 1988)

In the Matter of BABY M, a pseudonym for an actual person.

Supreme Court of New Jersey.

Argued Sept. 14, 1987.
Decided Feb. 3, 1988.

Natural father and his wife brought suit seeking to enforce surrogate parenting agreement, to compel surrender of infant born to surrogate mother, to restrain any interference with their custody of infant, and to terminate surrogate mother's parental rights to allow adoption of child by wife of natural father. The Superior Court, Chancery Division/Family Part, Bergen County, 217 N.J.Super. 313, 525 A.2d 1128, held that surrogate contract was valid, ordered that mother's parental rights be terminated and that sole custody of child be granted to natural father, and authorized adoption of child by father's wife. Mother

2. Infants ⬿19.4

Adoption of child through private placement is very much disfavored in New Jersey, although permitted.

3. Contracts ⬿105

Surrogate parenting contract's provision for payment of money to mother for her services and payment of fee to infertility center whose major role with respect to contract was as "finder" of mother whose child was to be adopted and as arranger of all proceedings that led to adoption, was illegal and perhaps criminal, under laws prohibiting use of money in connection with adoptions. N.J.S.A. 9:3–54.

4. Adoption ⬿7.3

Surrogate parenting contract's provision for termination of mother's parental rights violated laws requiring proof of parental unfitness or abandonment before termination of parental rights is ordered or

(b) A Digest

Baby M, Matter of, NJ, 537 A2d 1227, 109 NJ 396, on remand 542 A2d 52, 225 NJSuper 267.—Adop 7.3, 7.5, 7.6(1); App & E 843(2); Child 20; Const Law 82(10), 225.1; Contracts 105, 108(2); Infants 19.2(2), 19.3(2), 19.4, 85, 155, 156, 157, 232; Parent & C 2(16), 2(17).
Baby M, Matter of, NJSuperCh, 542 A2d 52, 225 NJSuper 267.—Child 20; Inj 96.
Baby M., Matter of, NJSuperCh, 525 A2d 1128, 217 NJSuper 313, certification gr 526 A2d 203, 107 NJ 140, aff in part, rev in part 537 A2d 1227, 109 NJ 396, on remand 542 A2d 52, 225 NJ-Super 267—Abort .50; Child 20; Const Law 70.1(9), 82(10), 224(1), 225.1, 274(5), 276(1); Contracts 1, 10(1), 94(1), 95(1), 110, 143.5, 147(2), 152, 169, 187(1); Fraud 3; Infants 155, 200;

Figure 1.13   Four Ways of Finding Parallel Citations (continued)

(c) *Shepard's* and Insta-Cite

```
                                    SHEPARD'S   (Rank 1 of 2)          Page 1 of 4
CITATIONS TO: 537 A.2d 1227
CITATOR: ATLANTIC REPORTER CITATIONS
DIVISION: Atlantic Reporter 2nd
COVERAGE: First Shepard's volume through Jan. 1993 Supplement
Retrieval                                                    Headnote
  No.    --Analysis--- -----Citation------      No.
            Same Text (109 N.J.  396)
            Same Text ( 77 A.L.R.4th 1)
   1    SC  Same Case 525 A.2d 1128
        SC  Same Case 526 A.2d 203
   2                  543 A.2d at 45          16
   3                  543 A.2d 925, 932        2
   4                  543 A.2d 925, 932        3
   5                  543 A.2d 925, 939        4
   6                  547 A.2d 691, 696       26
   7                  549 A.2d 792, 813
   8                  555 A.2d 1149, 1157     20
   9                  555 A.2d 1149, 1158     21
  10                  558 A.2d 1377, 1381      6

Note:  Check Shepard's PreView (SP), Insta-Cite (IC), and QuickCite (QC).
Copyright (C) 1993 McGraw-Hill, Inc.; Copyright (C) 1993 West Publishing Co.
```

```
                                    INSTA-CITE              PAGE   1 OF    2
CITATION: 537 A.2d 1227
                                    Direct History
    1  Matter of Baby M., 217 N.J.Super. 313, 525 A.2d 1128, 55 U.S.L.W. 2544
          (N.J.Super.Ch., Mar 31, 1987) (NO. FM-25314-86E)
          Certification Granted by
    2  Matter of Baby M., 107 N.J. 140, 526 A.2d 203 (N.J., Apr 07, 1987)
          AND Judgment Affirmed in Part, Reversed in Part by
 => 3  Matter of Baby M, 109 N.J. 396, 537 A.2d 1227, 56 U.S.L.W. 2442,
          77 A.L.R.4th 1 (N.J., Feb 03, 1988) (NO. A-39 SEPT TERM 1987)
          On Remand to
    4  Matter of Baby M, 225 N.J.Super. 267, 542 A.2d 52
          (N.J.Super.Ch., Apr 06, 1988) (NO. FM-25314-86E, A-39-87)

Related References
    5  Matter of Baby M., 107 N.J. 49, 526 A.2d 138 (N.J., Nov 21, 1986)
    6  Matter of Baby M., 107 N.J. 66, 526 A.2d 150 (N.J., Dec 16, 1986)

Note: This result is for the highlighted citation.  To view history for another
      case in this display, type IC and its number and press ENTER.  For
      indirect history prior to 1972 use Shepard's.  See SCOPE for more info.
(C) Copyright West Publishing Company 1993
```

(d) The *National Reporter Blue Book*

Official

Unofficial

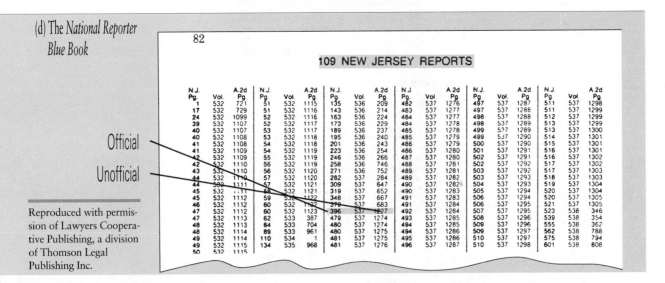

82

109 NEW JERSEY REPORTS

N.J. Pg.	Vol.	A.2d Pg.	N.J. Pg.	Vol.	A.2d Pg.	N.J. Pg.	Vol.	A.2d Pg.	N.J. Pg.	Vol.	A.2d Pg.	N.J. Pg.	Vol.	A.2d Pg.	N.J. Pg.	Vol.	A.2d Pg.	N.J. Pg.	Vol.	A.2d Pg.
1	532	721	51	532	1115	135	536	209	482	537	1276	497	537	1287	511	537	1298
17	532	729	51	532	1116	143	536	214	483	537	1277	497	537	1288	511	537	1299
24	532	1099	52	532	1116	163	536	224	484	537	1277	498	537	1288	512	537	1299
39	532	1107	52	532	1117	173	536	229	484	537	1278	498	537	1289	513	537	1299
40	532	1107	53	532	1117	189	536	237	485	537	1278	499	537	1289	513	537	1300
40	532	1108	53	532	1118	195	536	240	485	537	1279	499	537	1290	514	537	1301
41	532	1108	54	532	1118	201	536	243	486	537	1279	500	537	1290	515	537	1301
41	532	1109	54	532	1119	223	536	254	486	537	1280	501	537	1291	516	537	1301
42	532	1109	55	532	1119	246	536	266	487	537	1280	502	537	1291	516	537	1302
42	532	1110	56	532	1119	258	536	746	488	537	1281	502	537	1292	517	537	1302
43	532	1110	56	532	1120	271	536	752	489	537	1281	503	537	1292	517	537	1303
44	532	1110	57	532	1120	282	537	284	489	537	1282	503	537	1293	518	537	1303
44	532	1111	57	532	1121	309	537	647	490	537	1282	504	537	1293	519	537	1304
45	532	1111	58	532	1121	319	537	652	490	537	1283	505	537	1294	520	537	1304
45	532	1112	59	532	1122	348	537	667	491	537	1283	506	537	1294	520	537	1305
46	532	1112	60	532	1122	379	537	683	491	537	1284	506	537	1295	521	537	1305
47	532	1112	60	532	1123	396	537	1227	492	537	1284	507	537	1295	523	538	346
47	532	1113	62	533	387	479	537	1274	493	537	1285	508	537	1296	539	538	354
48	532	1113	84	533	704	480	537	1274	494	537	1285	509	537	1296	555	538	362
48	532	1114	89	533	961	480	537	1275	494	537	1286	509	537	1297	562	538	788
49	532	1114	110	534	1	481	537	1275	495	537	1286	510	537	1297	575	538	794
49	532	1115	134	535	968	481	537	1276	496	537	1287	510	537	1298	601	538	808
50	532	1115															

Parts of a Case

Since you will be spending most of your waking moments, or at least your semiconscious moments, in law school reading cases, it is important that you understand the structure of a case. We will discuss the parts of a case in a reporter and on WESTLAW (Figure 1.14).

Court

Particular reporters generally correspond to particular courts. When you choose a particular reporter, for instance, the *Federal Supplement,* you will be choosing a particular court of jurisdiction; that is, cases from the federal district court. Generally, the reporters are organized by jurisdiction.

Case Name or Title

Every case has a name. Most cases are named for the parties (usually two) involved in the lawsuit to indicate who is suing whom (e.g., *Bergman v. Unit-*

Figure 1.14   Parts of a Case

(a) Parts of a Case on WESTLAW

Citation · Case Name or Title · Docket Number · Court · Date · Synopsis

Headnote Number · Topic · Digest Classification Hierarchy · Key Number · Headnote

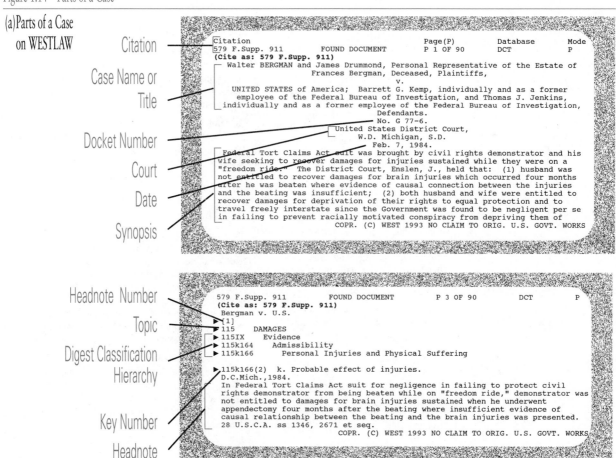

Figure 1.14   Parts of a Case (continued)

(b) Parts of a Case
       in a West Reporter

Citation

Case Name or Title

Docket Number

Court

Date

Synopsis

Key Number
Topic

Headnote

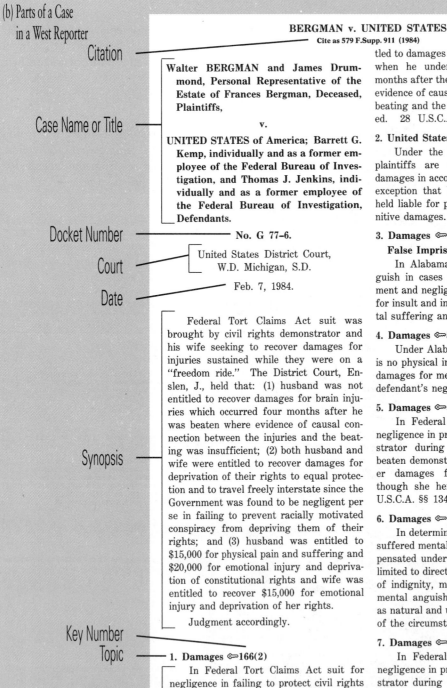

BERGMAN v. UNITED STATES   **911**
Cite as 579 F.Supp. 911 (1984)

Walter **BERGMAN** and James Drum-
mond, Personal Representative of the
Estate of Frances Bergman, Deceased,
Plaintiffs,

v.

UNITED STATES of America; Barrett G.
Kemp, individually and as a former employee of the Federal Bureau of Investigation, and Thomas J. Jenkins, individually and as a former employee of
the Federal Bureau of Investigation,
Defendants.

No. G 77–6.

United States District Court,
    W.D. Michigan, S.D.

Feb. 7, 1984.

Federal Tort Claims Act suit was
brought by civil rights demonstrator and
his wife seeking to recover damages for
injuries sustained while they were on a
"freedom ride." The District Court, Enslen, J., held that: (1) husband was not
entitled to recover damages for brain injuries which occurred four months after he
was beaten where evidence of causal connection between the injuries and the beating was insufficient; (2) both husband and
wife were entitled to recover damages for
deprivation of their rights to equal protection and to travel freely interstate since the
Government was found to be negligent per
se in failing to prevent racially motivated
conspiracy from depriving them of their
rights; and (3) husband was entitled to
$15,000 for physical pain and suffering and
$20,000 for emotional injury and depriva-
tion of constitutional rights and wife was
entitled to recover $15,000 for emotional
injury and deprivation of her rights.

Judgment accordingly.

1. **Damages** ⚖︎166(2)

In Federal Tort Claims Act suit for
negligence in failing to protect civil rights
demonstrator from being beaten while on
"freedom ride," demonstrator was not enti-

tled to damages for brain injuries sustained
when he underwent appendectomy four
months after the beating where insufficient
evidence of causal relationship between the
beating and the brain injuries was presented.   28 U.S.C.A. §§ 1346, 2671 et seq.

2. **United States** ⚖︎78(14), 110, 142

Under the Federal Tort Claims Act,
plaintiffs are entitled to compensatory
damages in accordance with state law, with
exception that United States may not be
held liable for prejudgment interest or pu-
nitive damages.   28 U.S.C.A. § 2674.

3. **Damages** ⚖︎52, 54

False Imprisonment ⚖︎34

In Alabama, damages for mental anguish in cases of assault, false imprisonment and negligence, include compensation
for insult and indignity, hurt feelings, mental suffering and fright.

4. **Damages** ⚖︎50

Under Alabama law, even where there
is no physical injury, plaintiff may recover
damages for mental anguish occasioned by
defendant's negligence.

5. **Damages** ⚖︎51

In Federal Tort Claims Act suit for
negligence in protecting civil rights demonstrator during "freedom ride," wife of
beaten demonstrator was entitled to recover damages for mental anguish even
though she herself was not beaten.   28
U.S.C.A. §§ 1346, 2671 et seq.

6. **Damages** ⚖︎48

In determining whether or not plaintiff
suffered mental anguish which can be com-
pensated under Alabama law, court is not
limited to direct testimony relating feelings
of indignity, mental suffering and fright;
mental anguish may properly be inferred
as natural and usual consequences from all
of the circumstances.

7. **Damages** ⚖︎49.10

In Federal Tort Claims Act suit for
negligence in protecting civil rights demonstrator during "freedom ride," demonstrators were entitled to damages for mental
anguish.   28 U.S.C.A. §§ 1346, 2671 et seq.

ed States). Some cases may have only one name with a Latin phrase attached (e.g., *In re Seiferth*). In a criminal case, since the state brings the action, the first party will often be the jurisdiction itself (e.g., *State v. Birditt*).

When a case begins in the trial court, the first name is the plaintiff, or the party bringing the suit, and the name after the "v." is the defendant. On appeal, the name of the petitioner or appellant will be listed first, the name of the respondent or appellee will be listed second. Therefore, if the defendant in the trial court brings an appeal, his or her name may be listed first in the appellate case.

When you read a case in one of the reporters or on WESTLAW, you will often find several plaintiffs, defendants, or cross-complainants. Correct citation form requires that only the first-named plaintiff and the first-named defendant be listed. The case name that appears at the top of each page in the reporters is not in correct citation format and should not be followed as an example of *Bluebook* format. For example, the following appears at the top of the page for the case at 441 F.2d 1061:

Local 13, Int. Longshoremen's & W.U. v. Pacific Mar. Ass'n

The correct *Bluebook* format for the case name would be *Local 13, Int'l Longshoremen's & Warehousemen's Union v. Pacific Maritime Ass'n.*

Docket Number

When a case is filed in the court clerk's office, it is assigned a docket number that remains with the case until it is decided. Typically, the first two numbers indicate the year that the case was filed. The docket number is printed below the name of the case.

Date

A reporter or WESTLAW will indicate the exact month, day, and year that the case was decided. For citation purposes, cite only the year.

Synopsis

Editors at West write a synopsis or brief description of each case that appears in the West reporters. You will find the synopsis below the date. Most synopses contain the following information: the facts of the case, the name and holding of the lower court judge, the holding of the court, and the name of the judge writing the opinion. If you have many cases to read, you can quickly scan the synopses to weed out the irrelevant cases, but be advised that the synopsis is not part of the opinion. It is a helpful editorial enhancement prepared by the publisher. If you are looking in a jurisdiction that has an official reporter in which the court writes a synopsis, you may get *two* synopses—one from West and one from the court.

Judge

The judge is listed both in the synopsis or syllabus of a case and on a separate line preceding the opinion. There is no manual index of judges' names that

lists all cases decided by specific judges, but you can search for opinions written by a particular judge by using an on-line service. On WESTLAW, you can retrieve cases in which a particular judge wrote the majority, dissenting, or concurring opinion.

Headnotes

Court decisions typically contain at least one legal issue. An issue is the question raised where the rules of law impinge on the facts of the case. The West editors decipher the legal issues from cases and summarize each issue in a headnote. Each headnote is usually one sentence. Headnotes appear in the case in West reporters and on WESTLAW after the synopsis, but before the opinion. A headnote in a West reporter begins with a number in boldface type followed by a topic and then by a key number (Figure 1.15a). A headnote screen on WESTLAW contains additional information showing the full digest classification hierarchy for a key number (Figure 1.15b).

Figure 1.15   Headnote Numbers

(a) Headnote
at Beginning
of Case

912   **579 FEDERAL SUPPLEMENT**

8. Conspiracy ☞13

In Federal Tort Claims Act suit for negligence in protecting civil rights demonstrators during "freedom ride," demonstrators were entitled to damages for deprivation of their constitutional rights to equal protection and freedom of interstate travel where United States was found to be negligent per se under Alabama law in part because it violated its statutory duty to prevent racially motivated conspiracy from depriving freedom riders of equal protection.   42 U.S.C.A. § 1986.

9. Civil Rights ☞13.17(5, 6)
Damages ☞130(1)

In Federal Tort Claims Act suit for negligence in protecting civil rights demonstrator from being beaten while on "freedom ride," demonstrator was entitled to damages of $15,000 for his physical pain and suffering, $20,000 for emotional injury and deprivation of constitutional rights.   28 U.S.C.A. §§ 1346, 2671 et seq.

OPINION ON DAMAGES

ENSLEN, District Judge.

Plaintiffs in this action under the Federal Tort Claims Act (FTCA) are Dr. Walter Bergman and the personal representative of the estate of his late wife, Frances Bergman. Both Walter and Frances Bergman were among the "freedom riders" who traveled by bus into the South in May, 1961 to test a recent pronouncement by the United States Supreme Court that the Constitution required racial equality in interstate transportation facilities. Their encounter with a conspiracy of violent racism in Alabama was described in detail by this Court in an earlier opinion. *Bergman v. United States,* 565 F.Supp. 1353 (W.D.MI. 1983). That decision followed upon trial of the United States' liability for the injuries plaintiffs suffered during their journey into Alabama.[1] I held that the federal Government was negligent in failing to take steps available to it to avoid the violence, and concluded that,

Figure 1.15   Headnote Numbers (continued)

(b) Headnote Screen
on WESTLAW

```
579 F.Supp. 911       FOUND DOCUMENT       P 14 OF 90      DCT      P
(Cite as: 579 F.Supp. 911)
Bergman v. U.S.
▶ [8]
▶ 91       CONSPIRACY
▶ 91I        Civil Liability
▶ 91I(A)        Acts Constituting Conspiracy and Liability Therefor
▶ 91k12         Persons Liable

▶ 91k13   k. In general.
D.C.Mich.,1984.
In Federal Tort Claims Act suit for negligence in protecting civil rights
demonstrators during "freedom ride," demonstrators were entitled to damages for
deprivation of their constitutional rights to equal protection and freedom of
interstate travel where United States was found to be negligent per se under
Alabama law in part because it violated its statutory duty to prevent racially
motivated conspiracy from depriving freedom riders of equal protection.  42
U.S.C.A. s 1986.
                    COPR. (C) WEST 1993 NO CLAIM TO ORIG. U.S. GOVT. WORKS
```

Headnotes are numbered so you can use them as a table of contents to the case. Numbers, corresponding to the headnote numbers, appear in brackets in the text of the opinion. The number in brackets indicates that this is covered by that particular headnote. On WESTLAW, you can "jump" from a headnote to the discussion of the point of law in the text of the opinion. To jump from a numbered headnote to the related text in the opinion, use the Tab key to move the cursor to the > symbol preceding the headnote number and press **Enter.**

The next part of the headnote after the number is a term or phrase, which is the broad topic under which West has classified that particular legal issue. After the topic is a key number in the West reporters. (Remember that on WESTLAW the full digest classification hierarchy appears between the broad topic and the very specific key number.) The key number represents a specific aspect or subsection of the topic. For example, under the topic Conspiracy, key number 13 covers "Conspiracy—In general." The West editors classify a case under all the applicable topics and key numbers. To find out what the key number stands for, consult either a West digest or the Key Number service on WESTLAW. Digests are books that group headnotes from cases under different topics of law; they are arranged by topics and key numbers. Once you find a relevant topic and key number, you can continue with the digests, or you can search for the topic on WESTLAW (as explained in the next chapter). The lines of text in the digest are actually the headnote itself; that is, they are an annotation of one of the legal issues in the case.

Writing headnotes is an art, not a science. Two different editors will see different sets of legal issues in a case. As in the debate over whether Hank Aaron or Babe Ruth was the greater ballplayer, there is no "correct" answer. Look at the headnotes in each of the three versions of a U.S. Supreme Court case (from the three reporters discussed earlier in this chapter) and see how different they are (Figure 1.16a–c). Note that the West reporter contains thirteen short headnotes while the Lawyers Cooperative reporter contains two longer headnotes and a set of references to other related materials. The official *United States Reports* does not contain any headnotes *per se,* but it does include a long synopsis of the case.

Figure 1.16   Variations in Headnotes

(a) United States Reports

Syllabus   485 U. S.

CITY OF ST. LOUIS *v.* PRAPROTNIK

CERTIORARI TO THE UNITED STATES COURT OF APPEALS FOR THE EIGHTH CIRCUIT

No. 86–772.   Argued October 7, 1987—Decided March 2, 1988

Two years after respondent, a management-level employee in one of petitioner city's agencies, successfully appealed a temporary suspension to petitioner's Civil Service Commission (Commission), he was transferred

1. Petitioner's failure to timely object under Federal Rule of Civil Procedure 51 to a jury instruction on municipalities' § 1983 liability for their employees' unconstitutional acts does not deprive this Court of jurisdiction to determine the proper legal standard for imposing such liability.   The same legal issue was raised by petitioner's motions for summary judgment and a directed verdict, was considered and decided by the Court of Appeals, and is likely to recur in § 1983 litigation against municipalities.   Review in this Court will not undermine the policy of judicial efficiency that underlies Rule 51.   Pp. 118–121.

2. The Court of Appeals applied an incorrect legal standard for determining when isolated decisions by municipal officials or employees may expose the municipality to § 1983 liability.   The identification of officials having "final policymaking authority" is a question of state (including local) law, rather than a question of fact for the jury.   Here, it appears that petitioner's City Charter gives the authority to set employment policy to the Mayor and Aldermen, who are empowered to enact ordinances,

Topic

As we have just seen, topics are the main classifications for cases. In a library, you would look at a West digest volume for the topic that you need. Cases may be searched on WESTLAW by digest topic.

Attorneys

The names of counsel are found preceding the opinion in a decision. If you need the briefs for a case at some time during your legal career, you may want

Figure 1.16   Variations in Headnotes (continued)

(b) Supreme Court Reporter

916   **108 SUPREME COURT REPORTER**

findings that decisions of supervisors were not individually reviewed for substantive priority by higher supervisory officials and that civil service commission decided appeals from such decisions in some circumscribed manner that gave substantial deference to original decision maker were insufficient to support conclusion that supervisors were authorized to establish employment policy for city with respect to transfers and layoffs.

Reversed and remanded.

Justice Brennan filed opinion concurring in judgment in which Justices Marshall and Blackmun joined.

Justice Stevens filed dissenting opinion.

Justice Kennedy took no part in the consideration or decision of the case.

1. Federal Courts ☞461

City's failure to timely object to jury instruction on municipalities' liability for their employees' unconstitutional acts did not deprive Supreme Court of jurisdiction to determine proper legal standard for im-

curring in the judgment.)   42 U.S.C.A. § 1983.

3. Civil Rights ☞13.7

Municipalities may be liable under § 1983 only for acts for which municipality itself is actually responsible, that is, acts which municipality had officially sanctioned or ordered. (Per Justice O'Connor with the Chief Justice and two Justices concurring and three Justices concurring in the judgment.) 42 U.S.C.A. § 1983.

4. Civil Rights ☞13.7

Only those municipal officers who have final policymaking authority may by their actions subject municipal government to § 1983 liability. (Per Justice O'Connor with the Chief Justice and two Justices concurring and three Justices concurring in the judgment.) 42 U.S.C.A. § 1983.

5. Civil Rights ☞13.7

Whether particular official has final policymaking authority for purposes of § 1983 liability is question of state law. (Per Justice O'Connor with the Chief Justice and two Justices concurring and three Justices concurring in the judgment.) 42 U.S.C.A. § 1983.

(c) United States Supreme Court Reports, Lawyers' Edition

ST. LOUIS v PRAPROTNIK
(1988) 485 US 112, 99 L Ed 2d 107, 108 S Ct 915

HEADNOTES

Classified to U.S. Supreme Court Digest, Lawyers' Edition

Appeal § 1677; Civil Rights § 27; Trial § 165 — reversal — liability of city — retaliatory employment actions — supervisors — jury question
1a-1c. The United States Supreme Court will reverse a Federal Court of Appeals decision, which affirmed a Federal District Court judgment finding a city liable under 42 USCS § 1983 for the violation of a city employee's federal constitutional rights through retaliatory employee transfer and layoff actions taken by

city agency supervisors in response to the employee's appeal of his suspension to the city's grievance review board, where (1) four Justices are of the opinion that the Federal Court of Appeals applied an incorrect legal standard in concluding that the supervisors were city "policymakers" whose actions could subject the city to liability under § 1983, in that (a) the identification of officials with such final policymaking authority is a question of state and local law, rather than a question of

to contact one of the attorneys. Since WESTLAW adds the city and state where the attorney practices, it is very easy to contact the attorney. When you begin your legal career, you may also want to search on WESTLAW for cases handled by a particular attorney to prepare for an interview with that attorney.

Opinion

We are now to the actual text of the judge's decision, which is called the opinion. An opinion is a court's written explanation of why it did what it did. The structure of an opinion includes the nature of the case, a general statement of the issues presented, the facts, the errors assigned, and a dispositional section.

Opinions may be unanimous. That used to be good form, but today it is less frequent. This means that you may find other opinions after the majority's statement. A dissenting opinion is written by a single judge or a minority of judges who disagree with the result. There may also be concurring opinions when a judge or judges agree with the result of the main opinion but not with the reasoning. Because of the doctrine of precedent, this policy is important. In complex cases, a judge may concur in part and dissent in part. Especially in U.S. Supreme Court cases, this can be very hard to sort out.

You may also encounter a few other kinds of opinions. A per curiam opinion is an opinion written anonymously that includes the reasoning of the entire court. Such opinions are generally short and are weak precedent. Memorandum decisions report routine decisions.

In reading *any* opinion, remember that only the issues of law that are resolved by the opinion are the "stuff" of the law. Much of the opinion will not be resolving such issues. Opinions may contain factual summaries, the judge's opinions on the state of civilization, or anything else. Judges can write what they like, but everything that does not resolve a legal issue is dictum. You will find that dicta, though not binding precedent, may be "persuasive." That is, the dicta may still be helpful to your case.

The last paragraph in a majority opinion is the mandate of the court. It states what action is being taken on appeal. For example, the court may indicate that the decision is affirmed, reversed, remanded, modified, or dismissed.

Conclusion

You should now feel familiar with cases. They are not really like the cryptic, heavily edited versions that lurk in your casebooks. In their fully reported form, they have lots of editorial enhancements and useful parts. In addition, they all follow a similar pattern, so you will find familiar aspects as you move from the state court system to the federal system.

This chapter has explained how to locate a case in a reporter from a legal citation and how to find and use parallel citations. At this point, you should also be able to recognize and understand the parts of a case in a reporter volume and on WESTLAW. Now that you understand the basics of reporters in print and on WESTLAW, we will proceed to finding particular cases.

2

FINDING CASES

F inding cases has been a challenge for lawyers for hundreds of years, and a variety of tools have been developed to help. In some ways every tool that you will encounter is designed to help you find cases. This chapter concentrates on print sources, called digests, and the on-line WESTLAW databases. Both the digests and WESTLAW try to be comprehensive. This means that they do not offer access to cases on just one topic, but instead provide access to *all* cases—a full-tilt blunderbuss approach. Given that some three million cases are already out there with perhaps another 130,000 being added each year, it is no surprise that these tools need some special instruction. This chapter will explain them.

Digests

Digests are research tools that arrange abstracts of cases by subject. They are built from the headnotes that we met in the last chapter. Every digest has three things: (1) a base of headnotes; (2) a subject arrangement that divides legal issues into a logical structure; and (3) an editor to put the headnotes into the subject arrangement.

To give you an example of how this works, suppose a child has been injured by an unleashed pit bull in the state of Washington. The child's parent wants you to file a claim against the dog's owner and against the local humane society for not enforcing the city's "leash law." You need to find cases regarding injuries from pit bulls. The only clue you have is that you remember reading about a "pit bull" case that took place in the state of Washington. How could you use this clue to find the cases you need?

The traditional answer has been to use a digest. A digest is a comprehensive subject index to cases. The digest contains a comprehensive list of legal topics, including some personal favorites of the authors, such as "Hawkers and Peddlers." Each legal topic is subdivided into issues and each issue is assigned a digest classification number called a key number. Then, the headnotes addressing issues in reported cases are dropped into their proper location in this digest classification scheme or hierarchy. As a result, the headnotes of decisions on the same point of law appear together.

Figure 2.1   The Descriptive-Word
Index in the *Washington Digest*

Figure 2.1   The Descriptive-Word
Index in the *Washington Digest*

Therefore, to find the pit bull cases, you would use the state of Washington digest and begin searching for cases by using the Descriptive-Word Index (Figure 2.1). We will discuss this index later in the chapter.

A digest is *one* way of locating a case by its subject. Digests are particularly useful for finding cases involving legal issues or concepts, such as ownership of property or various contract theories. Often, you will get maximum results by using digests in conjunction with WESTLAW, but for the time being, let's examine how to use a digest alone to find the information we need.

The digests that we will discuss are published by West, although other companies also publish digests. West has the largest system, the only one that covers *all* jurisdictions. West organizes its digests according to the West Key Number System. The paragraphs in the digests are basically the headnote paragraphs from the cases in the reporters rearranged according to subject (Figure 2.2 a and b).

Understanding the relationship between the headnotes and the digests is crucial to using the digests. Remember that the West editors create headnotes by isolating every issue of law that appears in the opinion. West then assigns topics and key numbers to every headnote. Each headnote is assigned at least one key number, and some headnotes are assigned several.

Figure 2.2   Headnote Paragraph in the Reporter and in the Digest

(a) Headnote in
    Pacific Reporter

1280   Wash.   **737 PACIFIC REPORTER, 2d SERIES**

5. Municipal Corporations ⬅723

Special relationship exception to public duty doctrine arises where relationship develops between individual and agents of entity performing governmental function, such that duty is created to perform mandated act for benefit of particular person or class of persons.

6. Municipal Corporations ⬅723

Before entity may be held liable under

[1888]John H. Loeffler, Olson, Loeffler & Landis, Spokane, for appellants.

Jonathan C. Rascoff, Spokane, for respondents.

MUNSON, Judge.

John and Roxie Champagne brought this action on behalf of their minor son, John, against the Spokane Humane Society for personal injuries resulting from the attack

9. Animals ⬅54

Although owner of pit bulls was negligent in allowing them to run loose, humane society, which had been contractually delegated authority to enforce animal regulations of city's ordinance, could be liable for its later negligence, if any, in failing to apprehend the pit bulls.

and to enforce the animal regulatory provisions of the Spokane city ordinances. Spokane city ordinance C13835 [1889]provides in pertinent part:

Section 1. Dogs at Large. It shall be unlawful for any person to cause, permit, or allow any dog or dogs, owned, harbored, controlled or kept by him, in the

1. Mr. Mason subsequently disappeared and is not a party to this action.

Figure 2.2 Headnote Paragraph in the Reporter and in the Digest (continued)

(b) Identical
Headnote in
*Washington
Digest*

1 Wash D 2d—515   **ANIMALS** ⚷➙68

For references to other topics, see Descriptive-Word Index

value of use and occupation thereof. RCW 16.24.070.

　MacKenzie-Richardson, Inc. v. Allert, 272 P.2d 146, 45 Wash.2d 1.

Wash. 1927. To recover for dog bite, it must be shown that dog was wrongfully on sidewalk.

　Shelby v. Seung, 257 P. 838, 144 Wash. 317.

Recovery for injuries for dog bite held improperly allowed without showing dog was wrongfully on street.

　Shelby v. Seung, 257 P. 838, 144 Wash. 317.

Wash. 1906. The owner of a steer who has knowledge of its dangerous character is liable for injuries inflicted by the steer while running at large, irrespective of whether the owner was negligent in securing the steer.

　Harris v. Carstens Packing Co., 86 P. 1125, 43 Wash. 647, 6 L.R.A., N.S., 1164.

⚷➙**54. —— Persons liable for injuries.**

　Wash.App. 1987. Although owner of pit bulls was negligent in allowing them to run loose, humane society, which had been contractually delegated authority to enforce animal regulations of city's ordinance, could be liable for its later negligence, if any, in failing to apprehend the pit bulls.

　Champagne v. Spokane Humane Soc., 737 P.2d 1279, 47 Wash.App. 887, review denied.

Evidence that defendant was running in excess of 300 head of cattle on approximately 12,000 acres of leased pasture, that county road ran through the pasture for four miles, that there was no fence separating pasture from the road, that it was necessary for cattle to cross road to reach watering place, that cattle were frequently observed on the road with no herdsman tending them and that herdsman, who patrolled the entire tract, ordinarily made only one daily check of the road, warranted misdemeanor conviction of owner for permitting his cattle to run at large and not under the care of a herder. West's RCWA 16.13.010.

　State v. Dear, 638 P.2d 85, 96 Wash.2d 652.

⚷➙**58–66. *For other cases see the Decennial Digests and WESTLAW.***

Library references

　C.J.S. Animals.

⚷➙**66. Personal injuries.**

Library references

　C.J.S. Animals §§ 170, 177.

⚷➙**67. —— Domestic animals in general.**

　Wash. 1980. Negligence cause of action against animal owner arises when there is ineffective control of an animal in a situation where it would reasonably be expected that an injury could occur and injury does proximately result from the negligence; amount of control required is that which would be exercised by a reasonable person based on the total situation at the time, including the past behavior of the

West developed the Key Number System to organize the digest paragraphs. In this system, the entire body of law has been broken down into general topics. Each topic has been further divided into a number of points of law. A separate number, the "key number" is assigned to each point of law.

Animals ⚷➙ 54

You must have both parts, the topic and the key number, in order to use the digests.

In the digests, the paragraphs under each key number are arranged by jurisdiction, and under each jurisdiction, they are arranged by date of decision. The cases are listed in reverse chronological order with the most recent at the beginning (Figure 2.3).

The beauty of the key number system is that the key number assigned is uniform throughout all West's digests. As a result, when you find a relevant case in the *Georgia Digest,* you can look under the identical key number in all

Figure 2.3 Cases Arranged by Jurisdiction in Reverse Chronological Order in the *Federal Practice Digest*

13 F P D 4th—115   **CIVIL RIGHTS** ⟜112

For references to other topics, see Descriptive-Word Index

constitutional wrong, for § 1983 purposes. 42 U.S.C.A. § 1983; U.S.C.A. Const.Amend. 14.

    Davis v. Bucher, 853 F.2d 718.

C.A.7 (Wis.) 1989. Deprivation of civil rights claim based on due process clause of Fourteenth Amendment does not translate every tort committed by state actor into a constitutional wrong. 42 U.S.C.A. § 1983; U.S.C.A. Const.Amend. 14.

    Erwin v. County of Manitowoc, 872 F.2d 1292.

C.A.7 (Wis.) 1987. Fact that tort-feasor is municipal employee is not sufficient alone to make his or her tort "abuse of power" in violation of due process clause which is redressable in action brought under § 1983. 42 U.S.C.A. § 1983.

    Archie v. City of Racine, 826 F.2d 480, rehearing granted, vacated 831 F.2d 152.

C.A.7 (Wis.) 1985. Section 1983 imposes liability for violations of rights protected by the Constitution, not for violations of duties of care arising out of tort law. U.S.C.A. Const. Amend. 14.

    Gumz v. Morrissette, 772 F.2d 1395, certiorari denied 106 S.Ct. 1644, 475 U.S. 1123, 90 L.Ed.2d 189.

C.A.7 (Wis.) 1985. General principles of tort liability govern the liability imposed under 42 U.S.C.A. § 1983.

    Hibma v. Odegaard, 769 F.2d 1147.

States so as to be actionable under 42 U.S.C.A. § 1983.

    Metcalf v. Long, 615 F.Supp. 1108.

M.D.Ga. 1988. Under Georgia law, payment of a higher salary to male comanager of restaurant than to female comanager, removal of some of female comanager's supervisory duties, and her proposed demotion were not so terrifying or insulting as to cause female comanager the humiliation, embarrassment or fright necessary to justify recovery from employer for intentional infliction of emotional distress.

    Thompson v. John L. Williams Co., Inc., 686 F.Supp. 315.

N.D.Ga. 1988. Defendant cannot be held liable under § 1983 merely for commission of common-law tort, instead, § 1983 plaintiff must show that defendant's conduct was constitutionally tortious and violated plaintiff's federal constitutional or legal right. 42 U.S. C.A. § 1983.

    Terrell v. Shope, 687 F.Supp. 579.

D.C.Ga. 1985. A negligent deprivation of a constitutional right is actionable under 42 U.S.C.A. § 1983 if requirements of the statute are met.

    Gravitt v. Graves, 609 F.Supp. 925, affirmed in part, reversed in part 797 F.2d 980.

other jurisdictions and find relevant cases. A particular regional or state digest may not list cases under every topic and key number. When you see the statement "For other cases see the Decennial Digest® and WESTLAW" in a digest, you should follow those directions.

Figure 2.4 lists the digests published by West. As you can see, there are different digests, each designed to fill specific needs. Logically, you would retrieve federal cases (including Supreme Court cases) from one of the various federal digests, and you would use the Supreme Court digest to retrieve only Supreme Court cases. If you want all cases from all jurisdictions, use the American Digest System®, which consists of the *Decennial Digest* and the *General Digest*®. This system has enormous scope: it includes all reported American cases, state and federal, from 1658 to the present. To make this digest manageable, West has divided it into five- or ten-year periods. West updates the *Decennial Digest* with a series of bound volumes known as the *General Digest* (eighth series); a volume is published approximately every month.

If you are researching state law, you should select a state digest since it will provide you with the quickest way to determine case law in one state. A

Figure 2.4   West's Digests

State	All states except Delaware, Nevada, and Utah. For Delaware, use the *Atlantic Digest®;* for Nevada and Utah, use the *Pacific Digest®.*
Region	Only four current regional digests: *Atlantic, North Western, Pacific,* and *South Eastern.* Use the state digests for states not covered in the regional digests.
Federal (both lower federal courts and Supreme Court)	*Federal Digest,* red, all cases prior to 1939 *Modern Federal Practice Digest®,* green, 1939–1960 *Federal Practice Digest®* 2d, blue, 1961–1975 *Federal Practice Digest®* 3d, red, 1976–1988 *Federal Practice Digest®* 4th, blue, 1989– (volumes are in the process of being published)
Supreme Court only	*United States Supreme Court Digest®,* 1790–date
American Digest System (all cases, both federal and state)	*Century Digest,* 1658–1896 *First–Tenth (Part 1) Decennial Digests,* 1897–1991 *General Digest®* 8th, 1991–date

Always Use the Smallest Digest

regional digest would be useful when you need cases from neighboring jurisdictions. A good rule of thumb is to always use the smallest possible digest.

Now that you have the correct digest for your jurisdiction, you need to learn how to use it.

Finding a Case in a Digest

If you are lucky enough to know one relevant case, perhaps obtained from a classmate or a textbook, for example, you should read the case and determine the key numbers that are relevant to your legal issue. Once you have relevant key numbers, you can go directly to the digest volume that indexes additional cases on point. For example, your client is charged with importing cocaine into the United States. He claims that the customs officer unlawfully searched his suitcase while it was in the baggage hold of the aircraft. A colleague suggests that you read the case *United States v. Franchi-Forlando,* 838 F.2d 585 (1st Cir. 1988). From this case, you can determine the appropriate topic and key numbers and head to the digest to retrieve other pertinent cases (Figure 2.5a and b). Legal research skills revolve around the finding of one good case, and you will encounter many methods of doing so.

Figure 2.5 Key Numbers from One Relevant Case Can Lead to Others

(a) Key Numbers
    in a Case

586   838 FEDERAL REPORTER, 2d SERIES

1. Drugs and Narcotics ⟨74, 124⟩

The Government did not have to prove that defendant knew that airplane en route from Colombia to Spain would stop in the United States in order for defendant to be convicted of unlawfully importing cocaine into the United States when airplane made scheduled stop in Puerto Rico and, in any event, evidence was sufficient for jury to find that defendant knew he would land in the United States. Comprehensive Drug Abuse Prevention and Control Act of 1970, § 1002(a), 21 U.S.C.A. § 952(a).

2. Customs Duties ⟨126(7)⟩

Customs officer could lawfully search suitcase of passenger who was in transit from Colombia to Spain, while suitcase was in baggage hold during scheduled stop in Puerto Rico. Tariff Act of 1930, §§ 467, 496, 581(a), 19 U.S.C.A. §§ 1467, 1496, 1581(a).

3. Customs Duties ⟨126(7)⟩

Customs regulation providing that customs officers are not to open baggage but are to detain it until owner opens or refuses to open it did not preclude search of suitcase which was not accompanying passenger through customs but which was in baggage hold of aircraft en route from Colombia to Spain, during scheduled stop in Puerto Rico.

6. Criminal Law ⟨200(1)⟩

Convictions for both unlawfully importing cocaine into the United States and unlawfully possessing cocaine on an aircraft arriving in the United States without proper listing in the aircraft's documents did not violate double jeopardy, in that the applicable statutory provisions each required proof of a fact which the other did not, in that the undocumented importation offense applied to approved as well as unapproved controlled substances. Comprehensive Drug Abuse Prevention and Control Act of 1970, §§ 1002(a), 1005, 21 U.S.C.A. §§ 952(a), 955; U.S.C.A. Const. Amend. 5.

―――――

Rafael F. Castro–Lang, San Juan, P.R., by Appointment of the Court, for defendant, appellant.

Jose R. Gaztambide, Asst. U.S. Atty., with whom Daniel F. Lopez–Romo, U.S. Atty., Hato Rey, P.R., was on brief for appellee.

Before CAMPBELL, Chief Judge, TIMBERS,* Senior Circuit Judge, and BREYER, Circuit Judge.

BREYER, Circuit Judge.

The appellant, Orlando Franchi–Forlando, is an Italian citizen, living in Colombia. He was flying on Iberia Airlines from Co-

Descriptive-Word Index

If you do not have one great case by which to find other cases, your gateway into the digest can be the Descriptive-Word Index (DWI). The DWI is a long list of everyday words, legal terms, and phrases. In a way, it is an index to the collected headnotes (this may sound odd, but don't worry—it is very useful). Under these DWI terms, you can find relevant topics and key numbers.

Before you use the DWI, analyze your fact situation thoroughly in order to generate sufficient words to look up in the DWI. You cannot use the DWI effectively if you do not fully understand your fact situation; you may overlook important terms.

Let's return to our problem involving the pit bull. West suggests that before consulting a Descriptive-Word Index, you should analyze your problem

Figure 2.5 Key Numbers from One Relevant Case Can lead to Others (continued)

(b) Digest Entries under a Key Number

36 F P D 4th—385

CUSTOMS DUTIES ⚷126(7)

For references to other topics, see Descriptive-Word Index

"Reasonable suspicion" standard for justifying an "extended border search" was not applicable to search of package at Pittsburgh airport, where package was searched while still under customs bond and prior to its delivery to addressee, even though package had stopped in New York and Chicago before reaching Pittsburgh.
U.S. v. Caminos, 770 F.2d 361.

C.A.1 (Puerto Rico) 1990. Search conducted by customs officials of baggage of aircraft passengers proceeding from Columbia to Europe was a "border search" irrespective of passengers' in-transit status or their lack of knowledge that stop would be made in the United States.
U.S. v. Garcia, 905 F.2d 557.

C.A.1 (Puerto Rico) 1988. Customs officer could lawfully search suitcase of passenger who was in transit from Colombia to Spain, while suitcase was in baggage hold during scheduled stop in Puerto Rico. Tariff Act of 1930, §§ 467, 496, 581(a), 19 U.S.C.A. §§ 1467, 1496, 1581(a).
U.S. v. Franchi–Forlando, 838 F.2d 585.

Customs regulation providing that customs officers are not to open baggage but are to detain it until owner opens or refuses to open it did not preclude search of suitcase which was not accompanying passenger through customs but which was in baggage hold of aircraft en route from Colombia to Spain, during scheduled stop in Puerto Rico.
U.S. v. Franchi–Forlando, 838 F.2d 585.

intent to unlade and also includes planned stops of commercial airplanes whatever their passengers' final destinations. Tariff Act of 1930, § 496, 19 U.S.C.A. § 1496.
U.S. v. McKenzie, 818 F.2d 115.

C.A.6 (Tenn.) 1986. Customs officials have authority to conduct border-type search of aircraft pursuant to Anti-Smuggling Act where they are reasonably certain that aircraft entered from foreign country. Anti-Smuggling Act, § 3(a), 19 U.S.C.A. § 1703(a).
U.S. v. One (1) 1966 Beechcraft Baron, No. N242BS, 788 F.2d 384.

Customs officials had authority to conduct border-type search of abandoned aircraft, even though unidentified aircraft that crossed border while operating without navigation lights, which officials had been tracking on radar, evaded surveillance and disappeared and there was one-hour time lapse between disappearance of monitored aircraft and discovery of abandoned aircraft. Anti-Smuggling Act, § 3(a, c), 19 U.S.C.A. § 1703(a, c).
U.S. v. One (1) 1966 Beechcraft Baron, No. N242BS, 788 F.2d 384.

C.A.5 (Tex.) 1988. Border patrol agents' detention of defendant's suitcase for approximately an hour and a half after seizure of suitcase when agents could have employed more diligent, less intrusive investigatory techniques and when there was an absence of probable cause was unreasonable. U.S.C.A. Const.Amend. 4.
U.S. v. Cagle, 849 F.2d 924.

and determine very specific words or phrases to be searched by breaking the problem down into the following elements common to every case:

1. The *parties* involved: In our case, the owner of the pit bull; the injured child; and the humane society.

2. The *places* where the facts arose and the *objects* or *things* involved: The facts took place in the city; the pit bull or the vicious dog was involved.

3. The *acts* or *omissions* that form the *basis of action* or *issue:* The owner of the pit bull was negligent in allowing the dog to run loose, and the humane society was negligent in failing to apprehend the loose pit bull.

4. The *defense* to the action or issue: The defendant, the humane society, claims that it never saw the pit bull running loose.

5. The *relief* sought: The owner and the humane society are liable for personal injuries.

Therefore, you would begin with the Descriptive-Word Index in the *Washington Digest* and might look under the term "Pit Bulls." You would find that "Pit Bulls" is not listed; this term is too restrictive and you must think of alternative terms. You should broaden your search term to "Animals." When you look under "Animals," you will find the subtopic "Injuries—Running at Large." This entry will lead you to Animals key numbers 52–55 (Figure 2.6a). Next you will pull the digest volume marked "Animals" off the shelf and turn to key numbers 52–55. You will then note that key number 54 is applicable (Figure 2.6b).

Topic Method

The digests can also be used in other ways. If you had analyzed your legal problem in terms of subject areas, such as animals, you could then go directly to the volume of the digest entitled "Animals." Next you would read through the summary of contents or analysis that appears at the beginning of the text of each topic until you find the appropriate entry (Figure 2.7). The topic approach is only useful for someone who knows the legal topics involved in the problem, however. As a beginning researcher, if you use the topic method, you probably will not select the proper topic and key numbers because you are not yet well acquainted with all of the subject possibilities.

Figure 2.6 Using the Descriptive-Word Index to Find Key Numbers

(a) Listings in Descriptive Word Index

37 Wash D 2d—79

ANIMALS

References are to Digest Topics and Key Numbers

ANIMALS—Cont'd
DESTRUCTION of diseased animals. **Anim 32**
DETINUE, killing or injuring animals. **Anim 44**
DISEASES. **Anim 28–37**
　Lessee's liability for destruction of barn used for
　　glandered horses. **Land & Ten 134**
　Vaccination by stockyards company. **Wareh 8**
DISTRAINING trespassing animals. **Anim 95, 100(5)**
DRIVING from range of pasture. **Anim 14**
DRIVING off trespassing animals. **Anim 94**
DUTIES of owners, stock laws. **Anim 50(3)**
ELECTIONS, stock law election. **Anim 50(2)**
ESTRAYS, see this index Estrays
EVIDENCE—
　Actions for—
　　Damages caused by trespassing animals. **Anim 100(4)**
　　Personal injuries caused by animals. **Anim 74(3–5)**
　Condition of animal. **Evid 477(5)**
　Damages for loss or injury. **Damag 174(2)**
　Judicial notice of—
　　Phenomena of animal life. **Evid 13**
　Ownership. **Anim 3, 10**
　Value or market price. **Evid 113(22)**

ANIMALS—Cont'd
INJURIES by or to animals—Cont'd
　Railroads injuring animals, see this index **Railroads**
　Running at large. **Anim 52–55**
　　Evidence, similar transactions. **Evid 141**
　Statutory regulations. **Anim 79**
　Street railroad injuring animals, see this index **Street
　　Railroads**
　Trespassing animals. **Anim 96**
INSPECTION—
　Officers. **Inspect 4**
INSTRUCTIONS to jury—
　Personal injuries. **Anim 74(7)**
INSURANCE of livestock. **Insurance 426**
JUDGMENT in actions for injuries caused by tres-
　　passing animals. **Anim 100(9)**
JUDICIAL notice—
　Phenomena of animal life. **Evid 13**
KEEPING and use, municipal regulations. **Mun Corp 604,
　　631(3)**
KILLING. **Anim 43–45**
　Animals running at large. **Anim 52**
　Trespassing animals. **Anim 96**
　Vicious animals. **Anim 73, 84**

Figure 2.6   Using the Descriptive-Word Index to Find Key Numbers (continued)

(b) Digest
Entries
under a
Key Number

---

1 Wash D 2d—515   **ANIMALS** ☞68

For references to other topics, see Descriptive-Word Index

value of use and occupation thereof.   RCW 16.24.070.
    MacKenzie-Richardson, Inc. v. Allert, 272 P.2d 146, 45 Wash.2d 1.

Wash. 1927.   To recover for dog bite, it must be shown that dog was wrongfully on sidewalk.
    Shelby v. Seung, 257 P. 838, 144 Wash. 317.

Recovery for injuries for dog bite held improperly allowed without showing dog was wrongfully on street.
    Shelby v. Seung, 257 P. 838, 144 Wash. 317.

Wash. 1906.   The owner of a steer who has knowledge of its dangerous character is liable for injuries inflicted by the steer while running at large, irrespective of whether the owner was negligent in securing the steer.
    Harris v. Carstens Packing Co., 86 P. 1125, 43 Wash. 647, 6 L.R.A., N.S., 1164.

☞**54. —— Persons liable for injuries.**

Wash.App. 1987.   Although owner of pit bulls was negligent in allowing them to run loose, humane society, which had been contractually delegated authority to enforce animal regulations of city's ordinance, could be liable for its later negligence, if any, in failing to apprehend the pit bulls.
    Champagne v. Spokane Humane Soc., 737 P.2d 1279, 47 Wash.App. 887, review denied.

Evidence that defendant was running in excess of 300 head of cattle on approximately 12,000 acres of leased pasture, that county road ran through the pasture for four miles, that there was no fence separating pasture from the road, that it was necessary for cattle to cross road to reach watering place, that cattle were frequently observed on the road with no herdsman tending them and that herdsman, who patrolled the entire tract, ordinarily made only one daily check of the road, warranted misdemeanor conviction of owner for permitting his cattle to run at large and not under the care of a herder.   West's RCWA 16.13.010.
    State v. Dear, 638 P.2d 85, 96 Wash.2d 652.

☞**58–66.**   *For other cases see the Decennial Digests and WESTLAW.*

Library references
    C.J.S. Animals.

☞**66. Personal injuries.**

Library references
    C.J.S. Animals §§ 170, 177.

☞**67. —— Domestic animals in general.**

Wash. 1980.   Negligence cause of action against animal owner arises when there is ineffective control of an animal in a situation where it would reasonably be expected that an injury could occur and injury does proximately result from the negligence; amount of control required is that which would be exercised by a reasonable person based on the total situation at the time, including the past behavior of the animal and the injuries that could have been

---

Finding a Case by Case Name

If you know the name of the case that you want to read, you have only to look in the Table of Cases in any digest. This table is easy to use and will lead you to the correct reporter and page number (Figure 2.8).

When you know the jurisdiction, use the Table of Cases volumes at the end of the digest for that jurisdiction. Every digest has its own Table of Cases. If you do not know the jurisdiction, but do know the approximate year, use the Table of Cases in West's American Digest System, which consists of the *Decennial Digest* and the *General Digest*.

In addition to providing you with the correct citation to the case, the Table of Cases also lists all key numbers under which that case has been digested. Note that the entry for *Champagne v. Spokane Humane Society* in the Table of Cases in Figure 2.8 lists Animals key number 54. Therefore, from

Figure 2.7   Using the Topic Method to Find Key Numbers

ANIMALS   1 Wash D 2d—504

20. —— Right to offspring.
21. Agistment, keeping, and care.
22. —— Rights and duties in general.
23. —— Loss of or injuries to animals.
   (1). In general.
   (2). Actions.
24. —— Injuries by animals.
25. —— Compensation.
26. —— Lien.
   (1). Existence, nature and incidents.
   (2). Persons entitled to lien.
   (3). Persons liable and property subject to lien.
   (4). Waiver and extinguishment.
   (5). Enforcement.

51. —— Impounding animals at large.
52. —— Killing or injuring animals at large.
53. —— Injuries by animals at large.
54. —— Persons liable for injuries.
55. —— Actions.
56. —— Penalties for violations of regulations.
57. —— Criminal prosecutions.
58. Estrays.

Figure 2.8   Finding a Case in the Table of Cases

40 Wash D 2d—87   **CHAPMAN**

References are to Digest Topics and Key Numbers

Chamberlain v. Cobb, Wash, 225 P 414, 129 Wash 549.—Bills & N 398.
Chamberlain v. Geer, Wash, 237 P 719, 135 Wash 340.—Bills & N 342, 378.
Chamberlain v. Piercy, Wash, 143 P 977, 82 Wash 157.—Bankr 3066(1), 3066(5); Corp 228, 259(7).
Chamberlain v. Winn, Wash, 24 P 446, 1 Wash 259.—Replev 91.
Chamberlain & Co. v. French, Wash, 230 P 837, 131 Wash 394.   See Northern Cedar Co v. French.
Chamberlain & Co v. Gloyd 46 SCt 204, 270 US 625, 70 LEd 767.   Mem.
Chamberlin v. Chamberlin, Wash, 270 P2d 464, 44 Wash2d 689, 68 ALR2d 457.—Divorce 145, 146, 151, 184(5); Pretrial Proc 713, 722, 724.
Chamberlin v. Winn, Wash, 24 P 446, 1 Wash 259. See Chamberlain v. Winn.
Chamberlin v. Winn, Wash, 20 P 780, 1 Wash 501, aff Chamberlain v. Winn, 24 P 446, 1 Wash 259.—Replev 69(4); Sales 147.
Chambers v. Calvin Philips & Co., Wash, 312 P2d 659, 50 Wash2d 413.—Corp 1.6(3); Trusts 167, 262.
Chambers v. Carlyon, Wash, 62 P2d 726, 188 Wash 352.—Corp 123(24); Plgs 56(4).
Chambers v. City of Mount Vernon, WashApp, 522 P2d 1184, 11 WashApp 357.—Health & E 25.15(10); Mun Corp 722; Nuis 85.

Chamness v. Marquis, Wash, 383 P2d 886, 62 Wash2d 509.—App & E 717, 1071.1(1); Brok 56(3), 84(1), 85(2), 86(4).
Chamness Realty v. Marquis 62 Wash2d 509, 383 P2d 886. See Chamness v. Marquis.
Champa v. Washington Compressed Gas Co., Wash, 262 P 228, 146 Wash 190.—Damag 62(1); Nuis 3(6), 4, 50(5), 54.
Champagne v. Birnot, Wash, 254 P 829, 143 Wash 187.—App & E 415; Chat Mtg 138(2).
Champagne v. Department of Labor and Industries, Wash, 156 P2d 422, 22 Wash2d 412.—Trial 182, 260(1); Work Comp 1853, 1911, 1929.
Champagne v. Hygrade Food Products, Inc., DCWash, 79 FRD 671.—Fed Civ Proc 1372.
Champagne v. McDonald, Wash, 251 P 874, 141 Wash 617.—Accord 8(1).
Champagne v. Spokane Humane Soc., WashApp, 737 P2d 1279, 47 WashApp 887, review den.—Anim 54; Judgm 181(33); Mun Corp 723, 751(1); Neglig 61(1).
Champ Arcade v. City of Seattle 86 Wash2d 395, 544 P2d 1242. See Bitts, Inc v. City of Seattle.
Champion v. Shoreline School Dist. No. 412 of King County, Wash, 504 P2d 304, 81 Wash2d 672.—Schools 63(1), 130, 147.34(1); Statut 181(1), 208, 223.-2(1).

Contracts 176(1); Damag 76, 78(1); Evid 80(1); Frds St of 130(1), 130(2); Impl & C C 81; Motions 51; Plead 34(1), 53(2), 214(2), 214(4), 354.
Chandler v. Gallemore, Wash, 43 P2d 968, 181 Wash 345.—Corp 80(12), 261, 263(2).
Chandler v. Humphrey, Wash, 31 P2d 1012, 177 Wash 402.—Corp 217; Lim of Act 2(1).
Chandler v. Miller, Wash, 19 P2d 1108, 172 Wash 252.—Corp 80(12), 247, 262(1), 262(2), 269(2); Plead 147.
Chandler v. Miller, Wash, 13 P2d 22, 168 Wash 563.—Corp 262(1), 563(2); Judgm 822(3).
Chandler v. Otto, Wash, 693 P2d 71, 103 Wash2d 268.—Mun Corp 159(5); Offic 70½.
Chandler v. Washington Toll Bridge Authority, Wash, 137 P2d 97, 17 Wash2d 591.—Bridges 5, 20(1), 20(2), 20(4), 20(5), 20(6); Contracts 4, 5, 187(1); Impl & C C 1, 2, 3, 4.
Chaney v. Chaney, Wash, 105 P 229, 56 Wash 145.—App & E 655(1), 1074(3); Divorce 161, 167.
Chantler v. Hubbell, Wash, 75 P 802, 34 Wash 211.—Fraud Conv 176(2); Trusts 96.
Chantry, In re, Wash, 524 P2d 909, 84 Wash2d 153.—Atty & C 61.
Chantry, In re, Wash, 407 P2d 160, 67 Wash2d 190.—Atty & C 32(2), 58.
Chaoussis' Estate, In re, Wash, 247 P 732, 139 Wash 479.—Ex & Ad 24.

Figure 2.9   A Table of Cases Reported in an Advance Sheet

CUMULATIVE CASES REPORTED

793 P.2d

(Cases in bold type appear in this issue)

ALASKA
(Cases in this issue, pp. 1025–1085)

	Page		Page
A., In re—Alaska	1033	**D.J.A., In re**—Alaska	1033
Alam v. State—Alaska App.	1081	F/V Chicamin—Alaska	69
Alascom, Inc. v. Alaska Public Utilities Com'n—Alaska	1028	**Gutierres v. State**—Alaska App.	1078
		McCormick v. Smith—Alaska	1042
Alaska Consumer Advocacy Program v. Alaska Public Utilities Com'n—Alaska	1028	Murat v. F/V Shelikof Strait—Alaska	69
		Napayonak v. State—Alaska App.	1059
		Russell v. State—Alaska App.	1085
Caucus Distributors, Inc. v. State, Dept. of Commerce and Economic Development, Div. of Banking, Securities and Corporations—Alaska	1048	Shapiro v. State—Alaska App.	535
		State v. Chryst—Alaska App.	538
		State v. Echols—Alaska App.	1066
City of Valdez v. State, Dept. of Community & Regional Affairs—Alaska	532	**State, Dept. of Revenue v. Gazaway**—Alaska	1025
		Taylor v. State—Alaska App.	1078
Davis v. State—Alaska App.	1064	Valdez, City of, v. State, Dept. of Community & Regional Affairs—Alaska	532

the entry in the Table of Cases, you can go to the digest and find related cases under the appropriate topic and key number.

If the case was decided during the previous year, you may find the citation through the pocket parts to the Table of Cases in the digests, or you may have to check the Cases Reported tables in the advance sheets to the reporter in which you expect the case to appear (Figure 2.9).

What if you only know the defendant's name in a case? Check the Defendant-Plaintiff Table in the state and federal digests (Figure 2.10). The regional digests do not contain Defendant-Plaintiff Tables.

Searching for Cases Using WESTLAW

Now that you understand how to find a case through the West digests, let's look at different ways of finding cases using WESTLAW: finding a case with a citation; retrieving cases using either the WIN Natural Language or the Terms and Connectors search method; and topic and key number searching. You may find it helpful to read or review the appendix at the end of this book to learn how to search for cases using WIN or Terms and Connectors. In the rest of this chapter, our focus will be on how to apply each of these different methods of searching.

Figure 2.10   A Defendant-Plaintiff Table

SPOKANE

References are to Digest Topics and Key Numbers

41 Wash D 2d—404

AND FOR—State, Wash, 177 P 654, 105 Wash 49.

SPOKANE COUNTY, SUPERIOR COURT OF WASHINGTON IN AND FOR—State, Wash, 174 P 646, 103 Wash 402.

SPOKANE COUNTY, SUPERIOR COURT OF WASHINGTON IN AND FOR—State, Wash, 147 P 436, 85 Wash 72.

SPOKANE COUNTY, SUPREME COURT OF—State, Wash, 34 P 930, 7 Wash 234.

SPOKANE COUNTY, TAXPAYERS OF—Spokane County, 85 Wash2d 216, 533 P2d 128.

SPOKANE COUNTY, TAXPAYERS OF—Spokane County, 84 Wash2d 475, 527 P2d 263.

SPOKANE COUNTY, TAXPAYERS OF, AND WITHIN, SCHOOL DIST. NO. 81 OF—School Dist. No. 81 of Spokane County, Wash, 225 P2d 1063, 37 Wash2d 669.

SPOKANE COUNTY, WASH.—Dodd, CAWash, 393 F2d 330.

SPOKANE CULVERT & FABRICATING CO.—Novenson, Wash, 588 P2d 1174, 91 Wash2d 550.

SPOKANE CYCLE & AUTO SUPPLY CO.—Maskell, Wash, 170 P 350, 100 Wash 16.

SPOKANE DAIRY PRODUCTS CO.—Royal Dairy Products Co., Wash, 225 P 412, 129 Wash 424.

SPOKANE DRUG CO.—Adams, CCWash, 57 F 888.

SPOKANE DRY GOODS CO.—Spokane Merchants' Ass'n, Wash, 299 P 371, 162 Wash 577.

SPOKANE DRY GOODS CO.—U.S., DCWash, 264 F 209.

SPOKANE, EACH AND EVERY LOT IN CITY OF—Spokane County, Wash, 13 P2d 1084, 169 Wash 355.

SPOKANE FALLS & N. RY.—Williams, Wash, 87 P 491, 44 Wash 363.

SPOKANE FALLS & N. RY. CO.—Fleutsch, Wash, 6 Wash 623, 34 P 150.

SPOKANE FALLS & N. RY. CO.—Flutsch, Wash, 6 Wash 623, 34 P 150.

SPOKANE FALLS & N. RY. CO.—Allend, Wash, 58 P 244, 21 Wash 324.

SPOKANE FALLS & N. RY. CO.—Dunkle, Wash, 55 P 51, 20 Wash 254.

SPOKANE FALLS & NORTHERN RY. CO.—Taylor, Wash, 73 P 499, 32 Wash 450.

SPOKANE FALLS & N. RY. CO.—Williams, Wash, 84 P 1129, 42 Wash 597.

SPOKANE FALLS & N. RY. CO.—Williams, Wash, 80 P 1100, 39 Wash 77.

SPOKANE FALLS, CITY OF—Curry, Wash, 27 P 477, 2 Wash 541.

SPOKANE FALLS, CITY OF—Spokane St. Ry. Co., CCWash, 46 F 322.

SPOKANE FALLS, CITY OF—Spokane Street Railway Co., Wash, 33 P 1072, 6 Wash 521.

SPOKANE FALLS, CITY OF—State, Wash, 25 P 903, 2 Wash 40.

SPOKANE FALLS, CITY OF—Town of Denver, Wash, 34 P 926, 7 Wash 226.

SPOKANE FALLS GASLIGHT CO.—Theis, Wash, 95 P 1074, 49 Wash 477.

SPOKANE FALLS GASLIGHT CO.—Theis, Wash, 74 P 1004, 34 Wash 23.

SPOKANE FUEL DEALERS CREDIT ASS'N—U.S., DCWash, 55 FSupp 387.

SPOKANE GAS & FUEL CO.—City of Spokane, Wash, 47 P2d 671, 182 Wash 475.

SPOKANE GAS & FUEL CO.—City of Spokane, Wash, 26 P2d 1034, 175 Wash 103.

SPOKANE GAS & FUEL CO.—Cole, Wash, 119 P 831, 66 Wash 393.

SPOKANE GAS & FUEL CO.—Jobe, Wash, 131 P 235, 73 Wash 1, 48 LRANS 931.

SPOKANE GRAIN CO.—Frederick & Nelson, Wash, 91 P 570, 47 Wash 85.

SPOKANE HARDWARE CO.—Conlan, Wash, 201 P 26, 117 Wash 378.

SPOKANE, HOME TEL. & TEL. CO. OF—Cavers, Wash, 201 P 20, 117 Wash 299.

SPOKANE, HOME TEL. & TEL. CO. OF—State, Wash, 172 P 899, 102 Wash 196.

SPOKANE HUMANE SOC.—Champagne, WashApp, 737 P2d 1279, 47 WashApp 887.

SPOKANE HYDRAULIC CO.—Cunningham, Wash, 52 P 235, 18 Wash 524.

SPOKANE INTERN. RY. CO.—Neitzel, Wash, 141 P 186, 80 Wash 30.

SPOKANE INTERN. RY. CO.—Neitzel, Wash, 117 P 864, 65 Wash 100, 36 LRA,NS, 522.

SPOKANE INTERN. RY. CO.—Pierce, Wash, 131 P2d 139, 15 Wash2d 431.

SPOKANE-INTERNATIONAL RY. CO.—Schaefer, Wash, 188 P 530, 110 Wash 316.

SPOKANE INTERN. RY. CO.—Walters, Wash, 108 P 593, 58 Wash 293, 42 LRA,NS, 917.

SPOKANE INTERN. R. CO.—McEwen, CAWash, 325 F2d 491.

SPOKANE INTERSTATE FAIR—Polk, Wash, 132 P 401, 73 Wash 610.

SPOKANE INTERSTATE FAIR ASS'N—Fidelity & Deposit Co. of Md., CCAWash, 8 F2d 224, 44 ALR 468.

SPOKANE JOBBERS' ASS'N—Hoffman, Wash, 102 P 1045, 54 Wash 179.

SPOKANE KNITTING MILLS—Jantzen Knitting Mills, DCWash, 44 F2d 656.

SPOKANE, LOCAL NO. 400 OF COOKS AND HELPERS, WAITERS AND WAITRESSES OF—Adams, Wash, 215 P 19, 124 Wash 564.

SPOKANE LODGE NO. 228, BENEV. AND PROTECTIVE ORDER OF ELKS—Local Joint Executive Bd. of Spokane, CAWash, 443 F2d 403.

SPOKANE MERCANTILE CO.—Burnham, Wash, 51 P 363, 18 Wash 207.

SPOKANE MERCHANTS' ASS'N—Fidelity & Deposit Co. of Maryland, Wash, 157 P 464, 91 Wash 170.

SPOKANE MERCHANTS' ASS'N—Kasper, Wash, 151 P 800, 87 Wash 447.

SPOKANE MERCHANT'S ASS'N—Kriegler, Wash, 189 P 1004, 111 Wash 179.

SPOKANE MILL CO.—U. S., DCWash, 206 F 999.

SPOKANE MORTG. CO.—Ellingson, WashApp, 573 P2d 389, 19 WashApp 48.

SPOKANE NAT. BANK—Grant, CCWash, 47 F 673.

SPOKANE NAT. BANK—Weber, CCAWash, 64 F 208, 12 CCA 93.

SPOKANE NAT. BANK—Weber, CCAWash, 50 F 735.

Finding a Case on WESTLAW with a Citation

If you have a citation of a case in a reporter or a WESTLAW cite and you want to find the case on WESTLAW, it is easily retrievable by the Find service. Find allows you to retrieve a document from anywhere in WESTLAW by simply entering its citation. There is no need to access a database; just type Find. For example, if you know the citation of one of the Washington cases in which a pit bull bit a child, *Champagne v. Spokane Humane Society*, 47 Wash.App. 887, 737 P.2d 1279 (1987), type

```
fi 47 wash.app. 887
```

or

```
fi 737 p.2d 1279
```

Searching for Cases on WESTLAW by Subject

In our example of how to find a case through the digests, we started with the clue that you remembered reading about a relevant "pit bull" case that took place in the state of Washington. With the same clue, you can search WEST-LAW for relevant cases. Actually, with one specific piece of information about a case, you can easily retrieve cases by telling the computer to look for that unique term. To find Washington cases mentioning pit bulls, you simply access the Washington cases database **wa-cs** and type

pit-bull

using the Terms and Connectors search method. Figure 2.11 shows the results of your search.

Figure 2.11 Retrieving Cases Using the Terms and Connectors Method

```
Citation              Rank(R)         Page(P)          Database       Mode
791 P.2d 257          R 1 OF 3        P 1 OF 13        WA-CS          T
58 Wash.App. 32
(Cite as: 791 P.2d 257)
                          Marci J. CLEMMONS, Appellant,
                                       v.
                      Clarence FIDLER, et al., Respondents.
                              No. 12774-1-II.
                      Court of Appeals of Washington,
                               Division 2.
                              May 24, 1990.
   Guest of tenants brought action against landlord for harm caused by tenants'
dog, who bit face of guest's baby.  The Superior Court, Clallam County, James
I. Maddock, J. pro tem., entered summary judgment in favor of landlord, and
appeal was taken. The Court of Appeals, Worswick, J., held that landlord was
not liable for harm caused by tenants' dog irrespective of his knowledge of dog
and its tendencies.
   Affirmed.
```

```
791 P.2d 257          R 1 OF 3        P 5 OF 13        WA-CS          Term
(CITE AS: 791 P.2D 257, *258)
   *258 Lane J. Wolfley, Wolfley, Kogut & Herdt, Port Angeles, for
appellant.
   D. Michael Reilly, Lane, Powell, Moss & Miller, Seattle, for respondents.

   WORSWICK, Judge.
   We are asked to extend the common law rule concerning liability for dog
bites by holding that a landlord is liable for harm caused by his tenant's dog
if the landlord knows that the dog has vicious tendencies.  We decline, and we
affirm a summary judgment dismissing Marci Clemmons' claim against Clarence
Fidler.
   Terry Calhoun had no pets when she rented a single family house in Forks from
Clarence Fidler on an oral month-to-month tenancy.  Later, she married Mike
Philbrook and the Philbrooks acquired a PIT BULL named Popeye, which they kept
chained to a truck axle in the yard of the Fidler house.  Whether Popeye could
reach walkways to the house while chained is disputed.  The Philbrooks posted
warning signs in the yard, but the animal nevertheless apparently attacked
several neighborhood children before the incident that brought about this
suit.  Several neighbors claim that they complained to Fidler about the dog.
Fidler acknowledges that he knew the Philbrooks kept a dog, but he denies that
he knew the dog was vicious.
   On April 16, 1987, the Philbrooks had a beer party.  Marci Clemmons came,
                COPR. (C) WEST 1993 NO CLAIM TO ORIG. U.S. GOVT. WORKS
```

Rather than a specific piece of information, you may have an issue. In that case, use the WIN Natural Language search method. For example, to find cases about whether a humane society that failed to enforce the city's leash law is responsible for an injury to a child caused by a pit bull, simply type a description of your issue:

Is the humane society liable for not enforcing the city's leash law?

WESTLAW then retrieves the 20 cases in your database that have the highest statistical likelihood (that's a bit of computer jargon) of matching the concepts in your issue description, starting with the most relevant (Figure 2.12).

When using WESTLAW, it is not necessary to translate specific fact situations into legal concepts. This is a very important point that can be illustrated by an example. Assume that a student is distributing political literature on a private college campus. The college president has ordered her to stop these activities, and she refuses. To locate cases on this issue in the **NJ-CS** database, enter your WIN Natural Language description:

Can political literature be distributed on campus?

As you can see from the results of your search in Figure 2.13, it is not necessary to translate the specific fact situation of distributing political literature into the legal concept of the First Amendment right to free speech.

Searching for Cases on WESTLAW Using Fields

Almost all WESTLAW documents are divided into several parts called fields. For example, the title, synopsis, topic, and the name of the judge and attorneys in a case are each considered a separate field. You can narrow your search to look for terms in a specific field instead of in an entire case. The only

Figure 2.12   Retrieving Cases Using the WIN Natural Language Search Method

```
Citation                Rank(R)           Page(P)          Database      Mode
737 P.2d 1279           R 1 OF 20         P 1 OF 25        WA-CS         T
47 Wash.App. 887
(Cite as: 737 P.2d 1279)
John CHAMPAGNE and Roxie Champagne, husband and wife, as Parents and Guardians
of John Douglas Champagne, a Minor;   and Roger A. Felice, as Guardian Ad Litem
                    of John Douglas Champagne, Appellants,
                                    v.
SPOKANE HUMANE SOCIETY and Society for the Prevention of Cruelty to Animals, a
              Non-Profit Corporation, Respondents.
                          No. 7709-8-III.
                  Court of Appeals of Washington,
                            Division 3.
                          May 28, 1987.
                  Review Denied Sept. 1, 1987.
 Parents brought suit on behalf of their son against humane society for
personal injuries resulting from attack on their child by a pit bull.  The
Superior Court, Spokane County, Thomas Merryman, J., dismissed claim on summary
judgment holding that action was barred by public duty doctrine, and parents
appealed.  The Court of Appeals, Munson, J., held that there was issue of
material fact as to each element of special relationship exception to public
duty doctrine, and as to society's duty of care and whether such duty was met,
precluding summary judgment.
              COPR. (C) WEST 1993 NO CLAIM TO ORIG. U.S. GOVT. WORKS
```

Figure 2.13 Describing a Specific Fact Situation

```
Citation              Rank(R)          Page(P)         Database      Mode
423 A.2d 615          R 1 OF 20        P 1 OF 90       NJ-CS         T
(Cite as: 84 N.J. 535,  423 A.2d 615)
                     STATE of New Jersey, Plaintiff-Respondent,
                                         v.
                          Chris SCHMID, Defendant-Appellant.
                            Supreme Court of New Jersey.
                               Argued Feb. 4, 1980.
                               Decided Nov. 25, 1980.
        Defendant was found guilty in the Superior Court, Law Division, of trespass.
     Following certification of the case while defendant's appeal was pending in the
     Appellate Division, the Supreme Court, Handler, J., held that: (1) university,
     which was predominantly private, unregulated and autonomous in its character
     and functioning as institution of higher education, was not subject to First
     Amendment obligations by virtue of joint relationship with or direct regulation
     by State, but (2) private university's regulations which were devoid of
     reasonable standards designed to protect both legitimate interest of the
     university as institution of higher education and individual exercise of
     expressional freedom, could not constitutionally be invoked to prohibit
     otherwise noninjurious and reasonable exercise of such freedom, and thus the
     university violated state constitutional rights of defendant by evicting him
     and securing his arrest for distributing political literature upon its campus.
                COPR. (C) WEST 1993 NO CLAIM TO ORIG. U.S. GOVT. WORKS
```

limitation is that you must use the Terms and Connectors search method rather than WIN within each field. To find out which fields are available for a specific database, type **f** while you are in that database (Figure 2.14). We will illustrate a few of the case law field restrictions:

■ *Title field:* It is extremely easy to search for the text of a case by its case name on WESTLAW. Searching WESTLAW for recent cases is particularly efficient because the pocket part to the Table of Cases in the digests can be a year out of date depending on the time of year. When you wish to retrieve a case on WESTLAW, you can limit your search to the title field (**ti**) to retrieve a case by name. Since the title field includes the complete title, including first names and extra parties, you should select significant or unique names from the title and combine them with the "&" connector. For example, type

ti(champagne & spokane)

Figure 2.14 Fields for a Case Law Database

```
                              FIELDS
        TI  TITLE        CO  COURT       TO  TOPIC      DI  DIGEST
        CI  CITATION     JU  JUDGE       HE  HEADNOTE   IM  IMAGE
        SY  SYNOPSIS     AT  ATTORNEY    OP  OPINION

     If you wish to:
        Limit your search to a specific field or fields, use a field restriction
           in your query, e.g., TI(MIRANDA & ARIZONA)
        Limit your search by date, add a date restriction to your query with the
           & connector, e.g., DA(3/91) & your query
        Return to the Enter Query screen, press ENTER
```

to retrieve one of the Washington pit bull cases. If you do not use a title field restriction, you will probably retrieve your case, but you will also retrieve any case where your case was cited, plus many totally irrelevant documents.

■ *Synopsis field:* West's editors write a synopsis for each case published in the West reporters. This information appears in the synopsis field (**sy**) on WESTLAW. Generally, a synopsis includes a review of the facts presented in the case; the name and holding of the lower court judge; the holding of the court in the case; and the names of the dissenting and concurring judges. Since the synopsis summarizes the procedural issues of a case, use the synopsis field restriction when a procedural issue is important. For example, to retrieve cases where the opinions of a particular trial court judge have been reversed, access the **wa-cs** database and type

sy(merryman & reversed)

Slip opinions, unreported cases, and cases not published by West generally do not have synopses. The synopses are added to cases published by West within a few weeks. Therefore, if you wish to retrieve very recent opinions, do not use the synopsis field restriction—simply search in the database without using any field restrictions.

■ *Topic field:* Headnotes for cases published by West are classified by West editors under as many digest topics as apply. When searching on WESTLAW, you can retrieve all cases containing a headnote classified under a specific West digest topic by restricting your search to the topic field (**to**). All digest topics on WESTLAW are numbered; you can use the topic number in a topic field restriction to retrieve all cases with a headnote on your topic. For instance, **to(28)** would retrieve all cases with a headnote addressing issues involving animals. A list of the digest topics and their numerical equivalents is located in Appendix A of the *WESTLAW Reference Manual* and in the Key Number service on WESTLAW.

The topic field includes not only the West digest topic number, but also the topic name, the digest classification hierarchy, the key number, and the text of the key line for each key number (Figure 2.15). Consequently, topic searches are effective when you may not be certain which specific key number is relevant. You can still search the *language* describing your specific legal issue to which a key number has been assigned. Within the topic field, combine a topic name or number with words describing your issue. For example, access the **wa-cs** database and type

to(28 /p injur! /p liab!)

You will retrieve Washington cases with headnotes classified under West digest topic number 28, the number for "Animals," where the topic field paragraph also contains forms of the words "injury" and "liability" (Figure 2.16).

Figure 2.15 Elements Included in the Topic Field

Topic Number and Name
Digest Classification Hierarchy
Key Number
Key Line

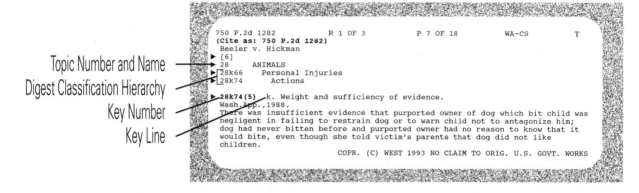

```
750 P.2d 1282            R 1 OF 3          P 7 OF 18        WA-CS        T
(Cite as: 750 P.2d 1282)
Beeler v. Hickman
[6]
28       ANIMALS
28k66       Personal Injuries
28k74          Actions

28k74(5)  k. Weight and sufficiency of evidence.
Wash.App.,1988.
There was insufficient evidence that purported owner of dog which bit child was
negligent in failing to restrain dog or to warn child not to antagonize him;
dog had never bitten before and purported owner had no reason to know that it
would bite, even though she told victim's parents that dog did not like
children.
                            COPR. (C) WEST 1993 NO CLAIM TO ORIG. U.S. GOVT. WORKS
```

■ *Digest field:* You may also want to restrict your search to the most important of fields, the digest field. The digest field contains all of the information provided in the topic field *plus* the text of the headnote. For searching purposes, all of the information in this field is considered to be in the same paragraph.

A digest search is particularly useful when your search contains common words, such as "contracts." By limiting your search to the digest field, you will avoid retrieving cases based on irrelevant occurrences of your search terms in the opinion.

Searching in the digest field also avoids the problem of judges who use idiosyncratic words or phrases. Since you use the computer to search for particular words, an unusual word usage by a judge can throw off your result. The editors at West use a standard vocabulary in the digest field to address this problem. For instance, if the judge refers to the "plaintiff" or "defendant" throughout a landlord-tenant opinion, West editors will use the words "landlord" or "tenant" in the headnotes.

Figure 2.16 Results of a Topic Field Search

```
613 P.2d 554            R 4 OF 8          P 3 OF 12        WA-CS        T
(Cite as: 613 P.2d 554)
Shafer v. Beyers
[2]
28       ANIMALS
28k66       Personal Injuries
28k72  k. Persons liable for injuries.
Wash.App., 1980.
Nonresident owners of rental property were not liable for injuries sustained by
pedestrian as result of attack by dog kept on premises by subtenant, even
though lease provided both that tenant was not to sublet apartment without
written consent of owners and that tenant was not to keep any dog on the
premises without owners' permission, where owners did not see or hear of the
dog until two or three days before date of the attack on the pedestrian.
West's RCWA 9.08.010, 16.08.040.
                            COPR. (C) WEST 1993 NO CLAIM TO ORIG. U.S. GOVT. WORKS
```

Searching in the digest field at the same time that you search the synopsis field can be very effective because the two fields contain summaries of the useful issues of the case. For example, if you are searching for cases involving the legal theory of assumption of risk in regard to a pit bull injury, you should search in the digest field and the synopsis field by typing

sy,di(assum! /p risk /p pit-bull)

- *Judge field:* On WESTLAW, you can search for cases authored by a particular judge by using the judge field (**ju**). The only catch is that the judge must have written the majority opinion. A judge field search does not retrieve an opinion where a judge dissented or concurred.
- *Attorney field:* If you are looking for cases that involve a particular attorney, you should search the attorney field. For example, to search for district court cases in which Griffin Bell represented a party, type

at(griffin +3 bell)

Searching for Cases on WESTLAW by Topic and Key Number

If you know a topic and key number, using WESTLAW in your search is a snap. Topic and key number searches let you quickly retrieve cases dealing with specific legal areas. With a topic and key number search, you can be sure of retrieving some cases that relate to your issue. Remember that the West digests are indexes of case law organized around topic and key numbers. A key number is a permanent number given to a specific point of law within an overall topic or area of law.

To perform a topic and key number search, you must find the relevant topic and key number using one of the following: the West digests, the on-line version of the digest topic and key number outline ("Key Number service"), or a known case. You must convert the topic name into the assigned topic number. Remember, to find the numerical equivalent of a West digest topic, you must first check Appendix. A of your *WESTLAW Reference Manual* or the Key Number service. For example, 28 is the number for the topic "Animals." After the topic number, add a **k** for the key number symbol. It is used on-line instead of the familiar key symbol in the digest. After the **k,** add the same key number that appeared in the digest or the Key Number service. For example, 54 stands for "Person liable for injuries." Thus, for your pit bull case, you would type **28k54** to retrieve cases on the issue of who is liable for injuries caused by animals (Figure 2.17).

You will find that by using topic and key number searches, you will retrieve cases dealing with very specific areas of law that will prove useful. These searches can be an effective supplement to word searches on WESTLAW.

Figure 2.17   Results of a Topic and Key Number Search

```
737 P.2d 1279          R 1 OF 1        P 11 OF 25        WA-CS        T
(Cite as: 737 P.2d 1279)
Champagne v. Spokane Humane Soc.
[9]
28      ANIMALS
28k47      Running at Large

28k54  k. Persons liable for injuries.
Wash.App.,1987.
Although owner of pit bulls was negligent in allowing them to run loose, humane
society, which had been contractually delegated authority to enforce animal
regulations of city's ordinance, could be liable for its later negligence, if
any, in failing to apprehend the pit bulls.
                        COPR. (C) WEST 1993 NO CLAIM TO ORIG. U.S. GOVT. WORKS
```

Choosing a Database

Once you have formulated your search a description of your issue for the WIN search method, a query for the Terms and Connectors method, or a topic and key number search—you are ready to sign on WESTLAW. Always spend time off-line preparing your search beforehand; it will prove to be time well spent in getting results once you sign on.

After signing on WESTLAW, the first thing you will do is choose a database. Use the WESTLAW Directory on-line and the Scope command to choose the best database for your search. The Directory provides the identifier for the databases in which you are interested. Use Scope to retrieve a detailed database description before accessing an unfamiliar database. Type **sc** followed by the database identifier to see the Scope information on your database. Once you have chosen a database, access the database simply by typing its identifier.

Browsing Cases on WESTLAW

Once you retrieve cases on WESTLAW, you must determine whether they are relevant to your issue. You can browse on-line in various ways.

When you run your search, your result will automatically be displayed in term mode. When you are in term mode, each time you press **Enter,** the next page or document portion containing your terms is displayed. The first page of each case is always displayed, whether it contains your search terms or not. You may choose to browse by page in page mode (**p**). If you have used the WIN search method to search for cases, you may also browse through your documents in best mode (**b**), stopping only at the statistically most relevant portion of each case. To move from one document to another, type **r** followed by the document rank number. The Locate command (**loc**) allows you to browse your result for a particular term, whether the term appeared in your original query or not.

Rather than viewing the text of the documents, you may want to print a list of the document citations. To do this, type **L**. Since your library will likely contain the reporters and other legal materials that you retrieve in WESTLAW, sign off the computer and turn to the books. It is very expensive to read the full text of the materials on-line.

You should be aware of a feature known as star paging. You may need to cite the exact page of the official *United States Reports*, even though you are using the unofficial *Supreme Court Reporter*. Star paging is a device used to indicate the precise word or letter with which the next page begins. In the printed *Supreme Court Reporter*, the number of the page in the official *United States Reports* is in the margin, and an upside down "T" symbol appears in the text at the point where the page break occurs in the official reporter (Figure 2.18).

Star paging is also available on WESTLAW where it allows you to view page numbers of cases as they appear in the bound volumes or the advance sheets of West's National Reporter System and the *United States Reports* or official reports from many states. Page numbers will appear highlighted within the text exactly where page breaks occur in the printed volumes (Figure 2.19).

Figure 2.18   Star Paging in the *Supreme Court Reporter*

1022   **105 SUPREME COURT REPORTER**   469 U.S. 559

eral labor regulation as applied to state railroad employees, 426 U.S., at 854, n. 18 [96 S.Ct., at 2475, n. 18], *National League of Cities* acknowledged that not all aspects of a State's sovereign authority are immune from federal control.'' 456 U.S., at 764, n. 28, 102 S.Ct., at 2153, n. 28.

tution itself. A unique feature of the United States is the *federal* system of government guaranteed by the Constitution and implicit in the very name of our country. Despite some genuflecting in the Court's opinion to the concept of federalism, today's decision effectively reduces the Tenth Amendment to meaningless rhetoric when

these cases.[3]

Whatever effect the Court's decision may have in weakening the application of *stare decisis*, it is likely to be less ⌐560⌐important than what the Court has done to the Consti-

2. Justice O'CONNOR, the only new member of the Court since our decision in *National League of Cities,* has joined the Court in reaffirming its principles. See *Transportation Union v. Long Island R. Co.,* 455 U.S. 678, 102 S.Ct. 1349, 71 L.Ed.2d 547 (1982), and *FERC v. Mississippi,* 456

the Court that *it* —an unelected majority of five Justices—today rejects almost 200 years of the understanding of the constitutional status of federalism. In doing so, there is only a single passing reference to

U.S. 742, 775, 102 S.Ct. 2126, 2145, 72 L.Ed.2d 532 (1982) (O'CONNOR, J., dissenting in part).

3. As one commentator noted, *stare decisis* represents "a natural evolution from the very nature of our institutions." Lile, Some Views on the Rule of *Stare Decisis,* 4 Va.L.Rev. 95, 97 (1916).

Figure 2.19   Star Paging on WESTLAW

```
105 S.Ct. 1005          FOUND DOCUMENT          P 55 OF 101          SCT          P
(Cite as: 469 U.S. 528, *559,   105 S.Ct. 1005, **1022)
      FN3. As one commentator noted, stare decisis represents "a natural
      evolution from the very nature of our institutions."  Lile, Some Views on
      the Rule of Stare Decisis, 4 Va.L.Rev. 95, 97 (1916).

      Whatever effect the Court's decision may have in weakening the application of
stare decisis, it is likely to be less *560 important than what the Court
has done to the Constitution itself.  A unique feature of the United States is
the federal system of government guaranteed by the Constitution and implicit
in the very name of our country.  Despite some genuflecting in the Court's
opinion to the concept of federalism, today's decision effectively reduces the
Tenth Amendment to meaningless rhetoric when Congress acts pursuant to the
Commerce Clause.  The Court holds that the Fair Labor Standards Act (FLSA)
"contravened no affirmative limit on Congress' power under the Commerce Clause"
to determine the wage rates and hours of employment of all state and local
employees.  Ante, at 1020.  In rejecting the traditional view of our federal
system, the Court states:
   "Apart from the limitation on federal authority inherent in the delegated
nature of Congress' Article I powers, the principal means chosen by the Framers
to ensure the role of the States in the federal system lies in the structure of
the Federal Government itself."  Ante, at 1018 (emphasis added).
   To leave no doubt about its intention, the Court renounces its decision in
                   COPR. (C) WEST 1993 NO CLAIM TO ORIG. U.S. GOVT. WORKS
```

Star Paging

Conclusion

You have just learned how to find cases using digests and on WESTLAW. We discussed how digests are put together and how to use them. We also introduced West topic and key numbers. The same topic and key numbers that appear in cases are the subject access points in the digests. We noted that West has individual sets of digests for almost all of the states in addition to several regional and federal digests and the mammoth *Decennial* and *General Digests*.

You also learned how to search on WESTLAW by entering a case law citation with the Find command, entering a description of your issue with WIN Natural Language, or restricting your Terms and Connectors search to particular case law fields. You learned how to conduct a topic and key number search on WESTLAW, using the advantages of the West digest indexing system on-line. WESTLAW gives you enormous flexibility in getting the best results.

3

Updating Case Law Research

F inding the law is only half of the legal research battle. Updating it is the second, and equally important, half. Because of the constant possibility of change in the law, systems have been created that help you determine the current status of any legal authority. The four methods that will be discussed in this chapter are *Shepard's Citations,* Shepard's PreView®, Quick-Cite™, and Insta-Cite.

Shepard's Citations

Case law is very dependent on precedent. Courts give deference to legal principles that have been established by prior decisions. Because of this respect for accumulated judicial wisdom, Frank Shepard developed a citation service more than one hundred years ago. It provides a method of historically tracking all references to a specific case in succeeding cases.

His service, *Shepard's Citations,* lists, in tabular form, all authority citing a specific authority. For case authority, it lists all cases (known as the *citing* cases) that have cited a specific case (known as the *cited* case). Figure 3.1 shows part of the table listing all cases that have cited the Supreme Court decision at 411 U.S. 1. For reasons given below, using *Shepard's* citators, a process called "Shepardizing™," is an essential part of legal practice. An eminent legal historian described the evolving dependence of the profession on *Shepard's Citations* thusly: "These red books, thick and thin, useful but unloved, became as familiar to lawyers as West's little keys."

Why *Shepard's Citations* Is Used

The first reason to use *Shepard's Citations* is to determine whether an authority—a U.S. Supreme Court decision, for example—on which you might be relying is still valid. Though the law is conservative, it does change at times; some of what was once "good law" is now "bad law." Thousands of cases in the two-hundred year history of American jurisprudence have been reversed or overruled by subsequent adjudications. These "bad" cases are still found in law books, and they are still in the on-line services.

Figure 3.1   A Portion of *Shepard's Citations* for *U.S. Reports*

Cited Case

Citing Cases

Vol. 410 — UNITED STATES SUPREME COURT REPORTS

501FS¹564	378A2d222	54CA3d801	495FS¹734	493FS1327	113Msc2d713	433US295	508F2d²498
Cir. 6	NM	115CaR311	e497FS¹400	546FS¹486	35NY185	433US410	d519F2d
473FS²338	96NM536	127CaR44	Cir. 2	Cir. 9	35NY191	434US¹381	[¹367
504FS474	632P2d1174	Colo	477F2d1115	540F2d1365	45NY808	434US391	537F2d564
Cir. 7	NY	193Col474	j498F2d807	591F2d¹1261	316NE862	435US221	554F2d¹497
h566F2d¹37	41Ap2d294	568P2d41	508F2d986	706F2d1527	316NE866	436US¹378	578F2d¹450
603F2d¹1269	41Ap2d297	Del	f532F2d¹873	358FS355	381NE337	436US¹663	614F2d2
419FS1310	83Ap2d92	314A2d212	575F2d382	390FS¹62	359S2d543	d438US¹290	638F2d¹268
Cir. 9	83Ap2d95	327A2d752	365FS¹52	88FRD¹542	359S2d549	j438US357	641F2d1012
559F2d¹1144	78Msc2d318	Mo	366FS793	Cir. 10	388S2d472	j438US¹357	649F2d²77
d613F2d¹183	116Msc2d990	574SW361	374FS248	f631F2d¹711	408S2d772	439US²70	659F2d¹282
613F2d²185	32NY240	NJ	379FS77	Cir. 11	409S2d130	j439US1053	671F2d4
j613F2d187	56NY310	74NJ353	382FS984	435FS1094	453S2d598	440US²97	699F2d²6
643F2d653	56NY315	378A2d222	382FS¹985	Ariz	Ohio	j440US114	e373FS635
f403FS⁴356	298NE71	NY	388FS253	132Az163	53@A217	440US¹199	373FS¹648
Cir. 11	437NE1092	41Ap2d297	394FS¹590	132Az167	373NE1278	j440US597	377FS621
719F2d1087	437NE1095	78Msc2d318	d402FS¹184	644P2d899	Pa	441US¹77	d377FS¹622
Ala	342S2d582	32NY240	f417FS845	644P2d903	255PaS365	j441US398	379FS²49
294Ala577	342S2d585	56NY311	417FS¹846	Calif	387A2d92	442US¹272	385FS¹400
319So2d704	356S2d993	298NE71	e443FS323	131CA3d104	PR	446US¹76	388FS²393
Ariz	444S2d963	437NE1093	457FS¹299	182CaR234	110DPR261	j446US113	388FS²1035
135Az151	444S2d965	342S2d585	f497FS¹423	Colo	Tenn	447US¹462	390FS1316
25AzA146	452S2d335	344S2d890	e550FS¹1034	184Col76	633SW307	448US¹323	390FS¹1317
541P2d937	452S2d338	356S2d993	Cir. 3	186Col63	Wash	j448US341	392FS¹302
659P2d1296	456S2d935	452S2d336	502F2d¹1128	518P2d810	93W2d703	448US¹518	e392FS¹1141
Calif	RI	SD	552F2d538	525P2d466	611P2d1258	448US¹588	395FS²627
32CA3d64	433A2d174	260NW641	365FS363	Conn	Wis	448US¹1329	396FS¹1296
40CA3d659	SD	287NW484	382FS¹387	175Ct561	93Wis2d504	449US¹174	396FS²1298
51CA3d678	260NW641	Wyo	d393FS123	400A2d720	287NW532	j449US188	406FS¹855
54CA3d801	287NW484	575P2d1112	j393FS¹126	DC	W Va	450US¹230	415FS²495
17C3d666	Tex	656P2d1145	399FS¹1262	324A2d189	233SE423	j450US243	j415FS¹505
17C3d670	636SW489		501FS782	Fla	270SE645	450US²478	j415FS²506
32C3d800	Utah	**– 752 –**	501FS¹783	295So2d292		j451US35	f423FS¹1265
107CaR850	614P2d1239	(36LE1)	83FRD¹477	351So2d46	**Vol. 411**	457US9	435FS¹262
115CaR311	Wash	(93SC1245)	Cir. 4	Haw		457US¹217	439FS1128
124CaR655	87W2d547	US reh den	513F2d242	60H289	**– 1 –**	457US230	465FS²660
127CaR44	554P2d1067	in411US959	710F2d¹1181	588P2d920	(36LE16)	457US232	522FS206
131CaR658		e406US937	477FS¹323	Idaho	(93SC1278)	e457US¹235	536FS¹1388
131CaR660	**– 743 –**	s458F2d649	Cir. 5	97Ida202	US reh den	e457US¹239	561FS¹1057
187CaR412	(35LE675)	413US¹567	e498F2d¹247	541P2d626	in411US959	j457US245	Cir. 2
552P2d442	(93SC1237)	d414US¹59	506F2d819	Ill	s406US966	457US¹963	476F2d¹405
552P2d444	Wyo	j414US¹62	508F2d¹777	57Il2d84	s411US980	457US²969	j476F2d¹826
654P2d182	s490P2d1069	j414US¹65	526F2d288	309NE591	s337FS280	458US¹200	j476F2d¹828
Colo	cc500FS1323	414US530	541F2d1154	Ind	411US208	j458US214	d482F2d
193Col474	439US¹69	j414US535	580F2d752	422NE716	j411US928	458US¹486	[¹1336
568P2d41	451US¹364	j414US¹537	717F2d¹1493	Iowa	412US458	51USLW	489F2d¹1091
Del	j451US377	415US715	d377FS¹1020	211NW341	j412US461	[4170	489F2d²1091
314A2d212	Cir. 2	e415US¹731	d382FS¹807	Mass	413US462	j51USLW	e507F2d¹1068
327A2d752	497F2d728	j415US760	382FS¹816	368Mas823	j414US²432	[4322	j507F2d¹1073
Idaho	f503F2d1189	415US770	d396FS¹812	385Mas1206	414US656	51USLW	f508F2d¹1028
99Ida503	j503F2d1191	415US¹786	e402FS¹927	388Mas194	415US²271	[4585	554F2d¹538
584P2d648	d520F2d¹802	416US¹126	531FS764	389Mas937	j415US¹278	j51USLW	562F2d843
Ill	379FS¹1165	j418US¹68	546FS¹454	333NE382	415US375	[4779	562F2d²844
371Il2d940	382FS¹1233	419US¹401	Cir. 6	434NE963	415US¹539	4MJ802	j562F2d¹865
117Il2d566	385FS¹225	d421US¹300	519F2d¹404	446NE46	415US713	12MJ910	576F2d462
75Il2d582	427FS¹1191	j421US¹304	664F2d561	452NE1142	417US¹612	77TCt872	j579F2d181
347NE44	Cir. 3	424US30	666F2d¹1027	Mich	d418US²742	97FRD614	584F2d²604
389NE1167	493FS¹88	431US403	362FS¹32	412Mch582	j418US¹760	Cir. D.C.	601F2d¹1234
453NE943	Cir. 4	435US775	387FS¹1128	317NW4	j419US420	477F2d1182	601F2d²1238
Kan	d456FS¹1155	442US300	f419FS¹1007	Mo	j419US¹586	483F2d¹1317	696F2d¹223
231Kan642	Cir. 5	450US115	e424FS¹592	504SW88	420US¹538	525F2d561	715F2d¹783
648P2d715	485F2d¹1304	450US¹122	496FS209	Mont	426US324	593F2d¹1125	717F2d¹41
Mo	496F2d¹111	j450US131	499FS134	177Mt78	426US¹602	665F2d1233	357FS¹763
574SW361	498F2d¹1235	Cir. D.C.	d499FS¹137	580P2d448	426US²814	674F2d10	357FS²763
NJ	538F2d¹1083	378FS¹1235	Cir. 7	NJ	427US¹312	676F2d730	359FS²971
70NJ572	396FS¹813	Cir. 1	542F2d1280	81NJ70	j427US¹318	j676F2d753	360FS232
74NJ353	Cir. 7	f482F2d98	370FS68	81NJ78	427US506	686F2d²980	f361FS¹440
129Su244	f482F2d98	f482F2d¹100	73FRD112	149Su490	j429US¹216	d386FS1326	361FS¹1053
145Su375	h566F2d¹37	519F2d1366	Cir. 8	374A2d63	j429US¹259	430FS²822	f361FS²1327
152Su499	Cir. 9	358FS1198	637F2d1162	405A2d353	j430US515	426FS²136	362FS²660
322A2d844	559F2d1149	373FS¹631	385FS¹705	405A2d357	431US¹503	468FS²690	363FS669
362A2d24	613F2d¹183	417FS448	387FS¹402	NY	j432US15	488FS¹133	365FS²78
367A2d1195	j613F2d187	437FS443	404FS¹646	54Ap2d266	j432US459	Cir. 1	365FS²1167
378A2d67	Calif	460FS1044	424FS¹954	64Ap2d878	f432US¹470	482F2d¹99	366FS²739
	40CA3d660				433US291		*Continued*

36

You can find, for instance, the 1942 Supreme Court case of *Betts v. Brady* in any of the reporters for U.S. Supreme Court cases or in the **sct-old** database on WESTLAW. The case held that the Sixth Amendment did not apply to the states and that there is no absolute right to counsel in a state criminal trial. Nothing in those reports says *"This case has been overruled and is no longer good law."* If you found *Betts* in the court reports and stopped researching at this point, you would be convinced that a state has no obligation to provide an attorney for an indigent defendant in a criminal trial. If you Shepardize® *Betts v. Brady,* however, you will find that the case was overruled twenty years later by the Supreme Court in *Gideon v. Wainwright* (Figure 3.2 a and b).

Nothing is more damaging to your client's interests or your own professional reputation than to rest your arguments firmly on bad law. The first reason to Shepardize is to avoid such damage.

The second reason to Shepardize is to determine how a case has been *treated* by other cases. Aside from the question of being "good law" or "bad law," the value of a case may be strengthened or weakened by the interpretation subsequently given it by the same court and/or other courts. It may be that every court that has confronted a situation similar to the one in the cited case has chosen to construe that case narrowly. Although the case is still "good law," subsequent interpretations of it may make it less compelling authority. The precedential value of a case greatly depends on the treatment it has received by later cases.

A third, and final, reason to Shepardize is simply to find more cases. Citators are not comprehensive case-finding tools in the same way that West digests are, but because cases tend to cite the seminal case in a particular area of law, if you find the seminal case and Shepardize it, you are likely to discover numerous cases on the same issue.

Figure 3.2 Shepardizing *Betts v. Brady*

(a) Shepardizing on WESTLAW

```
                                    SHEPARD'S   (Rank 1 of 1)        Page 5 of 39
CITATIONS TO: 62 S.Ct. 1252
CITATOR: UNITED STATES CITATIONS
DIVISION: Supreme Court Reporter
Retrieval                                               Headnote
No.      -----Analysis------  ------Citation------       No.
  1    J   Dissenting Opin  81 S.Ct. 473, 495
  2    J   Dissenting Opin  81 S.Ct. 954, 977
  3                         82 S.Ct. 501, 507            7
  4                         82 S.Ct. 884, 891            6
  5    Q   Questioned       82 S.Ct. 884, 892            6
  6                         82 S.Ct. at 1259
  7                         83 S.Ct. 768, 770            7
  8                         83 S.Ct. 792, 793            7
  9    O   Overruled        83 S.Ct. 792, 794
 10                         83 S.Ct. 792, 799            7
 11    E   Explained        83 S.Ct. 792, 799            7
 12    J   Dissenting Opin  84 S.Ct. 80, 81              7
 13    Q   Questioned       84 S.Ct. 1489, 1492          7
 14    J   Dissenting Opin  84 S.Ct. 1489, 1503          6
 15    J   Dissenting Opin  84 S.Ct. 1774, 1797

Copyright (C) 1993 McGraw-Hill, Inc.; Copyright (C) 1993 West Publishing Co.
```

Figure 3.2 Shepardizing *Betts v. Brady* (continued)

(b) Shepardizing in the Hard Copy Volume

Citing Case—*Gideon v. Wainwright*

"o" indicates overruling.

Cited Case—*Betts v. Brady*

Vol. 316 **UNITED STATES SUPREME COURT REPORTS**

– 450 –	321US[7]115	e385US399	184FS[6]542	c381F2d[4]641	256F2d[4]378	88FS[4]950	Calif
(86LE1591)	j322US[4]495	385US[4]564	200FS[4]907	c415F2d1325	256F2d[6]382	112FS[3]443	114CA2d844
(62SC1144)	322US[4]602	q386US[7]43	205FS[6]514	f443F2d[5]1095	j256F2d[6]386	154FS[5]238	154CA2d236
s315US793	324US[7]46	j388US[6]172	209FS[7]530	f443F2d[6]1095	q317F2d[5]783	154FS[7]238	174CA2d826
s41FS537	324US[7]764	q389US[6]134	210FS[3]277	j443F2d[5]1100	q371F2d[3]667	177FS[7]390	200CA2d24
s94CCL699	324US[1]768	395US[4]794	f210FS[3]279	447F2d[5]57	q558F2d[6]337	230FS[3]178	242CA2d728
4TCt216	325US[4]95	q395US[4]795	212FS[5]880	447F2d[6]57	666F2d[4]1054	268FS[4]1008	260CA2d526
18TCt12	325US[7]97	c405US[7]484	212FS[7]928	483F2d[3]655	137FS[6]536	553FS[4]1318	12CA3d763
24TCt637	326US[3]326	j405US[7]485	214FS[4]646	q561F2d[4]542	q313FS[3]1060	Cir. 10	17CA3d20
29TCt271	327US[1]85	q407US[7]31	219FS[4]153	47FS[1]366	q357FS[3]81	156F2d[6]941	80CA3d439
36TCt282	329US[6]665	q407US[4]65	e219FS[4]266	165FS[3]24	522FS[6]763	170F2d[7]741	82CA3d204
58TCt911	j332US[7]83	408US287	q219FS[6]268	176FS[7]954	9FRD348	269F2d[3]487	112CA3d116
59TCt74	332US[7]137	q411US[4]788	261FS[5]400	201FS[6]447	Cir. 7	315F2d[6]617	132CA3d99
66TCt356	j332US[7]140	j419US255	q327FS[6]546	206FS[6]302	146F2d[4]247	j315F2d[6]620	22C2d575
77TCt63	j332US[7]141	422US[6]807	24FRD79	q216FS[5]290	155F2d[6]912	508F2d[4]149	24C2d338
Cir. D.C.	333US[7]281	j422US[6]844	39FRD284	227FS[5]2	157F2d[6]808	77FS[1]555	28C2d851
707F2d[2]561	333US[6]656	q440US[7]371	Cir. 3	q227FS[5]3	158F2d[4]350	126FS[5]568	28C2d863
Cir. 1	333US[4]659	j440US378	130F2d[4]657	251FS[4]665	166F2d[7]980	171FS[7]390	47C2d359
61FS[1]1016	333US[5]660	q452US[7]25	175F2d[2]254	e257FS[7]808	167F2d[3]803	195FS[4]196	51C2d795
Cir. 2	333US[3]666	j452US35	203F2d[5]426	q307FS[4]206	172F2d[7]696	202FS[3]78	57C2d166
158F2d[2]161	333US[7]676	9MJ305	203F2d[7]806	j310FS[4]563	173F2d[3]670	223FS[6]596	64C2d17
306F2d[1]827	j333US[3]677	15MJ116	224F2d[4]508	q312FS[4]310	189F2d[6]768	q224FS[7]866	65C2d205
199FS458	j333US[5]677	Cir. D.C.	224F2d[5]512	324FS[5]697	238F2d[7]312	Cir. 11	66C2d625
199FS[2]466	j333US[6]677	139F2d[7]367	f310F2d[4]724	355FS[6]344	241F2d[3]108	46FS[4]421	28C3d345
Cir. 3	j333US[7]677	148F2d[7]875	j310F2d[4]735	Cir. 5	281F2d[7]786	79FS[3]916	18CaR59
181F2d[2]405	j333US[4]679	j177F2d[4]87	329F2d[4]858	158F2d[7]617	q329F2d[6]358	209FS[5]302	19CaR459
Cir. 4	334US[7]684	259F2d[5]790	e329F2d[5]858	194F2d[7]865	q402F2d309	h209FS[4]303	48CaR699
205F2d[1]342	j334US[7]685	j419F2d[6]1174	q334F2d[3]529	205F2d[3]668	q403F2d701	222FS872	51CaR742
Cir. 5	334US[7]730	421F2d1160	355F2d[7]313	j205F2d[4]675	j440F2d839	222FS[6]872	53CaR289
562F2d978	334US[7]739	485F2d[1]957	j359F2d[7]947	224F2d[4]905	719F2d[6]904	234FS[3]1010	58CaR591
Cir. 6	335US[7]441	584F2d488	j430F2d[5]469	228F2d[6]659	52FS[7]270	237FS[3]274	67CaR249
151F2d[1]1000	337US[6]780	624F2d[3]201	74FS[1]848	228F2d[7]664	54FS[7]925	239FS[4]142	90CaR834
229F2d[2]698	c337US782	624F2d[3]218	74FS[3]848	250F2d[3]647	54FS[4]980	q273FS[5]843	92CaR513
400F2d[1]823	339US661	146FS[4]882	74FS[5]848	258F2d[6]941	54FS[7]1000	357FS[3]1081	94CaR914
270FS[1]939	339US[4]666	Cir. 1	81FS[3]870	j258F2d[7]944	60FS[2]657	q442FS[5]264	113CaR746
Cir. 7	342US[6]64	181F2d[3]602	81FS[6]871	261F2d[7]233	60FS[3]821	q442FS[7]264	135CaR855
160FS[1]328	342US[6]179	d191F2d[6]965	84FS[3]940	j263F2d[4]44	60FS[6]821	Ala	145CaR734
Cir. 8	d348US[7]9	203F2d[7]935	85FS[3]787	j263F2d[6]46	74FS[1]993	254Ala541	147CaR43
266F2d69	348US[3]108	204F2d[7]362	88FS[3]780	330F2d[4]525	77FS[4]21	277Ala156	168CaR636
Cir. 9	349US[4]391	96FS[4]707	97FS[7]939	341F2d[4]98	86FS[4]384	34AlA196	169CaR84
172FS[2]938	350US[6]118	f101FS[4]165	148FS[6]684	c341F2d[6]776	Cir. 8	41AlA494	182CaR891
Cir. 10	j351US336	f105FS[6]529	187FS[3]715	341F2d[5]780	144F2d[1]918	41AlA558	133P2d462
80FS[2]344	354US[4]77	111FS[3]418	196FS[3]53	e353F2d[3]107	161F2d[3]304	41AlA656	133P2d466
CCPA	355US[6]159	123FS[3]443	208FS[6]639	366F2d[4]27	308F2d[4]72	42AlA425	140P2d28
j359F2d[2]885	j356US[6]83	124FS[3]37	226FS[3]420	q400F2d[3]596	q407F2d[5]128	42AlA453	149P2d701
CtCl	d357US[6]441	141FS[4]606	q226FS[6]582	q400F2d[5]596	435F2d[6]371	42AlA505	172P2d689
f97CCL262	j357US[7]442	332FS[6]834	243FS[7]700	410F2d335	e55FS[6]961	42AlA551	172P2d696
99CCL570	358US[7]636	377FS1341	271FS[4]409	j416F2d[5]1027	103FS[7]149	44AlA104	250P2d371
99CCL571	361US[4]246	432FS[4]115	33FRD424	422F2d[3]301	119FS[4]784	38So2d288	303P2d761
101CCL743	j361US[7]255	Cir. 2	33FRD438	430F2d[5]1117	241FS[5]1013	49So2d290	316P2d15
104CCL122	j363US[3]704	e137F2d[1]1010	33FRD454	430F2d[6]1117	281FS[5]797	136So2d576	336P2d950
179CCL610	j364US[5]275	190F2d[6]253	38FRD463	496F2d[4]1058	313FS[4]205	141So2d208	345P2d538
208CCL579	365US[3]117	221F2d[4]629	Cir. 4	j505F2d[3]1344	q313FS[4]206	148So2d253	367P2d699
223CCL430	q365US[3]119	d250F2d[7]354	128F2d[7]1013	j505F2d[6]1344	q421FS[7]673	167So2d179	409P2d923
375F2d[1]838	j365US[3]208	263F2d[3]943	129F2d[7]110	525F2d933	Cir. 9	167So2d914	417P2d873
530F2d869	j366US[3]158	292F2d[4]323	130F2d[7]881	c618F2d[4]384	198F2d[7]471	167So2d915	427P2d191
620F2d855	368US[6]459	303F2d[4]885	133F2d[2]477	j618F2d388	j253F2d[3]847	169So2d313	618P2d182
f47FS[1]119	369US[4]517	d313F2d460	155F2d[7]5	j640F2d608	258F2d[4]306	203So2d286	Colo
e48FS[1]358	q369US[4]519	315F2d[4]866	280F2d[4]539	126FS[3]546	259F2d[6]280	342So2d956	120Col5
55FS[1]624	q369US[4]520	j319F2d[3]318	280F2d[6]539	139FS[6]901	280F2d[4]735	409So2d897	131Col360
60FS[2]469	370US908	330F2d[4]304	280F2d[3]541	140FS[7]726	310F2d[4]37	Alk	206P2d339
Mass	372US[6]337	q330F2d[4]310	294F2d[6]396	185FS[5]936	q321F2d[7]712	438P2d230	281P2d810
378Mas273	o372US339	j330F2d[4]315	294F2d[3]609	q217FS[7]172	q372F2d[6]370	487P2d840	Conn
391NE263	372US[6]348	332F2d[4]891	297F2d853	236FS[7]240	403F2d860	604P2d1108	1Cir358
PR	e372US[6]349	q333F2d[7]610	d299F2d[7]173	238FS[5]595	j425F2d617	Ariz	1Cir423
74PRR922	372US[6]478	398F2d[4]985	j310F2d[3]917	261FS[4]265	e490F2d366	96Az126	1Cir554
So C	j375US[6]3	q465F2d[7]121	315F2d[4]644	q270FS[6]51	q551F2d1166	392P2d786	1Cir560
233SoC48	q378US[6]6	j611F2d421	315F2d[5]644	272FS[4]511	586F2d1328	Ark	2Cir573
103SE427	j378US[4]26	694F2d[5]22	q319F2d[6]2	q298FS298	j586F2d1335	227Ark50	24CS17
	j378US[3]407	e709F2d[6]168	q319F2d[6]4	331FS[5]433	647F2d[4]880	243Ark354	24CS96
– 455 –	q379US[2]80	113FS[3]920	q319F2d[5]772	345FS[6]1030	j678F2d799	256Ark429	24CS271
(86LE1595)	q380US[3]414	171FS[6]561	c368F2d298	385FS[4]1047	60FS[3]853	296SW207	24CS276
(62SC1252)	j381US[4]512	177FS[1]507	375F2d628	Cir. 6	88FS[5]949	420SW536	25CS67
s315US791	381US[3]590	184FS[4]282	375F2d[6]628	163F2d[1]823	88FS[6]949	508SW56	135Ct273
317US[1]24	j381US[3]616						
317US[7]276	384US[4]469						*Continued*

54

Thus far we have talked about Shepardizing cases. This is probably the first and most frequent way you will use the citators. But, in fact, it is possible to Shepardize nearly any legal authority, primary or secondary. You can Shepardize cases, statutes, administrative regulations and decisions, law review articles, and other types of legal authority. The sheer abundance of citators creates the first problem in the mechanics of Shepardizing (Figure 3.3).

The initial step in Shepardizing is to make sure that you have the appropriate set of volumes to find the authority that you wish to Shepardize. A library collection of *Shepard's* citators contains literally hundreds of different volumes. They all have the same dark red bindings. You must read the titles carefully to find the correct set. This sounds simple, but novice users frequently start with the wrong set by accident. If you have a case from the *North Eastern Reporter,* you need to find *Shepard's North Eastern Reporter Citations;* even though *Shepard's North Western Reporter Citations* looks similar, it won't do the job.

It is also possible to Shepardize the same case in more than one citator set, and the citing authority that you find will be different depending on the set that you use. For example, a state supreme court case can be Shepardized® in either a state citator or a regional reporter citator. In the state citator, the citing authority will include (1) federal cases, (2) state cases from that state, and (3) selected law review articles. The regional reporter citator has as citing authority (1) federal cases, (2) state cases *from all states,* but (3) *no* law review articles. The title page of every *Shepard's* lists the sources of citing authority for that set (Figure 3.4).

The second step in the process is getting all the volumes in the appropriate set of citators. Some sets of citators, such as *Shepard's United States Reports Citations,* may have several volumes, beginning with the initial hard-copy vol-

Figure 3.3   A Wide Variety of Citators

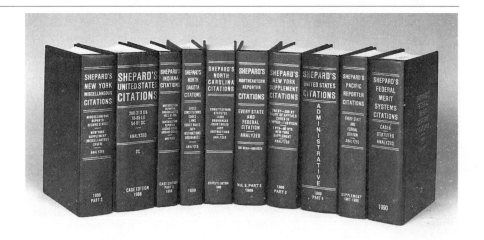

Figure 3.4   Title Pages from a State Citator and a Regional Reporter Citator

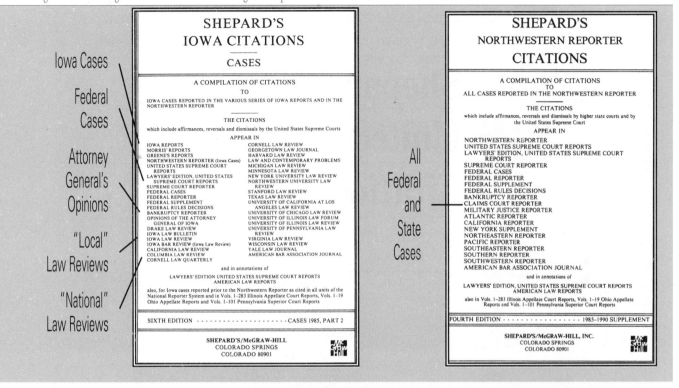

Source: Copyright © 1985 by McGraw-Hill, Inc. Reprinted with permission by Shepard's/McGraw-Hill, Inc. Further reproduction is strictly prohibited.

umes, followed by several supplements, and ending with a current advance sheet. To be comprehensive in your Shepardizing and to be as up-to-date as possible, you must have *all* the volumes of a particular *Shepard's* set.

The easiest way to make sure that you have all volumes in a citator set is to begin with the most recent advance sheet in the set. Normally (though not always), this will be a monthly *red* pamphlet, and it will have a current date (Figure 3.5). On the cover of this pamphlet will be an instructional guide of "WHAT YOUR LIBRARY SHOULD CONTAIN." Make sure that you have all the volumes that you need. (A corollary to Murphy's Law says that if you are missing one volume, it will be the one that includes a citing case that has overruled the case that you are Shepardizing.)

Figure 3.5 An Advance Sheet for *Shepard's United States Citations*

VOL. 91   FEBRUARY, 1993   NO. 9

Shepard's
United States
Citations

ADVANCE SHEET EDITION (IN TWO PARTS)
PART 1A CASES

(USPS 605470)

IMPORTANT NOTICE
Do not destroy the January, 1993 gold paper-covered
semiannual Cumulative Supplement (Parts 1A, 1B, 1C and 1D)
for Shepard's United States Citations, Cases.

WHAT YOUR LIBRARY SHOULD CONTAIN
PART 1, CASES

1988 Bound Volumes (Vols. 1A, 1B, 1C, 2A, 2B, 2C)*
1984 Bound Volumes (Vols. 3, 4, 5, 6)*
1984-1986 Bound Supplement (Vols. 7A and 7B)*
1986-1988 Bound Supplement (Vols. 8, 9, 10, 11, 12)*
1988-1990 Bound Supplement (Vols. 13, 14, 15, 16, 17)*
1990-1991 Bound Supplement (Vols. 18, 19)*
Supplemented with:
  –January, 1993 Semiannual Cumulative Supplement Vol. 91 No. 8
   (Parts 1A, 1B, 1C and 1D)
  –February, 1993 Advance Sheet Vol. 91 No. 9 (Parts 1A and 1B)
PART 2, STATUTES
  Please refer to the current supplement cover for Part 2, Statutes.

**RECYCLE YOUR
OUTDATED
SUPPLEMENTS**

When you receive new supplements
and are instructed to destroy the
outdated versions, please consider
taking these paper products to a local
recycling center to help conserve our
nation's natural resources. Thank you.

SHEPARD'S
McGRAW-HILL

Assume that you now have the right set of citators and all the volumes in the set. Next you must learn the very concise language of *Shepard's*.

First, you must become familiar with *Shepard's* abbreviations (Figure 3.6). *Shepard's* uses its own citation form; it does not use the *Bluebook*. For example, FS, not F.Supp., is *Shepard's* designation for the *Federal Supplement*. A table of these abbreviations appears at the beginning of every volume of *Shep-*

Figure 3.6 *Shepard's* Abbreviations of Reporters

ABBREVIATIONS—REPORTS

AA–Antitrust Adviser, Second Edition
(Shepard's, 1978)
AABA–Atwood & Brewster, Antitrust
and American Business Abroad
(Shepard's, 1958)
A2d–Atlantic Reporter, Second Series
Ab–Abstracts
AB–American Bankruptcy Reports
ABA–American Bar Association Journal
ABA(2)–American Bar Association
Journal, Part 2
AbD–Abbott's Court of Appeals
Decisions (N.Y.)
AbN–Abstracts, New Series
ABn–American Bankruptcy Reports,
New Series

Ark–Arkansas Reports
AS–American State Reports
At–Atlantic Reporter
Az–Arizona Reports
AzA–Arizona Court of Appeals Reports
Bar–Barbour's Supreme Court Reports
(N.Y.)
BCh–Barbour's Chancery Reports (N.Y.)
Binn–Binney's Reports (Pa.)
Blackf–Blackford's Reports (Ind.)
Bland–Bland's Chancery Reports (Md.)
Bos–Bosworth's Reports (N.Y.)
Boy–Boyce's Reports (Del.)
BP–Drake & Mullins, Bankruptcy
Practice (Shepard's, 1980)
Bradb–Bradbury's Pleading & Practice

Allen–Allen's Reports (Mass.)
AR –American Law Reports
ARF –American Law Reports, Federal
AN–Abbott's New Cases (N.Y.)
AntNP–Anthon's Nisi Prius Cases (N.Y.)
Ap–New York Appellate Division
Reports
Ap2d–New York Appellate Division
Reports, Second Series
AR–American Reports
ARD–Application for Review Decisions

Appeals Reports (Customs)
Cai–Caines' Reports (N.Y.)
CaiCs–Caines' Cases (N.Y.)
Cal–California Supreme Court Reports
CaR–California Reporter
CaU–California Unreported Cases
CCL–Court of Claims Reports (U.S.)
CCLM–Acret, California Construction
Law Manual (Shepard's, 1975)
CD–Decisions of the Commissioner
of Patents

(Continued)

ard's. Note also that the page numbers in a *Shepard's* list are to the page of the citing case where the citation occurs, not to the starting page of the case (Figure 3.7).

Shepard's also uses a second type of abbreviations, known as "history" and "treatment" abbreviations. The *Shepard's* editors read the citing cases to determine their relationship to the cited case and assign analytical abbreviations that describe the relationship. The *history* of the case is its direct procedural history. For example, on appeal the case may have been "affirmed" or "reversed" by a higher court. The *treatment* of the case is the way other cases (those not within the direct procedural history) have treated it. The *Shepard's*

Figure 3.7   Page Numbers in *Shepard's*

Vol. 410   UNITED STATES SUPREME COURT REPORTS

501FS¹564	378A2d222	54CA3d801	495FS¹734	493FS⅓327	113Msc2d713	433US295	508F2d²498
Cir. 6	NM	115CaR311	e497FS¹400	546FS¹486	35NY185	433US410	d519F2d
473FS²338	96NM536	127CaR44	Cir. 2	Cir. 9	35NY191	434US¹381	[¹1367
504FS474	632P2d1174	Colo	477F2d1115	540F2d1365	45NY808	434US391	537F2d564
Cir. 7	NY	193Col474	j498F2d807	591F2d¹1261	316NE862	435US221	554F2d¹497
h566F2d¹37	41Ap2d294	568P2d41	508F2d986	706F2d1527	316NE866	436US¹378	578F2d¹450
603F2d¹1269	41Ap2d297	Del	f532F2d¹873	358FS355	381NE337	436US¹663	614F2d2
419FS1310	83Ap2d92	314A2d212	575F2d382	390FS¹62	359S2d543	d438US¹290	638F2d¹268
Cir. 9	83Ap2d95	327A2d752	365FS¹52	88FRD¹542	359S2d549	j438US357	641F2d1012
559F2d¹1144	78Msc2d318	Mo	366FS793	Cir. 10	388S2d472	j438US¹357	649F2d²77
d613F2d¹183	116Msc2d990	574SW361	374FS248	f631F2d¹711	408S2d772	439US²70	659F2d¹282
613F2d²185	32NY240	NJ	379FS77	Cir. 11	409S2d130	j439US1053	671F2d4
j613F2d187	56NY310	74NJ353	382FS984	435FS1094	453S2d598	440US²97	699F2d²6
643F2d653	56NY315	378A2d222	382FS¹985	Ohio		j440US114	e373FS635
f403FS⁴356	298NE71	NY	388FS253	132Az163	53ΦA217	440US¹199	373FS¹648
Cir. 11	437NE1092	41Ap2d297	394FS¹590	132Az167	373NE1278	j440US597	377FS621
719F2d1087	437NE1095	78Msc2d318	d402FS¹184	644P2d899	Pa	441US¹77	d377FS¹622
Ala	342S2d582	32NY240	f417FS845	644P2d903	255PaS365	j441US398	379FS²49
294Ala577	342S2d585	56NY311	417FS¹846	Calif	387A2d92	442US¹272	385FS¹400
319So2d704	356S2d993	298NE71	e443FS323	131CA3d104	PR	446US¹76	388FS²393
Ariz	444S2d963	437NE1093	457FS¹299	182CaR234	110DPR261	j446US113	388FS²1035
135Az151	444S2d965	342S2d585	f497FS¹423	Colo	Tenn	447US¹462	390FS1316
25AzA146	452S2d335	344S2d890	e550FS¹1034	184Col76	633SW307	448US¹323	390FS¹1317
541P2d937	452S2d338	356S2d993	Cir. 3	186Col63	Wash	j448US341	392FS¹302
659P2d1296	456S2d935	452S2d336	502F2d¹1128	518P2d810	93W2d703	448US¹518	e392FS¹1141
Calif	RI	SD	552F2d538	525P2d466	611P2d1258	448US¹588	395FS²627
32CA3d64	433A2d174	260NW641	365FS363	Conn	Wis	448US¹1329	396FS¹1296
40CA3d659	SD	287NW484	382FS¹387	175Ct561	93Wis2d504	449US¹174	396FS²1298
51CA3d678	260NW641	Wyo	d393FS123	400A2d720	287NW532	j449US188	406FS¹855
54CA3d801	287NW484	575P2d1112	j393FS¹126	DC	W Va	450US¹230	415FS²495
17C3d666	Tex	656P2d1145	399FS¹1262	324A2d189	233SE423	j450US243	j415FS¹505
17C3d670	636SW489		501FS782	Fla	270SE645	450US²478	j415FS²506
32C3d800	Utah		501FS¹783	295So2d292		j451US35	f423FS¹1265
107CaR850	614P2d1239	**– 752 –**	83FRD¹477	351So2d46		457US9	435FS¹262
115CaR311	Wash	(36LE1)	Cir. 4	Haw	**Vol. 411**	457US¹217	439FS1128
124CaR655	87W2d547	(93SC1245)	513F2d242	60H289		457US230	465FS²660
127CaR44	554P2d1067	US reh den	710F2d¹181	588P2d920	**– 1 –**	457US232	522FS206
131CaR658		in411US959	477FS¹323	Idaho	(36LE16)	e457US¹235	536FS¹1388
131CaR660	**– 743 –**	s406US957	Cir. 5	97Ida202	(93SC1278)	e457US¹239	561FS¹1057
187CaR412	(35LE675)	s458F2d649	e498F2d¹247	541P2d626	US reh den	j457US245	Cir. 2
552P2d442	(93SC1237)	413US¹567	506F2d819	Ill	in411US959	457US¹963	476F2d¹405
552P2d444	Wyo	d414US¹59	508F2d¹777	57Il2d84	s406US966	457US²969	j476F2d¹826
654P2d182	s490P2d1069	j414US¹62	526F2d288	309NE591	s411US980	458US¹200	j476F2d¹828
Colo	cc500FS1323	j414US¹65	541F2d1154	Ind	s337FS280	j458US214	d482F2d
193Col474	439US¹69	414US535	580F2d752	422NE716	411US208	458US¹486	[¹1336
568P2d41	451US¹364	j414US1537	717F2d¹1493	Iowa	j411US928	51USLW	489F2d¹1091
Del	j451US377	415US715	d377FS¹1020	211NW341	412US458	[4170	489F2d²1091
314A2d212	Cir. 2	e415US¹731	d382FS¹807	Mass	j412US461	j51USLW	e507F2d¹1068
327A2d752	497F2d728	j415US760	j415FS¹816	368Mas823	413US462	[4322	j507F2d¹1073
Idaho	f503F2d1189	415US770	d396FS¹812	385Mas1206	j414US²432	51USLW	f508F2d¹1028
99Ida503	j503F2d1191	415US¹786	e402FS¹927	388Mas192	j414US656	[4585	554F2d¹538
584P2d648	d520F2d¹802	416US¹126	531FS764	389Mas937	415US²271	j51USLW	562F2d843
Ill	379FS¹1165	j418US¹68	546FS¹454	333NE382	j415US¹278	[4779	562F2d²844
371Il²940	382FS¹1233	419US¹401	Cir. 6	434NE963	415US375	4MJ802	j562F2d¹865
117Il²566	385FS¹225	d421US¹300	519F2d404	446NE46	415US¹539	12MJ910	576F2d462
75Il2d582	427FS¹191	j421US¹304	664F2d561	452NE1142	415US713	77TCt872	j579F2d181
347NE44	Cir. 3	424US30	666F2d¹1027	Mich	417US¹612	97FRD614	584F2d²604
389NE1167	493FS¹88	431US403	362FS¹32	412Mch582	d418US²742	Cir. D.C.	601F2d¹1234
433NE943	Cir. 4	435US775	387FS¹1128	317NW4	j418US¹760	477F2d1182	601F2d²1238
Kan	d456FS¹1155	442US300	f419FS¹1007	Mo	j419US²420	483F2d¹1317	696F2d¹223
231Kan642	Cir. 5	450US115	e424FS¹592	504SW88	j419US¹586	525F2d561	715F2d¹783
648P2d715	485F2d¹1304	450US¹122	496FS209	Mont	420US¹538	593F2d¹1125	717F2d¹41
Mo	496F2d¹111	j450US¹31	499FS134	177Mt78	426US324	665F2d1233	357FS1763
574SW361	498F2d¹1235	Cir. D.C.	d499FS¹137	580P2d448	426US¹602	674F2d10	357FS²763
NJ	538F2d¹1083	378FS¹1235	NJ	NJ	426US²814	676F2d730	359FS²971
70NJ572	396FS¹813	Cir. 1	542F2d1280	81NJ70	427US¹312	j676F2d753	360FS232
74NJ353	Cir. 7	f482F2d98	370FS68	81NJ78	427US¹318	686F2d²980	f361FS¹440
129Su244	h566F2d¹37	f482F2d¹100	73FRD112	149Su490	427US506	d386FS1326	361FS¹1053
145Su375	Cir. 9	519F2d1366	Cir. 8	374A2d63	j429US¹216	430FS²822	f361FS¹1327
152Su499	559F2d1149	358FS1198	637F2d1162	405A2d353	429US¹259	436FS²136	362FS²660
322A2d844	613F2d¹183	373FS¹631	385FS¹705	405A2d357	j430US515	468FS²690	363FS669
362A2d24	j613F2d187	417FS448	387FS¹402	NY	431US¹503	488FS¹133	365FS²78
367A2d1195	Calif	437FS443	404FS¹646	54Ap2d266	j432US15	Cir. 1	365FS²1167
378A2d67	40CA3d660	460FS1044	424FS¹954	64Ap2d878	j432US459	482F2d¹99	366FS²739
					f432US¹470		
					433US291		*Continued*

36

Page Where Citation Occurs, Not Initial Page of the Case

editors may, in their editorial judgment, find a citing case to have "explained" or "followed" or "distinguished" the cited case. A list of history and treatment abbreviations is also found at the beginning of each volume (Figure 3.8).

Another potentially confusing aspect of *Shepard's* language is the use of small, superscript numbers that refer to the *headnote of the cited case*. In the example in Figure 3.9, the small "2" means that the citing case has cited that portion of the cited case summarized by its second headnote. (You might want to re-read that sibilant sentence slowly. It does make sense—really.) As puzzling as this sounds, once you understand the function of these little numbers, you will find they are very time-saving. If you are Shepardizing a famous case that has been very frequently cited, such as *Miranda v. Arizona*, and you are interested in only one aspect of the case, using the headnote numbers is an

Figure 3.8 *Shepard's* History and Treatment Abbreviations

ABBREVIATIONS—ANALYSIS

History of Case

a	(affirmed)	Same case affirmed on rehearing.
cc	(connected case)	Different case from case cited but arising out of same subject matter or intimately connected therewith.
m	(modified)	Same case modified on rehearing.
r	(reversed)	Same case reversed on rehearing.
s	(same case)	Same case as case cited.
S	(superseded)	Substitution for former opinion.
v	(vacated)	Same case vacated.
US reh den		Rehearing denied by U. S. Supreme Court.
US reh dis		Rehearing dismissed by U. S. Supreme Court.

Treatment of Case

c	(criticised)	Soundness of decision or reasoning in cited case criticised for reasons given.
d	(distinguished)	Case at bar different either in law or fact from case cited for reasons given.
e	(explained)	Statement of import of decision in cited case. Not merely a restatement of the facts.
f	(followed)	Cited as controlling.
h	(harmonized)	Apparent inconsistency explained and shown not to exist.
j	(dissenting opinion)	Citation in dissenting opinion.
L	(limited)	Refusal to extend decision of cited case beyond precise issues involved.
o	(overruled)	Ruling in cited case expressly overruled.
p	(parallel)	Citing case substantially alike or on all fours with cited case in its law or facts.
q	(questioned)	Soundness of decision or reasoning in cited case questioned.

Figure 3.9   Headnote Numbers in *Shepard's*

Vol. 410

UNITED STATES SUPREME COURT REPORTS

501FS¹564	378A2d222	54CA3d801	495FS¹734	493FS1327	113Msc2d713	433US295	508F2d²498
Cir. 6	NM	115CaR311	e497FS¹400	546FS¹486	35NY185	433US410	d519F2d
473FS²338	96NM536	127CaR44	Cir. 2	Cir. 9	35NY191	434US¹381	[¹1367
504FS474	632P2d1174	Colo	477F2d1115	540F2d1365	45NY808	434US391	537F2d564
Cir. 7	NY	193Col474	j498F2d807	591F2d¹1261	316NE862	435US221	554F2d¹497
h566F2d¹37	41Ap2d294	568P2d41	508F2d986	706F2d1527	316NE866	436US¹378	578F2d¹450
603F2d¹1269	41Ap2d297	Del	f532F2d¹873	358FS355	381NE337	d438US¹290	614F2d2
419FS1310	83Ap2d92	314A2d212	575F2d382	390FS¹62	359S2d543	j438US357	638F2d¹268
Cir. 9	83Ap2d95	327A2d752	365FS¹52	88FRD¹542	359S2d549	j438US¹357	641F2d1012
559F2d¹1144	78Msc2d318	Mo	366FS793	Cir. 10	388S2d472	439US²70	649F2d²77
d613F2d¹183	116Msc2d990	574SW361	374FS248	f631F2d¹711	408S2d772	j439US1053	659F2d¹282
613F2d²185	32NY240	NJ	379FS77	Cir. 11	409S2d130	440US²97	671F2d4
j613F2d187	56NY310	74NJ353	382FS984	435FS1094	453S2d598	j440US114	699F2d²6
643F2d653	56NY315	378A2d222	382FS¹985	Ariz	Ohio	440US¹199	e373FS635
f403FS⁴356	298NE71	NY	388FS253	132Az163	530A217	440US597	373FS¹648
Cir. 11	437NE1092	41Ap2d297	394FS¹590	132Az167	373NE1278	441US¹77	377FS621
719F2d1087	437NE1095	78Msc2d318	d402FS¹184	644P2d899	Pa	j441US398	d377FS¹622
Ala	342S2d582	32NY240	f417FS845	644P2d903	255PaS365	442US¹272	379FS²49
294Ala577	342S2d585	56NY311	417FS¹846	Calif	387A2d92	446US¹76	385FS¹400
319So2d704	356S2d993	298NE71	e443FS323	131CA3d104	PR	j446US113	388FS²393
Ariz	444S2d963	437NE1093	457FS¹299	182CaR234	110DPR261	447US¹462	388FS²1035
135Az151	444S2d965	342S2d585	f497FS¹423	Colo	Tenn	448US¹323	390FS1316
25AzA146	452S2d335	344S2d890	e550FS¹1034	184Col76	633SW307	j448US341	390FS¹1317
541P2d937	452S2d338	356S2d993	Cir. 3	186Col63	Wash	448US¹518	392FS¹302
659P2d1296	456S2d935	452S2d336	502F2d¹1128	518P2d810	93W2d703	448US¹588	e392FS¹1141
Calif	RI	SD	552F2d538	525P2d466	611P2d1258	448US¹1329	395FS²627
32CA3d64	433A2d174	260NW641	365FS363	Conn	Wis	449US¹174	396FS¹1296
40CA3d659	SD	287NW484	382FS¹387	175Ct561	93Wis2d504	j449US188	396FS²1298
51CA3d678	260NW641	Wyo	d393FS123	400A2d720	287NW532	450US¹230	406FS¹855
54CA3d801	287NW484	575P2d1112	j393FS¹126	DC	W Va	j450US243	415FS²495
17C3d666	Tex	656P2d1145	399FS¹1262	324A2d189	233SE423	450US²478	j415FS¹505
17C3d670	636SW489		501FS782	Fla	270SE645	Cir. 9	j415FS2506
32C3d800	Utah	**– 752 –**	501FS¹783	295So2d292		457US9	f423FS¹1265
107CaR850	614P2d1239	(36LE1)	83FRD¹477	351So2d46	**Vol. 411**	457US¹217	435FS¹262
115CaR311	Wash	(93SC1245)	Cir. 4	Haw		457US230	439FS1128
124CaR655	87W2d547	US reh den	513F2d242	60H289	**– 1 –**	457US232	465FS²660
127CaR44	554P2d1067	in411US959	710F2d¹181	588P2d920	(36LE16)	e457US¹235	522FS206
131CaR658		s406US957	477FS¹323	Idaho	(93SC1278)	e457US¹239	536FS¹1388
131CaR660	**– 743 –**	s458F2d649	Cir. 5	97Ida202	US reh den	j457US245	561FS¹1057
187CaR412	(35LE675)	413US¹567	e498F2d¹247	541P2d626	in411US959		Cir. 2
552P2d442	(93SC1237)	d414US¹59	506F2d819	Ill	s406US966	457US¹963	476F2d¹405
552P2d444	Wyo	j414US¹62	508F2d¹777	57Il2d84	s411US980	457US²969	j476F2d¹828
654P2d182	s490P2d1069	j414US¹65	526F2d288	309NE591	s337FS280	458US¹200	j476F2d¹828
Colo	cc500FS1323	414US530	541F2d1154	Ind	411US208	j458US214	d482F2d
193Col474	439US¹69	j414US535	580F2d752	422NE716	458US¹486	51USLW	[¹1336
568P2d41	451US¹364	j414US¹537	717F2d¹1493	Iowa	j411US928		489F2d¹1091
Del	j451US377	415US715	d377FS¹1020	211NW341	412US458	j51USLW	489F2d²1091
314A2d212	Cir. 2	e415US¹731	d382FS¹807	Mass	j412US461	[4170	e507F2d¹1068
337A2d752	497F2d728	j415US760	382FS¹816	368Mas823	413US462	j51USLW	507F2d¹1073
Idaho	f503F2d1189	415US770	d396FS¹812	385Mas1206	j414US²432	[4322	f508F2d¹1037
99Ida503	j503F2d1191	415US¹786	e402FS¹927	388Mas192	414US656	51USLW	554F2d¹538
584P2d648	d520F2d1802	416US¹126	531FS764	389Mas937	415US²271	[4585	562F2d843
Ill	379FS¹1165	418US¹68	546FS¹454	333NE382	j415US¹278	j51USLW	562F2d²844
37Il2d940	382FS¹1233	419US¹401	Cir. 6	434NE963	415US375	[4779	562F2d²865
117Il2d566	385FS¹225	d421US¹300	519F2d404	446NE46	415US¹539	4MJ802	576F2d462
75Il2d582	427FS¹191	j421US¹304	664F2d561	452NE1142	415US713	12MJ910	j579F2d181
347NE44	Cir. 3	424US30	666F2d¹1027	Mich	417US¹612	77TCt872	584F2d²604
389NE1167	493FS¹88	431US403	362FS¹32	412Mch582	j418US²742	97FRD614	Cir. D.C.
453NE943	Cir. 4	435US775	387FS¹1128	317NW4	j418US¹760	Cir. D.C.	601F2d¹1234
Kan	d456FS¹1155	442US300	f419FS¹1007	Mo	j419US²420	477F2d1182	601F2d²1238
231Kan642	Cir. 5	450US115	e424FS¹592	504SW88	j419US¹586	483F2d¹1317	696F2d¹223
648P2d715	485F2d¹1304	450US¹122	496FS209	Mont	420US¹538	525F2d561	715F2d¹783
Mo	496F2d¹111	j450US131	499FS134	177Mt78	426US324	593F3d¹1125	717F2d¹41
574SW361	498F2d¹1235	Cir. D.C.	d499FS¹137	580P2d448	426US¹602	665F2d1233	357FS²763
NJ	538F2d¹1083	378FS¹1235	Cir. 7	NJ	426US²814	674F2d10	359FS²971
70NJ572	396FS¹813	Cir. 1	542F2d1280	81NJ70	427US¹312	676F2d730	360FS232
74NJ353	Cir. 7	f482F2d98	370FS68	81NJ78	j427US¹318	j676F2d753	365FS232
129Su244	h566F2d¹37	f482F2d¹100	73FRD112	149Su490	427US506	686F2d²980	f361FS¹440
145Su375	Cir. 9	519F2d1366	Cir. 8	374A2d63	j429US¹216	d386FS1326	361FS¹1053
152Su499	559F2d1149	358FS1198	637F2d1162	405A2d353	429US¹259	430FS²822	f361FS²1327
322A2d844	613F2d¹183	373FS¹631	385FS¹705	405A2d357	436FS²136	436FS²136	362FS²660
362A2d24	j613F2d187	417FS448	387FS¹402	NY	j430US515	468FS²690	363FS669
367A2d1195	Calif	437FS443	404FS¹646	54Ap2d266	431US¹503	488FS¹133	365FS278
378A2d67	40CA3d660	460FS1044	424FS¹954	64Ap2d878	j432US15	Cir. 1	365FS²1167
					j432US459	482F2d¹99	366FS2739
					f432US¹470		
					433US291		Continued

Parallel Cites

Headnote Number

History/Treatment of Case

Court

36

excellent way to winnow a very long list of citing cases into a much shorter one. If you are just interested in cases citing *Miranda* for the legal issue summarized in its second headnote, you only need to read the cases that have that particular headnote reference number in the *Shepard's* display. Remember, however, that the same case is often published in more than one reporter and by more than one publisher. Different publishers write different headnotes. In order to use the *Shepard's* headnote numbers correctly, you must Shepardize with the citator that corresponds to the reporter volume you are reading. Thus, if you are Shepardizing a Supreme Court case as you read it in the *Supreme Court Reporter,* you must use the *Shepard's* table for S.Ct. cites.

In summary, *Shepard's* is a unique and essential research tool. Before you can use the citators effectively, however, you need to understand what they do, how they do it, and the language they use. Once you have accomplished that, Shepardizing is a relatively easy and very mechanical process.

Shepardizing Made Simple: WESTLAW Access to Shepard's

WESTLAW provides on-line access to most *Shepard's* case law citators. On-line Shepardizing offers several significant advantages over the manual version: First, when you Shepardize on WESTLAW, you retrieve a single, cumulative list of citing cases. You no longer need to worry about finding the right set of *Shepard's* or missing a volume in a *Shepard's* set. Second, as will be discussed later, you can manipulate the display to limit it to your research specifications. Third, and perhaps most important, Shepard's on WESTLAW is interactive with the rest of the WESTLAW databases. You can go back and forth from the cited case to Shepard's to citing cases. For all of these reasons, Shepard's on WESTLAW is a great time-saver.

There are two ways to enter Shepard's on WESTLAW. If you are viewing a case on WESTLAW and wish to Shepardize it, simply type **sh.** The second way is to type **sh** followed by the citation of the case you want to Shepardize.

A Shepard's display on WESTLAW is shown in Figure 3.10. Note that the top of the screen says "Rank 1 of 2." This means that your citation is found in two different citator sets; if you type **r,** you will see the display in the second set. In this example, r1 (rank 1) is a regional reporter citator, r2 is a state citator. "Only page" means that there is only one screen of citing cases.

Next, the screen tells you the citation you have entered, the citator series you have displayed, and the coverage of that series in WESTLAW. The WEST-LAW coverage will always be as current as the hard-copy version of *Shepard's*—no more and no less.

Next comes the Shepard's information itself. Everything that you would find in the manual version is in the on-line version, with two significant additions. The analytical abbreviations (and what they mean) are to the left of the citations; the numbers that refer to headnotes of the cited case are to the right. Additionally, the on-line version not only lists the page of the citing case

Figure 3.10   A Shepard's Display on WESTLAW

```
                              SHEPARD'S  (Rank 1 of 2)           Only Page
CITATIONS TO: 250 N.W.2d 590
CITATOR: NORTHWESTERN REPORTER CITATIONS
DIVISION: Northwestern Reporter 2nd Series
COVERAGE: First Shepard's volume through Jan. 1993 Supplement
Retrieval                                      Headnote
   No.    ----Analysis----- -----Citation------   No.
                Same Text    (312 Minn. 1)
    1    SC  Same Case     268 N.W.2d 705
    2                      267 N.W.2d 730, 732      6
    3     D  Distinguished 283 N.W.2d 897, 901      4
    4                      345 N.W.2d 723, 731
    5                      392 N.W.2d 679, 683      5
    6                      392 N.W.2d 679, 683      6
    7                      414 N.W.2d 227, 231      1
    8                      415 N.W.2d 341, 345      3

Note:  Check Shepard's PreView (SP), Insta-Cite (IC), and QuickCite (QC).
Copyright (C) 1993 McGraw-Hill, Inc.; Copyright (C) 1993 West Publishing Co.
```

where the reference to the cited case occurs, it also usually lists the *initial* page of the citing case. (The printed version of *Shepard's* only gives the internal—citing—page.) And, most important, on the far left of the display is a "retrieval number." If you wish to view a citing case, simply enter its number. WESTLAW first displays the initial page of the citing case (Figure 3.11) and then, if you press **Enter** again, the first citing page (Figure 3.12). To return from a citing case to your Shepard's display, type **gb** or **goback.**

Narrowing a Shepard's Search on WESTLAW

WESTLAW offers great flexibility in the display of citing authority; that is, the citing list can be limited to certain types of authority. WESTLAW allows limitation by abbreviation and headnote number. For example, you can use the Locate command to find only those cases that have "followed" the cited case (**loc f**) or those cases that have cited the Shepardized case for its second headnote (**loc 2**). You can also use the Locate command to find cases by reporter

Figure 3.11   The Initial Page of the Citing Case on WESTLAW

```
Citation                           Page(P)         Database    Mode
283 N.W.2d 897      CITING CASE    P 1 OF 20       NW          T
(Cite as: 283 N.W.2d 897)
                        'STATE of Minnesota, Respondent,
                                    v.
                     David Allen ORSCANIN, Appellant.
                          Nos. 47431, 49368.
                       Supreme Court of Minnesota.
                            Aug. 17, 1979.
                     Certiorari Denied Nov. 26, 1979.
                          See 100 S.Ct. 464
   Defendant appealed from an order of the District Court, Rice County, Urban J.
Steimann, J., denying his request to have his judgment of conviction and
sentence vacated and set aside. The District Court decision was made following
a postconviction hearing held pursuant to remand of a prior appeal, 266
N.W.2d 880. The Supreme Court, Rogosheske, J., held that: (1) evidence
sustained trial court's finding that defendant's confession was voluntary and
that its admission at trial did not deny defendant due process; (2) defendant
was not promised leniency in exchange for a confession; and (3) defendant's
confinement did not induce defendant to confess.
   Affirmed.
   Wahl, J., dissented and filed opinion in which Yetka, J., joined.
                     COPR. (C) WEST 1993 NO CLAIM TO ORIG. U.S. GOVT. WORKS
```

Figure 3.12   The Citing Page on WESTLAW

```
283 N.W.2d 897        CITING CASE        P 19 OF 20        NW        T
(Cite as: 283 N.W.2d 897, *901)
     defendant were not legally detained for a parole violation, a confinement more
     than 36 hours without appearance before a judge generally would be illegal.
     See, Rule 4.02, subd. 5(1), Rules of Criminal Procedure. Given the fact that
     defendant does not claim that he was promised relief from his confinement
     conditions in exchange for a confession and the fact that defendant was legally
     detained for a parole violation, we agree with the postconviction court that
     defendant's confinement did not induce defendant to confess. Defendant surely
     must have realized that his confession of involvement in the Northfield
     burglary would not free him from some sort of confinement. The only authority
     defendant offers in support of his argument, State v. Weekes, 312 Minn. 1,
     250 N.W.2d 590 (1977), is distinguishable from the instant case. There the
     defendant was taken into custody and confined for "investigation" for more than
     34 hours, but was never arrested. In addition, the defendant in Weekes was
     repeatedly questioned until he finally confessed.
        [7][8] Defendant's final contention, that the trial court's instructions to
     the jury on the issue of the voluntariness of the confession were prejudicial,
     is without merit. In State v. Orscanin, 266 N.W.2d 880 (Minn.1978), we
     stated that it was error for the trial court to instruct the jury on the issue
     of the voluntariness of defendant's confession. Voluntariness is strictly a
     matter for the trial court at the omnibus hearing. Given our disposition of the
     voluntariness issue, the trial court's error in submitting the issue of
                       COPR. (C) WEST 1993 NO CLAIM TO ORIG. U.S. GOVT. WORKS
```

(**loc fs**) or jurisdiction (**loc cir9**). For a complete list, type **analysis** in Shepard's or see the *WESTLAW Reference Manual.*

It is also possible to use more than a single limit function at one time. For example, typing **loc fs,f2d** will display any citing case from either the *Federal Supplement* or the *Federal Reporter,* 2d. Likewise, **loc e,f** will display citing cases to which the *Shepard's* editors have assigned either an "explained" or a "followed" analytical abbreviation. Even more complicated and precise combinations are possible. For example, to find only *Federal Supplement* cases that have both been assigned an "explained" abbreviation and cite the case for its third headnote, type **loc fs,e,3.**

The flexibility of the Locate commands permits you to "fine-tune" your Shepardizing. By limiting your Shepard's display, you can deal very efficiently with a cited case that might have several columns or even several pages of citing authority in the hard-copy version of *Shepard's.*

Shepard's PreView

The main problem with *Shepard's Citations,* whether in its hard-copy or its on-line format, is currentness. The editors at Shepard's work from published advance sheets, and their editorial work takes some time. *Shepard's* pamphlets may be from two to nine months out of date by the time they reach your library.

To make the citators more current, Shepard's and West Publishing have jointly created a new service called Shepard's PreView. Shepard's PreView exists solely as an on-line service and is exclusive to WESTLAW. Shepard's PreView is created from the printed West advance sheets; citing cases will be listed in it about four to six weeks after they arrive at West.

Shepard's PreView contains *raw data,* offered to WESTLAW users before Shepard's has added its editorial enhancements. There is no "history" and "treatment" analysis or headnote numbers. Shepard's PreView is simply a citation list. The absence of editorial additions is the cost of currentness (Figure 3.13).

Figure 3.13   A Shepard's PreView Display on WESTLAW

```
                         SHEPARD'S PREVIEW              PAGE   1 OF   4
        Citations to:  109 S.Ct. 2207
                       South Carolina v. Gathers, (U.S.S.C.  1989)

        Retrieval
           No.    -------Citation------
                  ( 490 U.S. 805)          Same Text
                  ( 104 L.Ed.2d 876)       Same Text
            1      113 S.Ct. 838, 852

                        Cir. 4
            2      790 F.Supp. 594, 610

                        Ala
            3      601 So.2d 1062, 1079
            4      601 So.2d 1062, 1080
            5      603 So.2d 368, 381

        Note:  Citing references are only from West Reporters.  See SCOPE for a list.
               Check Shepard's (SH), Insta-Cite (IC), and QuickCite (QC).
        Copyright (C) 1993 Shepard's/McGraw-Hill, Inc. and West Publishing Company
```

The mechanics of Shepard's PreView are similar to those of the on-line version of Shepard's Citations. If you wish to see the Shepard's PreView display for a case you are viewing on WESTLAW, type **sp.** Or, from anywhere in WESTLAW, type **sp** and a citation. Like the on-line version of Shepard's Citations, Shepard's PreView is interactive: by entering a retrieval number from a citing list you can move instantaneously to the WESTLAW display of a citing case.

QuickCite

Shepard's PreView is created from the printed West advance sheets. That means that there is still a lag—usually about a month—between the loading of newly decided cases in WESTLAW and their appearance in Shepard's PreView. So, as current as Shepard's PreView is, it still isn't as current as yesterday. Quick*Cite* is.

Quick*Cite,* in fact, is the last word in timeliness. It literally can't get any faster than this. Quick*Cite* uses WESTLAW itself as a citator. Confused? That means that when you enter a citation in Quick*Cite,* it is reformulated as a search query and you select an "appropriate" database: if your case is a federal case, the search may be run in **allfeds;** if it is a state case, then it may be run in **allstates.** A date restriction is automatically included so that you only retrieve cases that are more recent than those in Shepard's and Shepard's PreView.

To use Quick*Cite,* you simply type **qc** while viewing a case (or the Shepard's, Shepard's PreView, or Insta-Cite display of a case). Select the **allstates** or **allfeds** database by pressing Enter. If you wish, you can customize your Quick*Cite* request to select a different database or date restriction. Figure 3.14a shows how you would do that and Figure 3.14b shows you what a Quick*Cite* display looks like.

Insta-Cite

Insta-Cite is West Publishing's case history and citation verification system. Insta-Cite is *very current.* Case history information is added to the system as

Figure 3.14 Using Quick*Cite*

(a) Instructions for Selecting a Database and Date Restriction

```
                            QUICKCITE
         Citation:  841 F.2D 282
                    Cohen v. Wedbush, Noble, Cooke, Inc. (9th Cir.(Cal.), Mar 02, 1988)

         COMMAND                    RESULT
         PRESS ENTER . . . . .      Updates Shepard's and Shepard's PreView by retrieving
                                    documents added to ALLFEDS after 10/92 that cite this
                                    decision.
         ALL . . . . . . . . .      Retrieves all ALLFEDS documents that cite this
                                    decision.
         DATABASE IDENTIFIER .      Retrieves documents added to WESTLAW after 10/92 that
         (e.g., SCT)                cite this decision in the selected database.
         Q . . . . . . . . . .      Displays the QuickCite query for editing in ALLFEDS.

            NOTE:  Your previous research will be discarded when you select a
                   QuickCite command.  For comprehensive citator information, also
                   use Insta-Cite (IC), Shepard's (SH) and Shepard's PreView (SP).


         If you wish to:
            Select a QuickCite command, type the COMMAND and press ENTER
            Go back to the previously accessed service, type GB and press ENTER
            Obtain further information on QuickCite, type HELP and press ENTER
```

soon as it arrives at West. This means that if an appellate court reverses a federal district court case, that reversal will be noted in the Insta-Cite display of the district court case within twenty-four to thirty-six hours of the receipt of the appellate decision by West. That's fast! Thus, Insta-Cite has the most up-to-date information possible on the history of a case.

Insta-Cite is *not* the same as Shepard's. Shepard's contains *all* the reported cases that have cited a particular case. Insta-Cite will give you the direct procedural history of the case ("direct history") *plus* later cases that have had a substantial negative impact on the precedential validity of the case ("negative indirect history"), but it is not a comprehensive citator. Thus, it will show overruling cases and questioning or limiting cases, but it will not show less consequential references. It will also give you *complete citation information*, including all parallel citations. Figure 3.15 illustrates all of these features; notice the distinction between "direct history" and "negative indirect history."

Figure 3.14 Using Quick*Cite* (continued)

(b) Quick*Cite* Result

```
Not Reported in F.Supp.         R 1 OF 1         P 6 OF 8         ALLFEDS         T
(Cite as: 1992 WL 392612, *3 (E.D.Pa.))
 the arbitration clause in the joint account agreement.  Therefore, according to
Gershman and Levitt, the clause should be rendered void because Defendants'
failure to disclose the existence and meaning of the arbitration clause
fraudulently induced them into signing the arbitration clause.
 In order to make a claim for fraudulent inducement, Gershman and Levitt must
show that there was either an affirmative misrepresentation or a failure to
disclose material information.  Marian Bank v. International Harvester
Credit Corp., 550 F.Supp. 456 (E.D.Pa.1982), aff'd, 725 F.2d 668 (3d
Cir.1983).  Gershman and Levitt contend that Defendants failed to disclose the
change in the arbitration clause in the joint account agreement, and therefore,
this matter should not be subject to arbitration.
 The contention of Gershman and Levitt is simply inaccurate.  The material
information--the arbitration clause in the joint account agreement--was
disclosed to Gershman and Levitt when they received it in the mail.  If
Gershman and Levitt would have taken the time to read the document they would
have become fully aware of the new arbitration clause.  It is absurd to think
that the election of Gershman and Levitt to sign the agreement without first
reading it constitutes a failure to disclose on the part of Defendants.
Cohen v. Wedbush Noble Cooke, Inc., 841 F.2d 282, 287-88 (9th Cir.1988).
This Court is unaware of any duty which requires brokers to orally highlight
the clauses of an agreement.
                       COPR. (C) WEST 1993 NO CLAIM TO ORIG. U.S. GOVT. WORKS
```

Figure 3.15   Insta-Cite Displays on WESTLAW

(a) Direct History

Parallel Citations

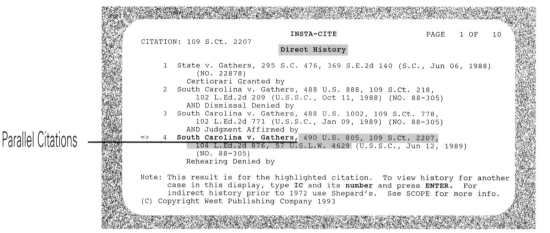

```
                              INSTA-CITE              PAGE   1 OF   10
      CITATION: 109 S.Ct. 2207
                             Direct History

          1  State v. Gathers, 295 S.C. 476, 369 S.E.2d 140 (S.C., Jun 06, 1988).
                (NO. 22878)
             Certiorari Granted by
          2  South Carolina v. Gathers, 488 U.S. 888, 109 S.Ct. 218,
                102 L.Ed.2d 209 (U.S.S.C., Oct 11, 1988) (NO. 88-305)
             AND Dismissal Denied by
          3  South Carolina v. Gathers, 488 U.S. 1002, 109 S.Ct. 778,
                102 L.Ed.2d 771 (U.S.S.C., Jan 09, 1989) (NO. 88-305)
             AND Judgment Affirmed by
    =>    4  South Carolina v. Gathers, 490 U.S. 805, 109 S.Ct. 2207,
                104 L.Ed.2d 876, 57 U.S.L.W. 4629 (U.S.S.C., Jun 12, 1989)
                (NO. 88-305)
             Rehearing Denied by

      Note: This result is for the highlighted citation.  To view history for another
            case in this display, type IC and its number and press ENTER.  For
            indirect history prior to 1972 use Shepard's.  See SCOPE for more info.
      (C) Copyright West Publishing Company 1993
```

(b) Negative Indirect History

```
                              INSTA-CITE              PAGE   2 OF   10
      CITATION: 109 S.Ct. 2207
                             Direct History

          5  South Carolina v. Gathers, 492 U.S. 938, 110 S.Ct. 24, 106 L.Ed.2d 636
                (U.S.S.C., Aug 30, 1989) (NO. 88-305)

                         Negative Indirect History

      Overruled by
          6  Payne v. Tennessee, 111 S.Ct. 2597, 115 L.Ed.2d 720, 59 U.S.L.W. 4814
                (U.S.Tenn., Jun 27, 1991) (NO. 90-5721)
      Overruling Recognized by
          7  Willie v. State, 585 So.2d 660 (Miss., Jul 24, 1991) (NO. 89-DP-1285)
          8  Pruett v. Thompson, 771 F.Supp. 1428 (E.D.Va., Aug 19, 1991)
                (NO. CIV.A.3:90CV00667)
          9  People v. Mickle, 54 Cal.3d 140, 284 Cal.Rptr. 511, 814 P.2d 290
                (Cal., Aug 19, 1991) (NO. S004708, CRIM. 25377, CRIM. 25540),
                rehearing denied (Oct 30, 1991)
         10  McWilliams (James Edmund) v. State, 1991 WL 184448
                (Ala.Cr.App., Aug 23, 1991) (NO. 6 DIV. 190)

      (C) Copyright West Publishing Company 1993
```

The statement at the bottom of the first screen describes the "depth" of Insta-Cite. Although the system has direct procedural history for federal cases as far back as 1754, it has indirect history only since 1972. To find indirect history before 1972, you must use Shepard's. Thus, the Insta-Cite display for *Betts v. Brady,* which was decided in 1942 and overruled in 1962, does not show the pre-1972 overruling case, *Gideon v. Wainwright,* but it does show two post-1972 cases that have noted its overruling (Figure 3.16a). The display for *Roe v. Wade,* which was decided in *1973,* shows complete direct *and* indirect negative history including the 1989 *Webster* case that limited the *Roe* holding (Figures 3.16b and 3.16c).

Like a Shepard's display, Insta-Cite displays are interactive with the WESTLAW databases. If, for example, you wished to view the *Webster* case in the *Roe v. Wade* example, you would type 20. Insta-Cite, Shepard's Citations,

Figure 3.16   Precedential History on Insta-Cite

(a) *Betts v. Brady*

```
                              INSTA-CITE            PAGE   1 OF    2
   CITATION: 62 S.Ct. 1252
                            Direct History

=>   1  Betts v. Brady, 316 U.S. 455, 62 S.Ct. 1252, 86 L.Ed. 1595
            (U.S.Md., Jun 01, 1942) (NO. 837)

                        Negative Indirect History

   Overruling Recognized by
       2  Murray v. Giarratano, 492 U.S. 1, 109 S.Ct. 2765, 106 L.Ed.2d 1,
            57 U.S.L.W. 4889 (U.S.Va., Jun 23, 1989) (NO. 88-411)
       3  Fletcher v. Armontrout, 725 F.Supp. 1075 (W.D.Mo., Nov 13, 1989)
            (NO. 89-0435-CV-W-JWO)
       4  Peltier v. State, 119 Idaho 454, 808 P.2d 373 (Idaho, Feb 27, 1991)
            (NO. 17214)
       5  U.S. v. Curtis, 32 M.J. 252, 59 U.S.L.W. 2742 (CMA, Apr 18, 1991)
            (NO. 63,044, NMCM 87-3856)

   Note: This result is for the highlighted citation.  To view history for another
         case in this display, type IC and its number and press ENTER.  For
         indirect history prior to 1972 use Shepard's.  See SCOPE for more info.
   (C) Copyright West Publishing Company 1993
```

(b) *Roe v. Wade*

```
                              INSTA-CITE            PAGE   1 OF    7
   CITATION: 93 S.Ct. 705
                            Direct History

       1  Roe v. Wade, 314 F.Supp. 1217 (N.D.Tex., Jun 17, 1970)
            (NO. CIV. 3-3690-B, CIV. 3-3691-C)
            Jurisdiction Postponed by
       2  Roe v. Wade, 402 U.S. 941, 91 S.Ct. 1610, 29 L.Ed.2d 108
            (U.S.Tex., May 03, 1971) (NO. 808)
            AND Judgment Affirmed in Part, Reversed in Part by
=>     3  Roe v. Wade, 410 U.S. 113, 93 S.Ct. 705, 35 L.Ed.2d 147
            (U.S.Tex., Jan 22, 1973) (NO. 70-18)
            For Concurring Opinion, see
       4  Roe v. Wade, 410 U.S. 179, 93 S.Ct. 755, 35 L.Ed.2d 147
            (U.S., Jan 22, 1973) (NO. 70-18, 70-40)
            AND For Concurring Opinion, see
       5  Roe v. Wade, 410 U.S. 179, 93 S.Ct. 756, 35 L.Ed.2d 147
            (U.S., Jan 22, 1973) (NO. 70-18, 70-40)

   Note: This result is for the highlighted citation.  To view history for another
         case in this display, type IC and its number and press ENTER.  For
         indirect history prior to 1972 use Shepard's.  See SCOPE for more info.
   (C) Copyright West Publishing Company 1993
```

(c) *Roe v. Wade*, continued

```
                              INSTA-CITE            PAGE   4 OF    7
   CITATION: 93 S.Ct. 705

   Related References
      17  Doe v. Bolton, 126 F.R.D. 85 (N.D.Ga., May 02, 1989) (NO. CIV A 13676)

                        Negative Indirect History

   Disagreement Recognized by
      18  People v. Berquist (Richard), 1993 WL 17818
              (Ill.App. 2 Dist., Jan 28, 1993) (NO. 2-91-0976, 2-91-0977,
              2-91-0978, 2-91-0970, 2-91-0971, 2-91-0972, 2-91-0973, 2-91-0974,
              2-91-0975)
   Called into Doubt by
      19  Coe v. Melahn, 958 F.2d 223 (8th Cir.(Mo.), Mar 02, 1992)
              (NO. 90-1552)
   Holding Limited by
      20  Webster v. Reproductive Health Services, 492 U.S. 490, 109 S.Ct. 3040,
              106 L.Ed.2d 410, 57 U.S.L.W. 5023 (U.S.Mo., Jul 03, 1989)
              (NO. 88-605)

   (C) Copyright West Publishing Company 1993
```

and Shepard's PreView are also interactive among themselves. You can move from one to another by typing **ic, sh, sp,** or **qc** as appropriate.

Conclusion

There is no legal research tool that first-year law students find more confusing at first glance than *Shepard's Citations.* If you find yourself baffled by the endless pages of numbers and letter abbreviations, you are not alone—generations of students have initially been baffled by "these red books, thick and thin." But after some practice, you will find that Shepardizing is really quite simple. WESTLAW access to Shepard's Citations makes it even simpler. If, after you have worked with *Shepard's,* you still do not understand the procedure or the result, ask a reference librarian for help or read the pamphlet prepared by Shepard's called *How to Use Shepard's Citations* or the *WESTLAW Reference Manual.*

Insta-Cite is a case history and citation verification service. It is the most up-to-date way of determining whether a case is still good authority. Many attorneys routinely use Insta-Cite as both the first step and the last step in the research process or even as the final check before submitting a brief or memo. Updating your research with Shepard's Citations, Shepard's PreView, Quick*Cite,* and Insta-Cite is an essential part of every research assignment. It is a good practice to start in law school.

4 LEGISLATION

If you suspect your issue involves a statute, you should begin your research with a check through the statutory codes. A practicing attorney is more likely to need a statute than a case, though this can vary from one legal specialty to another. Although you may become acquainted with the Uniform Commercial Code in Contracts and a few scattered constitutional provisions elsewhere, many first-year law students do not receive a systematic introduction to the legislative process and its resultant publications. This is changing as more courses concentrate on the legislative process, but case law still tends to receive more attention in law school. In this chapter, we will introduce you to the common forms of legislative publications, with a special focus on federal materials. Learn this and you will be ahead of the game.

Federal Laws

A federal law first appears in the information stream as a bill introduced in Congress by a representative or a senator. A bill is assigned its own unique number depending on the side of the legislature in which it originates and the order in which it is introduced. Then it is referred to the appropriate House or Senate committee. For example, an amendment to the Truth in Lending Act passed in 1980 began life as H.R. 4986, which means that it came from the House of Representatives (H.R.) and was the 4986th bill introduced in the House during that Congress. Once a bill is introduced and sent to the appropriate committee, it can meet several fates. Most bills sink from sight never to be seen again. Others are passed by the House but die in the Senate. The same fate awaits many bills that are passed by the Senate and are then sent to the House. Sometimes both the House and Senate pass a bill, but in different versions due to the process of amendment; in that case, a conference committee, with members from each house, is appointed to try to hammer out a compromise that can then be passed by each house. If both the House and Senate pass the same version of the bill, this process can be skipped, but in either case, the final version is sent to the president who can sign it into law or veto it and send it back to the house where it started. The House and Senate can then try to override the president's veto by mustering a two-thirds vote in each house (Figure 4.1).

Figure 4.1   The Legislative Process and Accompanying Documents

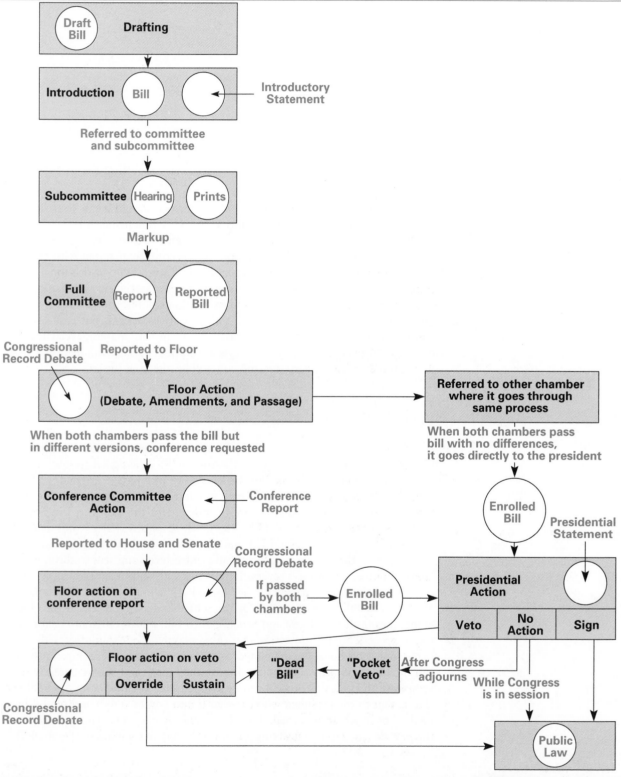

Source: Figure 4.1 is adapted from *A Research Guide to Congress: How to Make Congress Work for You, Second Edition* by Judith Manion, Joseph Meringolo and Robert Oakes and used with the permission of Legi-Slate, Inc.

Each step in the process can be repeated, and when a controversial or high-profile issue is involved, there may be a host of bills on the same issue. Only a few hundred bills survive to become law. Later in life you may have to do a legislative history, a process that is as enjoyable as root canal work. Fortunately, using the laws themselves is relatively easy.

A law, also called a statute or an act, is identified by a public law number, which is comprised of the number of the Congress in which it passed, followed by a number that reflects the order in which the bill was enacted; for example, P.L. 101–12 refers to the 12th law passed in the 101st Congress. As soon as they are enacted, federal laws are published separately in pamphlet form as "slip laws." Slip laws include valuable information in the headings and margin notes. From them, you can learn when the law was approved, the number of the bill that was enacted into law, and the short title or popular name of the law. The reference to the *United States Code* (U.S.C.) will tell you where the provision will be codified in the U.S.C. The *U.S. Statutes at Large* citation will tell you the initial page of the law in the permanent bound volume. At the end of the slip law, you will find references to House and Senate Reports as well as citations to the congressional debates. These "legislative history" references will tell you where you can find congressional materials that may help you determine the intent of the language of the law (Figure 4.2).

Although slip laws sound rather useful, you will not find them in most libraries. They are messy and hard to keep organized. But fear not, the slip laws are compiled into several much more useful formats. You can access current public laws on WESTLAW in the United States Public Laws database (**us-pl**).

At the end of each session of Congress, all of the slip laws for that year are compiled in numerical order and published in bound volumes. These laws are generically called "session laws" because they are compiled for each session of Congress. Similarly, each year's **us-pl** database is "recompiled" into a new database for session laws passed during that year. For example, to retrieve P.L. 101–265, the National Affordable Housing Act of 1990, enter the search **ci(101-265)** in the **us-pl90** database. You can also retrieve the same act by searching for words in the heading, which is included in the caption field, **ca(affordable)**.

The law as it is passed by Congress and as it appears in the session laws is useful if you are looking for the original version of an act before it has been codified by its subject areas or amended, or if you require the language of a particular amendment. You will also use the session laws if you need to find a law that has been repealed and deleted from the code. For example, assume that your client committed a crime for which she received a sentence and a fine. If the crime was committed in 1986 before the date on which a new law on the topic became effective, you would have to look for the language of the repealed law that has been deleted from the code. When new laws are printed in the session laws, they have a "preamble" that may explain what the law is designed to do. This preamble can be helpful in determining the legislative intent of the act.

Note: although session laws serve specific purposes, you cannot safely use the session law version of a statute to determine the *present* text of a law, since

Figure 4.2   A Slip Law: Headings, Margin Notes, and Legislative History References

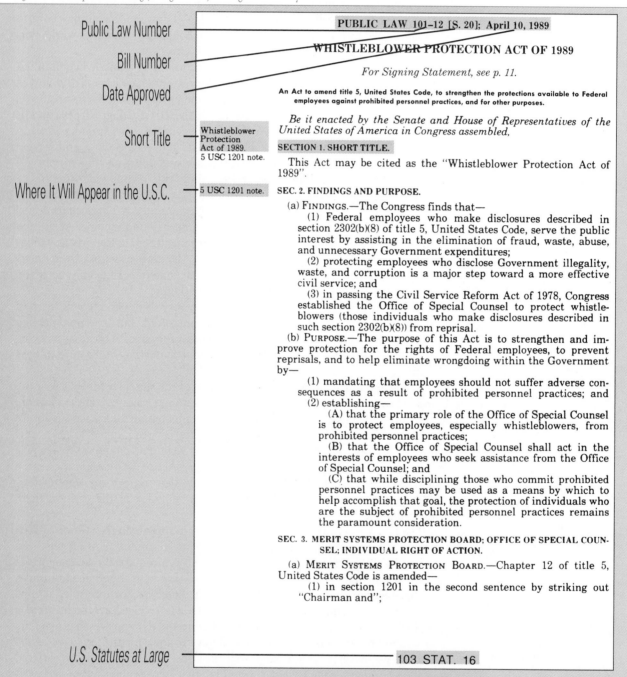

Public Law Number

Bill Number

Date Approved

Short Title

Where It Will Appear in the U.S.C.

U.S. Statutes at Large

PUBLIC LAW 101–12 [S. 20]; April 10, 1989

WHISTLEBLOWER PROTECTION ACT OF 1989

For Signing Statement, see p. 11.

An Act to amend title 5, United States Code, to strengthen the protections available to Federal employees against prohibited personnel practices, and for other purposes.

Be it enacted by the Senate and House of Representatives of the United States of America in Congress assembled,

Whistleblower
Protection
Act of 1989.
5 USC 1201 note.

SECTION 1. SHORT TITLE.

This Act may be cited as the "Whistleblower Protection Act of 1989".

5 USC 1201 note.

SEC. 2. FINDINGS AND PURPOSE.

(a) FINDINGS.—The Congress finds that—
(1) Federal employees who make disclosures described in section 2302(b)(8) of title 5, United States Code, serve the public interest by assisting in the elimination of fraud, waste, abuse, and unnecessary Government expenditures;
(2) protecting employees who disclose Government illegality, waste, and corruption is a major step toward a more effective civil service; and
(3) in passing the Civil Service Reform Act of 1978, Congress established the Office of Special Counsel to protect whistle-blowers (those individuals who make disclosures described in such section 2302(b)(8)) from reprisal.
(b) PURPOSE.—The purpose of this Act is to strengthen and im-prove protection for the rights of Federal employees, to prevent reprisals, and to help eliminate wrongdoing within the Government by—
(1) mandating that employees should not suffer adverse con-sequences as a result of prohibited personnel practices; and
(2) establishing—
(A) that the primary role of the Office of Special Counsel is to protect employees, especially whistleblowers, from prohibited personnel practices;
(B) that the Office of Special Counsel shall act in the interests of employees who seek assistance from the Office of Special Counsel; and
(C) that while disciplining those who commit prohibited personnel practices may be used as a means by which to help accomplish that goal, the protection of individuals who are the subject of prohibited personnel practices remains the paramount consideration.

SEC. 3. MERIT SYSTEMS PROTECTION BOARD; OFFICE OF SPECIAL COUN-SEL; INDIVIDUAL RIGHT OF ACTION.

(a) MERIT SYSTEMS PROTECTION BOARD.—Chapter 12 of title 5, United States Code is amended—
(1) in section 1201 in the second sentence by striking out "Chairman and";

103 STAT. 16

Figure 4.2   A Slip Law: Headings, Margin Notes, and Legislative History References (continued)

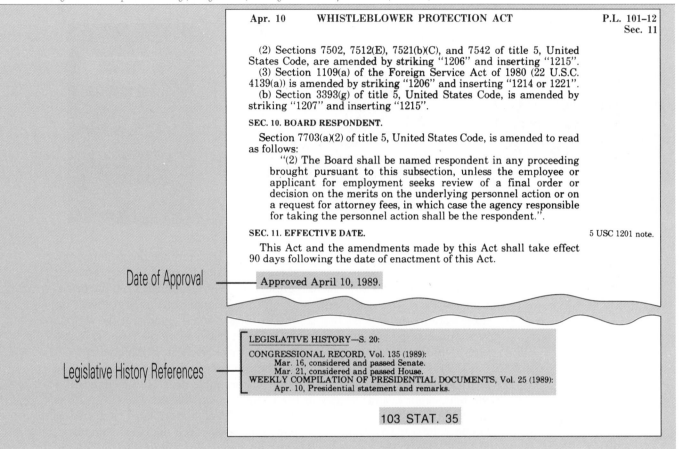

Date of Approval

Legislative History References

the original law may have been repealed or amended. You will find the present text of a law in a code, as explained later in this chapter.

Federal session laws can be located in three sources: *U.S. Statutes at Large* (Stat.) published by the U.S. Government Printing Office; *United States Code Congressional & Administrative News®* (U.S.C.C.A.N.) published by West; and *Advance* pamphlets to *United States Code Service®* (U.S.C.S.) published by Lawyers Cooperative (Figure 4.3). The *U.S. Statutes at Large* is the *official* session law publication produced by the U.S. Government Printing Office for federal laws. *Statutes at Large* is found in every law library, but, as is frequently true of government publications, it is very slow to arrive, lagging three to four years behind the end of the session covered.

One of the titles that publishes session laws also contains valuable information pertaining to the history of those laws. *U.S. Code Congressional and Administrative News* (U.S.C.C.A.N.), published by West, includes selective legislative history material. It lists the citations for the House, Senate, and conference committee reports and reprints the report or reports that it determines

Figure 4.3   The Three Sources of Session Laws

to be the most closely related to the public law. To determine the meaning of a statute, you may need to refer to these congressional committee reports. For example, assume that your client represents over fifty plaintiffs from the petroleum industry. The case revolves around the meaning of the term "well" in three statutory provisions. By reading the congressional reports for the various acts, you may be able to determine the exact meaning of the term. It is this type of information that is gleaned from the legislative history materials.

U.S.C.C.A.N. does not reprint all the congressional materials, such as the hearings and debates, but the legislative history table does list the citations to the bills, reports, and debates in the *Congressional Record*. U.S.C.C.A.N. is updated monthly in separate softbound pamphlets that are later published in bound volumes. To obtain the most current laws, check the latest pamphlets. On WESTLAW, the Legislative History (**lh**) database contains House, Senate, and conference committee reports as set forth in U.S.C.C.A.N. from 1978 to the present as well as all congressional committee reports on pending legislation after July 1990. If you want to access the congressional debates as reported in the *Congressional Record* on-line, you can search the **cr** database on WESTLAW.

Codes

Laws are classified or "codified" by subject or topic in volumes called "codes." These codes not only group the laws by subject, but also show all subsequent amendments. This makes life much simpler. Most often you will use one of the codes (actually, you will use an "annotated code," but that's in the next section) when you try to locate federal statutes with all of their amendments and deletions.

Codes are easy to use and are effective research tools if used correctly. To locate laws efficiently, you need a basic understanding of how the codes are organized. Federal laws are collected and organized by subject matter into fifty "titles" and compiled into a code. There is no magic to the number "50." Codes can be built around *any* subject arrangement. Some states use lots of

Figure 4.4   The Three Sources
of Federal Codes

Figure 4.4   The Three Sources of Federal Codes

topics, some only a few. The federal government decided on fifty topics in the 1920s and has retained the same arrangement ever since, even though a few of the topics are never used. For example, laws pertaining to age discrimination will be classified under Title 29, which is the title designated to laws concerning labor. Each title of the *U.S. Code* is further divided into subdivisions called chapters and sections. For age discrimination, the chapter would be 14 "Age Discrimination in Employment," and the section would be 623 "Prohibition of Age Discrimination." The citation to the code would read 29 U.S.C. 623; you omit the chapter number in the citation and retain the section number. Recall that in addition to placing similar laws together under topics, codes also incorporate amendments and indicate repeals. Some laws may apply to more than one subject, so you may have to check more than one place in the code.

There are three federal codes: the *United States Code* is the official code for federal laws, while the *United States Code Annotated*® and the *United States Code Service* are both unofficial annotated codes (Figure 4.4). Each of the codes is useful for certain purposes.

United States Code

The *United States Code* (U.S.C.) is published by the U.S. Government Printing Office. The whole set is recompiled every six years, using the same fifty subject categories or titles. Congress has deemed the U.S.C. prima facie evidence of the actual text, which means simply that the U.S.C. is sort of official. Ask your legal research instructor why we say "sort of."

The U.S.C. contains only the text of the law. It does not give citations to the cases that have interpreted the statutes; this information can only be found in one of the annotated codes. The U.S.C. is also very cumbersome to use. Although you can find material in the U.S.C. by checking the multivolume index, the material may not be as current as you need. As we noted, the U.S.C. is reissued every six years, with cumulative annual supplements between the new editions. In reality, the annual cumulative supplements do not appear in the library until eight months to two years have passed. Therefore, if you rely only on the U.S.C., you will miss the current laws, amendments, and deletions.

The reason that you may need to use the U.S.C. at all is that the *Bluebook* says "to cite the U.S.C. if therein." Therefore, the U.S.C. has the advantage of being official, but the two unofficial codes are much more helpful research tools than the U.S.C.

Federal Codes on WESTLAW

You may prefer the convenience of accessing the codes on computer rather than searching in the printed materials. Fortunately, the federal statutes in codified form are available on-line in the WESTLAW **usc** database, and the U.S.C.A.® is in the WESTLAW **usca** database. To survey the coverage of the titles, use the Scope command to check the currentness of each title. Each title is updated through a specific public law number. You can retrieve the text of

the code section by using the Find service with the citation of the code section. For example, type **fi 20 usca 60** or, in the WESTLAW **usca** database, use **ci(20 +5 60)**; the "+5" is an instruction to the computer to locate "60" within 5 characters of "20." If you are researching case law on-line and you see a citation to a code section, it is easy to "jump" to that section by using the Tab key, read the statutory language, and then go back (**gb**) to reading your case.

Generally speaking, the bound codes have good print indexes, but at times those indexes just don't seem to have the access points that you had expected. Then a full-text search of the WESTLAW **usc** or **usca** database can be especially helpful. Likewise, when you are searching for the interpretation of a particular word or phrase or want to see all of the occurrences of that word or phrase throughout the code, the print indexes may be of little use, and a WESTLAW search will be essential.

Annotated Codes

Annotated codes are more useful versions of the U.S.C. Not only do they contain the text of the U.S.C., they also refer to the cases that have interpreted the federal laws. For any statutory research, you will want to use one of the annotated codes—they are universally accepted. Both of the annotated codes— West's *United States Code Annotated* (U.S.C.A.) and Lawyers Cooperative's *United States Code Service* (U.S.C.S.)—contain basically the same text and title and section numbers as the official U.S.C. Both annotated codes contain references to cases that have construed the statutes, to administrative regulations, and to secondary sources. The annotated codes also contain cross-references to related sections within the code. Each annotated code refers to the research tools provided by its publisher; that is, U.S.C.A. cites to West's other publications, and U.S.C.S. cites to the publications of Lawyers Cooperative. You may have a preference for one publisher's materials, or you may simply use whatever is available at the time that you need it.

United States Code Annotated

The *United States Code Annotated* (U.S.C.A.) is an excellent example of West's publishing philosophy. West believes in providing as much information as possible, leaving it to the researcher to wade through the information and discard what is not relevant. Following this philosophy, U.S.C.A. occupies well over two hundred volumes and provides the researcher with citations to all the cases that it can locate and a wide variety of other references as well (Figure 4.5). If you like receiving as much information as possible, you will prefer using the U.S.C.A.

In essence, by enhancing the statutory text with notes and references to other research materials, West allows you to use the U.S.C.A. as an entryway to a statutory research system. In the U.S.C.A., directly following the text of the statute, you will find the history of the statute. It indicates, in parentheses, when the law was originally passed and when it was amended or repealed. It

Figure 4.5   Information Available in the U.S.C.A.

SUBCHAPTER I—HOUSING RENOVATION AND MODERNIZATION

CROSS REFERENCES

Insurance of mortgages, see 12 USCA § 1743.
Maintenance of records and public disclosure, see 12 USCA § 2803.
State constitutional and legal limits upon interest chargeable on loans, mortgages, or other interim financing arrangements, see 12 USCA § 1709–1a.

Cross-References

§ 1702. Administrative provisions

The powers conferred by this chapter shall be exercised by the Secretary of Housing and Urban Development (hereinafter referred to as the "Secretary"). In order to carry out the provisions of this subchapter and subchapters II, III, V, VI, VII, VIII, IX–A, IX–B, and

HISTORICAL AND STATUTORY NOTES

Revision Notes and Legislative Reports
   1941 Act. House Report No. 517, see 1941 U.S.Code Cong. Service, p. 570.

   1948 Act. House Report No. 2389, see 1948 U.S.Code Cong. Service, p. 2351.

   1949 Acts. House Report No. 854, see 1949 U.S.Code Cong. Service, p. 1757.

   House Report No. 1396, see 1949 U.S. Code Cong. Service, p. 2216.

   1950 Act. Senate Report No. 1286 and

   1988 Act. House Report No. 100–122 (I & II) and House Conference Report No. 100–426, see 1987 U.S.Code Cong. and Adm.News, p. 3317.

References in Text
   This chapter, referred to in text, was in the original "this Act", meaning Act June 27, 1934, c. 847, 48 Stat. 1246, as amended, known as the National Housing Act. For complete classification of this Act to the Code, see note under

U.S.C.C.A.N. References

EXECUTIVE ORDERS

EXECUTIVE ORDER NO. 7280

Ex.Ord. No. 7280, Jan. 28, 1936, was issued as evidence of the creation of the former Federal Housing Administration and validated and confirmed the creation thereof.

Executive Orders

CROSS REFERENCES

Construction of defense housing by private enterprise, see 42 USCA § 1591a.

Cross-References

LIBRARY REFERENCES

West Topic and Key Number

American Digest System
   Disbursements for housing, see United States ☜82(3 to 3.5, 7).
   Instrumentalities of United States for housing, see United States ☜53(9).
Encyclopedias
   Federal loans, grants and insurance of loans for housing, see C.J.S. United States § 70.

Library References

C.J.S. Reference

191

Figure 4.5   Information Available in the U.S.C.A. (continued)

Text and Treatise Reference

WESTLAW Reference

Notes of Decisions

Subdivision Index

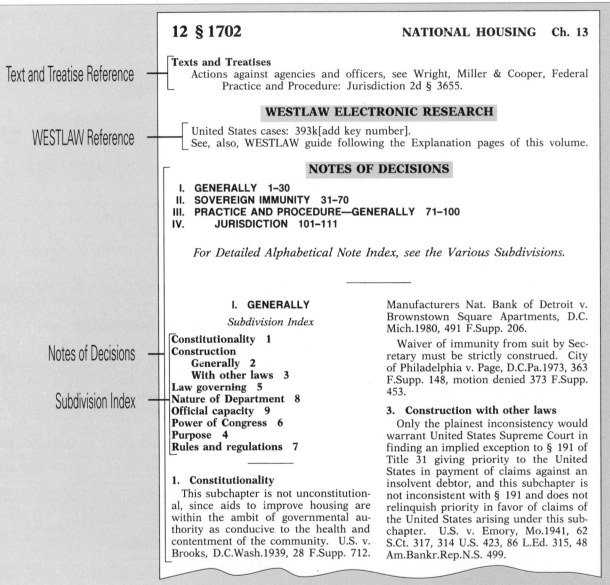

12 § 1702   **NATIONAL HOUSING   Ch. 13**

Texts and Treatises
  Actions against agencies and officers, see Wright, Miller & Cooper, Federal
  Practice and Procedure: Jurisdiction 2d § 3655.

WESTLAW ELECTRONIC RESEARCH

United States cases: 393k[add key number].
See, also, WESTLAW guide following the Explanation pages of this volume.

NOTES OF DECISIONS

  I.   GENERALLY   1–30
  II. SOVEREIGN IMMUNITY   31–70
  III. PRACTICE AND PROCEDURE—GENERALLY   71–100
  IV.   JURISDICTION   101–111

For Detailed Alphabetical Note Index, see the Various Subdivisions.

———

I.   GENERALLY

Subdivision Index

Constitutionality   1
Construction
    Generally   2
    With other laws   3
Law governing   5
Nature of Department   8
Official capacity   9
Power of Congress   6
Purpose   4
Rules and regulations   7

———

1.   Constitutionality
  This subchapter is not unconstitutional, since aids to improve housing are within the ambit of governmental authority as conducive to the health and contentment of the community. U.S. v. Brooks, D.C.Wash.1939, 28 F.Supp. 712.

Manufacturers Nat. Bank of Detroit v. Brownstown Square Apartments, D.C. Mich.1980, 491 F.Supp. 206.

  Waiver of immunity from suit by Secretary must be strictly construed. City of Philadelphia v. Page, D.C.Pa.1973, 363 F.Supp. 148, motion denied 373 F.Supp. 453.

3.   Construction with other laws
  Only the plainest inconsistency would warrant United States Supreme Court in finding an implied exception to § 191 of Title 31 giving priority to the United States in payment of claims against an insolvent debtor, and this subchapter is not inconsistent with § 191 and does not relinquish priority in favor of claims of the United States arising under this subchapter. U.S. v. Emory, Mo.1941, 62 S.Ct. 317, 314 U.S. 423, 86 L.Ed. 315, 48 Am.Bankr.Rep.N.S. 499.

will provide citations to the *U.S. Statutes at Large* origin of the text as well as to amendments. The historical notes provide detail on specific word changes. This information can be extremely helpful when a law has gone through several revisions. Cross-references to related and qualifying laws are included to prevent oversights. Other references indicate where the legislative history can be located in the *United States Code Congressional and Administrative News* (U.S.C.C.A.N.). You will also find citations to the *Code of Federal Regulations* (C.F.R.), which contains administrative regulations (Figure 4.6).

Figure 4.6 References to the Code of Federal Regulations in the U.S.C.A.

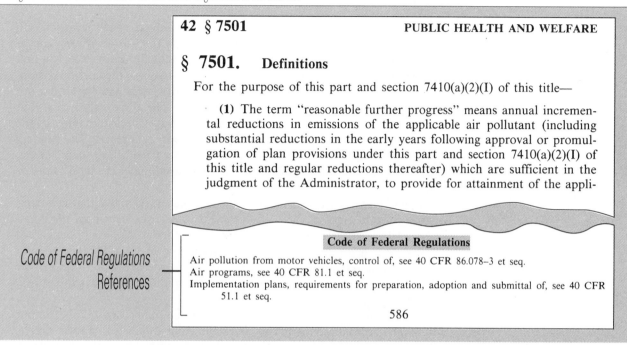

Code of Federal Regulations
References

The Library References section gives the applicable West topic and key numbers and citations to *Corpus Juris Secundum*® (C.J.S.), the West legal encyclopedia. The West topic and key numbers give you access points into the West digests. The U.S.C.A. also contains references to other relevant materials published by West, such as West's *Federal Forms* and West's *Federal Practice Manual*®.

As we observed earlier, the U.S.C.A. is known for its abundance of annotations of court and administrative decisions. Annotations are one-sentence summaries, written by West's editors, that indicate if, and how, courts or administrative bodies have interpreted a law. The case citation appears at the end of each annotation, so that you can find the case and read it yourself. At times, you will find an annotation to an opinion by the attorney general. Although these opinions are only persuasive, they could be useful and should be read. Some statutes have been interpreted by the courts so many times that West provides an index to the annotations so you can preselect cases involving your legal issue. Some statutes may not have been the subject of litigation and will not have any annotations.

To be absolutely sure that you have all the cases that cite a federal statute, you may want to search on WESTLAW for code references in case law. When you know the citation of a statute or code section, search for references to that citation. For example, to retrieve federal circuit court cases that cite 12 U.S.C. 1702, access the U.S. courts of appeals (**cta**) case law database and do the following Terms and Connectors search in the headnote field:

he(12 +5 1702)

How to Use the U.S.C.A.

If you need a specific statute but know only the subject of the law, you will need to use the multivolume general index for the U.S.C.A. It is very important to consider as many terms as possible when using the index. You will find the index includes many cross-references that lead you to the correct section. For example, your client has lost his credit card. Unfortunately, he did not report the loss to the bank that issued the card. The bank claims that your client is responsible for the unauthorized purchases. Check the index to the U.S.C.A. under "credit cards" to find the appropriate statutes. The heading "Credit Cards and Plates" refers you to "Consumer Credit Protection." Going to this heading, you will find the laws that you need under the term "Loss or theft" (Figure 4.7).

If you know the popular name of the act, that is, the name that it is commonly known by, such as Title VII or the FOIA Act, you can check the Popular Name Table located at the end of the General Index. We use "popular" in a special sense here—it is not as if these laws have been on MTV. The popular name of an act is sometimes just the author of the act—for example, the Gramm-Rudman-Hollings Act named after the authors of the act in the U.S. Senate.

If you approach the U.S.C.A. with either the public law number or the *Statutes at Large* citation, you can check the volumes labeled "Tables" at the end of the set. These tables translate the public law number and the *Statutes at Large* citation, broken down into its component section numbers, into its corresponding U.S.C.A. citation (Figure 4.8).

Updating the U.S.C.A.

The constant possibility of change in legislation makes it *mandatory* for you to check for the very latest amendments to a law. Always check the publication date (copyright date on the back of the title page) of the hard-copy volume to determine if your law needs updating. To check for amendments, deletions, and new annotations that have appeared since the bound volume was published, check the supplementary pamphlets inserted in the back of each volume; these are called "pocket parts" because they fit into pockets in the cover of each volume. *Always, always, check the pocket part.* Do you catch our drift? Check it. The pocket parts are arranged by the same section numbers as the bound volume.

Because pocket parts to the U.S.C.A. appear only once a year, there are many times when a new law or amendment is not yet included. To fill this gap, the U.S.C.A. issues bimonthly noncumulative pamphlets of the newest laws and amendments arranged in U.S.C.A. classification. All of the new annotations also appear in these pamphlets. Usually, two additional pamphlets, as needed, will also be issued. These are the *U.S.C.A. Statutory Supplements* containing all amendments to the code through the last law of the session signed by the president. These two pamphlets are not arranged in U.S.C.A. classification, but are in public law form. Late in any given year, you will have to check the main volume, the pocket part, and each of the year's pamphlets. An amazing number of people forget to check the pamphlets. Don't be one of them.

Figure 4.7   Using the U.S.C.A. Index

CREATIVE   972

CREATIVE WRITING
"Arts" as including, National Foundation on
  the Arts and the Humanities Act of
  1965, **20 § 952**

CREDIT (PAYMENT OF INDEBTEDNESS)
  —Cont'd
Regional Agricultural Credit Corporations,
  generally, this index

Cross-Reference

Equal credit opportunity. Consumer Credit
  Protection, generally, this index
Extortionate Credit Transactions, generally,
  this index
Fair credit billing. Consumer Credit Protec-
  tion, generally, this index
Farm credit,
  Agricultural Credit, generally, this index
  Farm Credit Administration, generally, this
    index
  Farm Credit Bank, generally, this index
  Farm Credit Banks, generally, this index
  Farm Credit System, generally, this index
Farm Credit Administration, generally, this

CREDIT CARD FRAUD ACT OF 1984
Text of Act, **18 §§ 1029, 1029 nt**
Credit cards or plates. Consumer Credit Pro-
  tection, generally, this index
Short title, **18 § 1001 nt**

CREDIT CARDS AND PLATES
Consumer Credit Protection, this index
Credit billing. Consumer Credit Protection,
  this index
Fair credit billing. Consumer Credit Protec-
  tion, generally, this index
System, person operating, financial records,
  maintenance of, **12 § 1953**

583   **CONSUMER**

CONSUMER CREDIT PROTECTION
  —Cont'd
Credit billing—Cont'd
  Statement,
    Effect of failure of timely mailing or de-
      livery of, **15 § 1666b**
    Required with each billing cycle, **15
      § 1637**
  Surcharge,
    Defined, prohibition, surcharge on card-
      holders, **15 § 1602**
    "Discount" as excluding, inducements to
      cardholders by sellers of cash dis-
      counts for payments by cash, etc., **15
      § 1602**
    On cardholder electing to use card pro-
      hibited, **15 § 1666f**
  Time, notice, correction of billing errors, **15
    § 1666**
  Transmit statement to last address of obli-
    gor, **15 § 1666**
  Treatment of credit balances, **15 § 1666d**
  Use of,
    Annual percentage rate in oral disclo-
      sures, exceptions, **15 § 1665a**
    Cash discounts, **15 § 1666f**
  Usury laws of State, etc., cash discounts
    not considered as finance charge or
    other charge for credit for sales trans-
    actions, **15 § 1666j**

Reference to the Statute

Credit cards and plates,
  Accepted credit card, defined, **15 § 1602**
  Access device,

CONSUMER CREDIT PROTECTION
  —Cont'd
Credit cards and plates—Cont'd
  "Credit device" existing for purpose of ob-
    taining money, property, etc., as mean-
    ing, **15 § 1602**
  Defined, **15 § 1602**
  Device-making equipment, defined, **18
    § 1029**
  Direct mail applications and solicitation,
    disclosure requirements, **15 § 1637**
  Exclusiveness of liability of cardholder, **15
    § 1643**
  Fraud,
    Access devices, **18 § 1029**
      Interception of wire, etc., communica-
        tions, authorization, **18 § 2516**
    Secret Service arrests, **18 § 3056**
  Fraudulent use, **15 § 1644**
  General information without specific term,
    applications and solicitations, disclosure
    requirements, **15 § 1637**
  Issuance, **15 § 1642**
  Issuers, access to open end consumer credit
    plans, disclosure requirements, **15
    § 1637**
  Liability of cardholder, **15 § 1643**
  Liability of issuer, violation of disclosure re-
    quirements, **15 § 1640**
  Limits on liability of cardholder, **15 § 1643**
  Loss or theft, liability of cardholder for un-
    authorized use in event of, **15 § 1643**
  Other laws or agreement with issuer, liabili-

Figure 4.8 Finding the U.S.C.A. Citation from the Tables

1968   **STATUTES AT LARGE**

1968—90th Cong.—82 Stat.   **U S C A**

Apr.	P.L.	Sec.	Page	Tit.	Sec.	Status
29	90–296	1	109	28	1407	
		2	110	28	prec. 1391	
	90–297	1	110	42	1958	Rep.
		2, 3	111	42	1958 nts	Elim.
	90–298	—	111	46	817	
May						
3	90–299	1	112	47	223	
		2	112	47	153	
4	90–300	—	113	12	355	
7	90–301	1(a)	113	38	1810	
		1(b)	113	38	1811	
		2(a)	113	38	1810	
		2(b)	113	38	1822	Rep.
		3(a)	113	12	1709—1	Rep.
		3(b)	114	12	1713	
		3(c)	114	12	1715e	
		3(d)	114	12	1715v	
		3(e)	114	12	1715y	
		4	114	12	1709—1 nt	
		5(a)	116	38	prec. 1827	
		5(b)	116	38	prec. 1801	
8	90–302	1	117	42	1752, 1752 nt	
		2(a)	117	42	1755	
		2(b)	117	42	1758	
		3	117	42	1761	
		4	119	42	1776	
		5	119	42	1773	
17	90–308	—	123	25	331 nt	
	90–309	2	123	25	396f nt	
18	90–311	1 to 3	124	43	615 to 615e nt	Elim.
	90–312	—	125	33	59f	
22	90–313	1–7	126–129	49	1653 nt	
23	90–314	—	129	22	2589	
24	90–318	—	131	16	1132 nt	
29	90–321	1, 101	146	15	1601 nt	
		102	146	15	1601	
		103	147	15	1602	
		104	147	15	1603	
		105	148	15	1604	
		106	148	15	1605	
		107	149	15	1606	
		108	150	15	1607	
		109	150	15	1608	
		110	151	15	1609	Rep.
		111	151	15	1610	
		112	151	15	1611	
		113	151	15	1612	
		114	151	15	1613	
		115	—	15	1614	Rep.
		121	152	15	1631	
		122	152	15	1632	
		123	152	15	1633	
		124	152	15	1634	
		125	152	15	1635	
		126	153	15	1636	Rep.
		127	153	15	1637	
		128	155	15	1638	
		129	156	15	1639	Rep.
		130	157	15	1640	
		131	157	15	1641	
		132	—	15	1642	
		133	—	15	1643	
		134	—	15	1644	
		135	—	15	1645	
		136	—	15	1646	
		141	158	15	1661	
		142	158	15	1662	
		143	158	15	1663	
		144	158	15	1664	
		145	159	15	1665	
		146	—	15	1665a	
		161	—	15	1666	
		162	—	15	1666a	
		163	—	15	1666b	

310

Public Law Number & Section No., and U.S.C.A. Citation

When we discussed the West publication U.S.C.C.A.N., we noted that the bound volumes were supplemented on a monthly basis. You can also use the softbound monthly supplements to U.S.C.C.A.N. to update the code. The laws in U.S.C.C.A.N. are arranged in chronological order as they were passed by Congress. Remember that you can also update the code by checking the U.S. Public Laws database (**us-pl**) on WESTLAW. Public laws are on WESTLAW within a few working days of approval by the president. The **Update** service on WESTLAW is a particularly easy method for updating the U.S. Code.

United States Code Service

The *United States Code Service* (U.S.C.S.) is published by Lawyers Cooperative. Like the U.S.C.A., the U.S.C.S. provides the researcher with references to authority, historical notes, cross-references, and case annotations. The U.S.C.S. also has a multivolume general index. The set is updated with annual pocket parts and quarterly cumulative supplements. The U.S.C.S. differs from the U.S.C.A. in that it is Lawyers Cooperative's philosophy to be selective in its notes of case decisions. Therefore, the U.S.C.S. excludes case annotations that the editors at Lawyers Cooperative deem to be obsolete, repetitive, or insignificant. On the other hand, the U.S.C.S. includes more notes of administrative decisions than the U.S.C.A. does. Therefore, if you are working on a subject area that is highly regulated, like occupational health and safety, you may want to check the U.S.C.S. (Figure 4.9), as well as administrative decision sources on WESTLAW.

State Codes

At times when you are using the federal codes, you will also need to refer to the state codes. For example, although most aspects of labor law are subject to extensive federal law, some matters are not covered by federal law but are regulated by comprehensive state statutes concerning labor relations. For instance, federal law specifically covers picketing by employees during labor controversies. Additionally, many states have comprehensive state statutes regulating violent conduct during picketing. It is this link between federal law and state law that may lead you to compare federal laws with state laws. If you search on WESTLAW, use the *U.S. Code* database (**usc**). As with case law research on WESTLAW, you can use either the WIN Natural Language or the Terms and Connectors search method for searching statutory databases. Run the following Terms and Connectors query:

picket! & violen! crim! & employ! labor

Figure 4.9   Citations to Decisions in the U.S.C.S.

OCCUPATIONAL SAFETY AND HEALTH   **29 USCS § 661**

Employer discharged employees as retaliation for filing safety charges, despite contention they were fired for taking extended lunch breaks, where there was no prior enforcement of tardiness rules and employees were not issued warnings. Donovan v Peter Zimmer America, Inc. (1982, DC SC) 557 F Supp 642.

plained to OSHA about health conditions in her workplace did not establish violation of nondiscrimination provisions (29 USCS § 660(c)), where no direct evidence of retaliation or employer animus was introduced and employer produced evidence that (1) it had taken actions to accommodate employee in resolving her com-

§ 661.   Occupational Safety and Health Review Commission

(a) Establishment; membership; appointment; Chairman. The Occupational Safety and Health Review Commission is hereby established. The Commission shall be composed of three members who shall be appointed by the President, by and with the advice and consent of the Senate, from among persons who by reason of training, education, or experience are qualified to carry out the functions of the Commission under this Act. The President shall designate one of the members of the Commission to serve as Chairman.

(b) Terms of office; removal by President. The terms of members of the Commission shall be six years except that (1) the members of the Commission first taking office shall serve, as designated by the President at the time of appointment, one for a term of two years, one for a term of four years, and one for a term of six years, and (2) a vacancy caused by the death, resignation, or removal of a member prior to the expiration of the term for which he was appointed shall be filled only for the remainder of such unexpired term. A member of the Commission may be removed by the President for inefficiency, neglect of duty, or malfeasance in office.

[(c)](d) Principal office; hearings or other proceedings at other places. The principal office of the Commission shall be in the District of Columbia.

243

Figure 4.9   Citations to Decisions in the U.S.C.S. (continued)

OCCUPATIONAL SAFETY AND HEALTH   29 USCS § 661, n 1

Law Review Articles:

Bangser, An Inherent Role for Cost-Benefit Analysis in Judicial Review of Agency Decisions: A New Perspective on OSHA Rulemaking. 10 Boston College Environmental Affairs L Rev 365, 1982.

Pleading and Practice Before the Occupational and Safety and Health Review Commission. 24 Labor LJ 779 (1973).

INTERPRETIVE NOTES AND DECISIONS

I. OSHRC

1. Judicial authority
2. Action by majority
3. Continuing jurisdiction of proceedings
4. Remand jurisdiction
5. Construction of rules and pleadings
6. Information subject to disclosure
7. Summary judgment
8. Evidence
9. Scope of review
10. —Final orders
11. —Constitutionality of Act
12. —Issues not raised before hearing examiner
13. —Withdrawal of citation
14. Assessment of attorneys' fees and costs
15. Disposition of proposed settlements
16. —Employee challenges
17. Statement of grounds for decision
18. Notice to respondent
19. Appearance in appellate court

II. ADMINISTRATIVE LAW JUDGE

20. Duties
21. Action after final disposition
22. Approval of settlement agreement
23. —Employee challenges
24. Enforcement of disclosure procedures
25. Order on withdrawal of notice of contest
26. Evidence
27. Acceptance of stipulations
28. When report is "made"
29. Required notice to respondent
30. Reopening hearing

I. OSHRC

1. Judicial authority

Commission's function is to act as a neutral arbiter and determine whether the Secretary's citations should be enforced over employee or union objections, and its authority does not extend to overturning the Secretary's decision not to issue or to withdraw a citation. Cuyahoga V.R. Co. v United Transp. Union (1985) 474 US 3, 88 L Ed 2d 2, 106 S Ct 286, on remand (CA6) 783 F2d 58.

Congress intended that occupational safety and health review commission would have nor-

mal complement of adjudicatory powers possessed by traditional administrative agencies such as Federal Trade Commission. Brennan v Gilles & Cotting, Inc. (1974, CA4) 504 F2d 1255, 27 ALR Fed 925 (disagreed with by Marshall v Sun Petroleum Products Co. (CA3) 622 F2d 1176) and (disagreed with by Marshall v Occupational Safety & Health Review Com. (CA6) 635 F2d 544) and (disagreed with by Oil, Chemical & Atomic Workers International Union v Occupational Safety & Health Review Com., 217 App DC 137, 671 F2d 643, 33 FR Serv 2d 1223, 65 ALR Fed 580) and (disagreed with by Donovan v A. Amorello & Sons, Inc. (CA1) 761 F2d 61) and (disagreed with by United Steelworkers of America, etc. v Schuylkill Metals Corp. (CA5) 828 F2d 314, 13 BNA OSHC 1393, 1987 CCH OSHD ¶ 28059) and (disagreed with by Re Perry (CA1) 882 F2d 534, 14 BNA OSHC 1113, 1989 CCH OSHD ¶ 28625).

Decision on general contractor's joint responsibility for subcontractors' workmen is vested in occupational safety and health review commission, guided by "economic realities" in interpreting terms "employer" and "employee" in manner to achieve statutory objectives. Brennan v Gilles & Cotting, Inc. (1974, CA4) 504 F2d 1255, 27 ALR Fed 925 (disagreed with on other grounds Marshall v Sun Petroleum Products Co. (CA3) 622 F2d 1176, cert den 449 US 1061, 66 L Ed 2d 604, 101 S Ct 784) and (disagreed with by Donovan v Oil, Chemical, etc. Local 4-23 (CA5) 718 F2d 1341) and (disagreed with by Donovan v United Transp. Union (CA6) 748 F2d 340) and (disagreed with by Marshall v Occupational Safety & Health Review Com. (CA6) 635 F2d 544) and (disagreed with by Oil, Chemical & Atomic Workers International Union v Occupational Safety & Health Review Com., 217 App DC 137, 671 F2d 643, 33 FR Serv 2d 1223, 65 ALR Fed 580) and (disagreed with by Donovan v A. Amorello & Sons, Inc. (CA1) 761 F2d 61) and (disagreed with by United Steelworkers of America, etc. v Schuylkill Metals Corp. (CA5) 828 F2d 314, 13 BNA OSHC 1393, 1987 CCH OSHD ¶ 28059) and (disagreed with by Re Perry (CA1) 882 F2d 534,

247

This query retrieves several documents in the **usc** database, including 18 U.S.C. 1231 (Figure 4.10). Run the same query in the multistate unannotated statutes database: type **sdb stat-all.** This query retrieves more than seventy documents from nearly thirty states (Figure 4.11).

At other times, you will need just state law. For example, your client feels it is unfair that she cannot pay for her legal education by scalping tickets at concerts. If you search this problem on WESTLAW in the New York Statutes–Unannotated database **ny-st** by typing

```
ticket /s scalp! resell! speculat!
```

you will retrieve statutes on this issue (Figure 4.12).

Figure 4.10   A Document Retrieved by Using the USC Database

```
Citation              Rank(R)         Page(P)          Database       Mode
18 USCA s 1231        R 1 OF 4        P 1 OF 4         USC            TERM
   18 U.S.C.A. s 1231

                         UNITED STATES CODE ANNOTATED
              TITLE 18.   CRIMES AND CRIMINAL PROCEDURE
                            PART I--CRIMES--
                            CHAPTER 57--LABOR
              COPR. (c) WEST 1993  No Claim to Orig. Govt. Works
                    Current through P.L. 103-30, approved 5/7/93

s 1231. Transportation of strikebreakers

  Whoever willfully transports in interstate or foreign commerce any person who
is EMPLOYED or is to be EMPLOYED for the purpose of obstructing or interfering
by force or threats with (1) peaceful PICKETING by EMPLOYEES during any LABOR
controversy affecting wages, hours, or conditions of LABOR, or (2) the exercise
by EMPLOYEES of any of the rights of self-organization or collective
bargaining;  or
  Whoever is knowingly transported or travels in interstate or foreign commerce
for any of the purposes enumerated in this section--
  Shall be fined not more than $5,000 or imprisoned not more than two years, or
both.
```

Figure 4.11   Documents Retrieved by Using the STAT-ALL Database

```
CITATIONS LIST (Page 1)              Search Result Documents: 72
Database: STAT-ALL

   1.  A.R.S. s 23-619.01   ARIZONA REVISED STATUTES ANNOTATED   TITLE 23.
       LABOR   CHAPTER 4.  EMPLOYMENT SECURITY   ARTICLE 1. DEFINITIONS   s
       23-619.01. Misconduct connected with the employment;  wilful misconduct;
       evaluation

   2.  A.R.S. s 23-1321   ARIZONA REVISED STATUTES ANNOTATED   TITLE 23.  LABOR
       CHAPTER 8.  LABOR RELATIONS   ARTICLE 2. PICKETING AND SECONDARY BOYCOTTS
       s 23-1321. Definitions

   3.  A.R.S. s 23-1385   ARIZONA REVISED STATUTES ANNOTATED   TITLE 23.  LABOR
       CHAPTER 8.  LABOR RELATIONS   ARTICLE 5. AGRICULTURAL EMPLOYMENT
       RELATIONS   s 23-1385. Unfair labor practices

   4.  West's Ann.Cal.Civ.Code s 51.7   WEST'S ANNOTATED CALIFORNIA CODES
       CIVIL CODE   DIVISION 1. PERSONS   PART 2. PERSONAL RIGHTS   s 51.7.
       Freedom from violence or intimidation
```

Figure 4.12   Retrieving a State Statute on WESTLAW

```
CITATIONS LIST (Page 2)                    Search Result Documents: 28
Database: NY-ST
  3.  McKinney's Arts and Cultural Affairs Law s 25.05   MCKINNEY'S
      CONSOLIDATED LAWS OF NEW YORK ANNOTATED   ARTS AND CULTURAL AFFAIRS LAW
      CHAPTER 11-C  OF THE CONSOLIDATED LAWS   TITLE G--REGULATION OF SALE OF
      THEATRE TICKETS   ARTICLE 25--THEATRE TICKETS [APPLICABILITY SUSPENDED
      UNTIL JAN. 1, 1995.  SEE, ALSO, ARTICLE 25 POST.]   s 25.05. Ticket
      speculators [Applicability suspended until Jan. 1, 1995.  See, also, s
      25.05 post.]

  4.  McKinney's Arts and Cultural Affairs Law s 25.13   MCKINNEY'S
      CONSOLIDATED LAWS OF NEW YORK ANNOTATED   ARTS AND CULTURAL AFFAIRS LAW
      CHAPTER 11-C  OF THE CONSOLIDATED LAWS   TITLE G--REGULATION OF SALE OF
      THEATRE TICKETS   ARTICLE 25--THEATRE TICKETS [APPLICABILITY SUSPENDED
      UNTIL JAN. 1, 1995.  SEE, ALSO, ARTICLE 25 POST.]   s 25.13. Printing
      price on ticket [Eff. Jan. 1, 1995.  See, also, s 25.13 post.]
```

You can also find the law in the hard-copy materials. Using the index to *McKinney's Consolidated Laws of New York Annotated*®, look under "Tickets-Sales," which leads you to "Ticket Speculators-Selling or soliciting tickets" and to the statute Arts & Cult Aff § 25.05 (Figure 4.13).

Figure 4.13   Finding a State Statute in the Hard-Copy Materials

Index Reference

97   **TICKETS**

TIANA BAY
Fish and wildlife, marine fisheries, nets, restrictions on use, **ECL 13–0343**
Nets, restrictions on use, **ECL 13–0343**

TIBBETTS BROOK
Grant of former bed, **PUB L 75**

TICKETS
Admission, excise tax in cities and villages for subsidies, **PUB HO 110**
Advertising sale of partially used non-transferable ticket, **GEN B 126**
Air transportation service, use of stolen or forged credit or debit card to obtain, pre-

TICKET AGENTS
Advertising, this index
Sporting Events, generally, this index
Theatre Tickets, generally, this index

TICKET SPECULATORS
Boxing and wrestling matches, **UNCON 8919**
Cities and Nassau county, selling or soliciting tickets in, misdemeanor, **ARTS&CA 25.05**
Selling or soliciting tickets, misdemeanor, **ARTS&CA 25.05**
Sporting Events, generally, this index
Theatre Tickets, generally, this index

Season, exemption, sales tax, **TAX 1105**
Soliciting, unauthorized, in behalf of civil service employees, purchase, etc., misdemeanor, **CIV S 156**
Sporting Events, generally, this index
Theatre Tickets, generally, this index
Theatrical Syndication Financing, generally, this index
Trade-Marks, Trade-Names and Service-Marks, generally, this index
Uniform Appearance Ticket and Simplified Information, generally, this index
Value of ticket or equivalent instrument, larceny provisions, **PEN 155.20**

In the statutory databases, it is most efficient to use a field restriction if you are using the Terms and Connectors search method. The fields are the same for both the U.S.C.A. and the state codes. When searching by subject, restrict your search to the prelim and caption fields. For example, type

```
pr,ca(ticket /s scalp! resell! speculat!)
```

in the **ny-st** database. This search uses the preliminary field (which includes the title, subtitle, chapter, and subchapter headings of each section) and the caption field (which includes the section number, followed by terms that generally describe its contents). Figure 4.14 shows the results of your search.

What we said earlier about the publications of federal legislation is true for state legislation. Most states publish their statutes initially in a slip law format. Many states publish slip laws in the form of an advance sheet service, which are softbound supplements to a code. All states publish bound session laws. Most states publish a bound official code, and at least one annotated code is published for every state. Court rules and constitutions, along with the laws, are usually included in state codes. State codifications may be called codes, revisions, compilations, or consolidations, and their format and numbering systems will vary from state to state.

Figure 4.14   The Results of a Search Using the Preliminary and Caption Fields

```
CITATIONS LIST (Page 1)                     Search Result Documents: 4
Database: NY-ST

 1.  McKinney's Arts and Cultural Affairs Law s 25.03    MCKINNEY'S
     CONSOLIDATED LAWS OF NEW YORK ANNOTATED    ARTS AND CULTURAL AFFAIRS LAW
     CHAPTER 11-C  OF THE CONSOLIDATED LAWS    TITLE G--REGULATION OF SALE OF
     THEATRE TICKETS    ARTICLE 25--THEATRE TICKETS [APPLICABILITY SUSPENDED
     UNTIL JAN. 1, 1995.  SEE, ALSO, ARTICLE 25 POST.]   s 25.03. Reselling of
     tickets of admission;  licenses;  fees [Applicability suspended until
     Jan. 1, 1995.  See, also, s 25.03 post.]

 2.  McKinney's Arts and Cultural Affairs Law s 25.05    MCKINNEY'S
     CONSOLIDATED LAWS OF NEW YORK ANNOTATED    ARTS AND CULTURAL AFFAIRS LAW
     CHAPTER 11-C  OF THE CONSOLIDATED LAWS    TITLE G--REGULATION OF SALE OF
     THEATRE TICKETS    ARTICLE 25--THEATRE TICKETS [APPLICABILITY SUSPENDED
     UNTIL JAN. 1, 1995.  SEE, ALSO, ARTICLE 25 POST.]    s 25.05. Ticket
     speculators [Applicability suspended until Jan. 1, 1995.  See, also, s
     25.05 post.]
```

When you practice law, you will find that on-line access to the full text of state laws is an enormous advantage since your law firm is unlikely to have the codes from all of the states. Statutes databases are being added or expanded all the time, so use the Scope command to see current coverage information. All state statutes can be searched on WESTLAW in either an annotated or an unannotated database. If you want to see the summaries of the cases that have interpreted the statute, you should search in the annotated databases. You can also search in the unannotated databases and use the Annos service to retrieve the annotations and references as well as the statute text. The unannotated database focuses on specific legislative terminology and narrows your search considerably.

You can search for laws from individual states or from many states simultaneously. Use either **st-ann-all,** for the annotated statutes from all states or **stat-all** for the unannotated statutes from all states. For example, assume you are searching for legislation on the placement of smoke or heat detectors in hotels. To retrieve statutes from all states containing specific language on smoke detectors in hotels, search in the multistate unannotated statutes database, **stat-all,** and type

fire heat smok! /5 detect! & hotel motel lodg!
"public accommodation"

Figure 4.15 shows the results of your search. Once you have retrieved the statute you want, read the statute and type **d** (the Documents in Sequence command) to view the documents preceding and following the displayed document.

The most important step in searching state statutes on-line is to use the Update service. This service allows you to quickly determine whether a statute or rule on WESTLAW has been amended or repealed. Use this service to retrieve legislation that has been enacted after the last compilation of statutes

Figure 4.15 Documents Retrieved by Searching All States Simultaneously

```
CITATIONS LIST (Page 1)              Search Result Documents: 115
Database: STAT-ALL

 1.  Code 1975 s 34-15-4   CODE OF ALABAMA 1975   TITLE 34. PROFESSIONS AND
     BUSINESSES.   CHAPTER 15. HOTELS, INNS AND OTHER TRANSIENT LODGING
     PLACES.   s 34-15-4 Duty of hotel owners, operators, etc., to maintain
     conditions, smoke detectors, etc.

 2.  A.R.S. T. 36, Ch. 13, Art. 3.1, Refs & Annos   ARIZONA REVISED STATUTES
     ANNOTATED   TITLE 36.  PUBLIC HEALTH AND SAFETY   CHAPTER 13.  SAFETY
     ARTICLE 3.1. HOTELS AND MOTELS;  SMOKE DETECTORS

 3.  A.R.S. s 36-1645   ARIZONA REVISED STATUTES ANNOTATED   TITLE 36.
     PUBLIC HEALTH AND SAFETY   CHAPTER 13.  SAFETY   ARTICLE 3.1. HOTELS
     AND MOTELS;  SMOKE DETECTORS   s 36-1645.  Definitions

 4.  A.R.S. s 36-1646   ARIZONA REVISED STATUTES ANNOTATED   TITLE 36.
     PUBLIC HEALTH AND SAFETY   CHAPTER 13.  SAFETY   ARTICLE 3.1. HOTELS
     AND MOTELS;  SMOKE DETECTORS   s 36-1646. Smoke detectors;  hotels and
     motels
```

in the statutes database. You can type **update** when you are viewing a statute to view session laws that amend or repeal the original section. Eventually, material in the Update service is incorporated into the statutory databases.

The Related Materials service lists materials related to the specific state statutory document that you are viewing. To see the Related Materials directory for a particular document, type **rm** from any screen.

The legislative service databases contain laws passed in the current or recent sessions. These materials are eventually incorporated into the statutory databases. This service is useful if you recently learned about a new law and want to view it on-line. We also recommend that you run previous searches in a legislative service database to assure that you have the most current information.

When you know a statute's citation, Find is the easiest method for retrieving the statute. For example, type **fi az st s 36–1646** to retrieve section 36-1646 from *Arizona Revised Statutes Annotated*®. Figure 4.16 shows the result of your search.

Figure 4.16 Retrieving a Statute When You Have a Citation

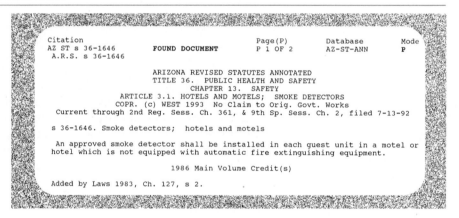

```
Citation                                Page(P)        Database        Mode
AZ ST s 36-1646      FOUND DOCUMENT      P 1 OF 2       AZ-ST-ANN        P
A.R.S. s 36-1646

                      ARIZONA REVISED STATUTES ANNOTATED
                       TITLE 36.  PUBLIC HEALTH AND SAFETY
                            CHAPTER 13.  SAFETY
                 ARTICLE 3.1. HOTELS AND MOTELS;  SMOKE DETECTORS
                 COPR. (c) WEST 1993  No Claim to Orig. Govt. Works
       Current through 2nd Reg. Sess. Ch. 361, & 9th Sp. Sess. Ch. 2, filed 7-13-92

       s 36-1646. Smoke detectors;  hotels and motels

        An approved smoke detector shall be installed in each guest unit in a motel or
       hotel which is not equipped with automatic fire extinguishing equipment.

                            1986 Main Volume Credit(s)

       Added by Laws 1983, Ch. 127, s 2.
```

Constitutions

The U.S. Constitution is the foundation of our judicial system. As you will learn in your course on constitutional law, the wording of the U.S. Constitution is very general. Consequently, most of the law in this area has been made by the courts, especially by decisions of the U.S. Supreme Court. Finding the Constitution is easy and keeping up with the amendments is not a problem, but locating these cases can be a trial, no pun intended. You can locate the Constitution in the *U.S. Code* and as separate volumes of the two annotated versions, U.S.C.A. and U.S.C.S. The two annotated codes are perhaps the easiest way to find citations to cases that have interpreted the Constitution. Most parts have been interpreted so frequently, however, that you will need more help than the cases alone can provide. Fortunately, there are many other materials that you can use, including treatises, encyclopedias, and periodicals.

The U.S.C.A. provides extensive coverage by including annotations to both the federal and state decisions regarding each article or amendment to the Constitution. Over four thousand annotations to the Fourth Amendment alone are listed in the U.S.C.A. The digests, either the one devoted to the U.S. Supreme Court or the federal digests, will also prove useful in locating cases that interpret the Constitution.

Additionally, WESTLAW can be useful in retrieving case law that interprets the Constitution. You can search by a particular section or by an amendment or perhaps combine the citation with relevant terms. WESTLAW also has specific First Amendment databases. For example, to obtain Supreme Court cases concerning a city's right to display religious scenes on public grounds, a topic that is constantly in the news, you would access the First Amendment-Supreme Court Cases database (**fcfa-sct**) and type a Terms and Connectors search

religio** nativity christmas hanukkah /s
display scene show

or, as a WIN search, you could simply ask:

can a city display religious scenes on public grounds

These searches will retrieve cases such as *County of Allegheny v. ACLU*, 109 S.Ct. 3086 (1989) that discuss the issue (Figure 4.17).

State constitutions also have provisions that parallel the basic rights guaranteed by the U.S. Constitution. There is an interrelationship between the state and federal constitutions that protects all of us regardless of our residence. State constitutions can usually be found in the state codes. The constitutions for most states are available on WESTLAW in the state statutes database.

Figure 4.17 Retrieving Case Law That Interprets the Constitution

```
Citation              Rank(R)           Page(P)          Database        Mode
109 S.Ct. 3086        R 2 OF 20         P 1 OF 207       FCFA-SCT        Page
 106 L.Ed.2d 472, 57 USLW 5045
(Cite as: 492 U.S. 573, 109 S.Ct. 3086)
                   COUNTY OF ALLEGHENY, et al., Petitioners
                                      v.
        AMERICAN CIVIL LIBERTIES UNION GREATER PITTSBURGH CHAPTER et al.
                          CHABAD, Petitioner,
                                      v.
                  AMERICAN CIVIL LIBERTIES UNION et al.
                      CITY OF PITTSBURGH, Petitioner,
                                      v.
        AMERICAN CIVIL LIBERTIES UNION GREATER PITTSBURGH CHAPTER et al.
                      Nos. 87-2050, 88-90 and 88-96.
                          Argued Feb. 22, 1989.
                          Decided July 3, 1989.
   Civil liberties organization and certain individuals brought action against
county and city to challenge constitutionality of creche in county courthouse
and Chanukah menorah outside city and county building as violations of
establishment clause.  The United States District Court for the Western
District of Pennsylvania, Barron P. McCune, J., entered judgment in favor of
defendants.  The Court of Appeals, 842 F.2d 655, reversed and remanded.
Certiorari was granted.  The Supreme Court, Justice Blackmun, held that:  (1)
              COPR. (C) WEST 1993 NO CLAIM TO ORIG. U.S. GOVT. WORKS
```

Court Rules

Court rules guide the operation of courts in solving legal controversies. Court rules typically cover such matters as selecting a proper court, commencing the action, pleadings, discovery, jury selection, the trial, and the judgment. The various federal court rules may be found in a variety of practitioners' manuals, rules services, and formbooks. The two most accessible sources are the two annotated codes, U.S.C.A. and U.S.C.S. Both of these annotated codes have special volumes containing the federal court rules, including the Federal Rules of Civil Procedure, Criminal Procedure, Appellate Procedure, and Evidence. In the U.S.C.A., you will find these rules in special volumes accompanying Title 28 "Judiciary and Judicial Procedure" and Title 18 "Crimes and Procedure." These forms of statutory publication are crucial parts of the research process. You should come to understand how they are created and organized—they are the real world.

On WESTLAW, the **us-rules** database contains rules from the *United States Code*. State court rules are in the state rules databases. For individual states, type the state identifier, followed by **–rules**. You would search the rules databases for the states using the same techniques as in statute databases. To retrieve motions to quash, for example, access the California Rules database (**ca-rules**) and type

quash! /p sub-poena!

The Documents in Sequence command (**d**) is useful when you are viewing a rule that contains a reference to a nearby rule that you want to see. In the preceding group of documents from California, Rule 307 contains a reference to Rule 305. To view this rule, type **d-2**.

Conclusion

This chapter has explained how to find federal laws as they are passed by Congress and then as they appear in a codified form. We discussed several titles and formats, including on-line databases, each of which is suited to a different purpose. We also discussed state legislative materials, with a special emphasis on state law on WESTLAW. Once you have taken a few legislative courses, you will want to review this chapter since you may not have the opportunity to use federal or state legislative materials during your first year.

5

ADMINISTRATIVE LAW

L egislatures, including the U.S. Congress, pass broadly written laws that need to be enforced. To make such broad and often highly technical laws work, the legislature has to delegate some of its power to administrative agencies. These agencies, which are part of the executive/administrative branch of government, are responsible for writing specific rules and regulations (these terms have the same meaning) that enforce the statutes that are written by the legislatures. Think of the Federal Aviation Administration (FAA). Congress knows that it wants to enforce rules to govern air travel, but it also knows that it needs people with technical expertise to do it. Hence, Congress turns to the FAA.

Federal agencies regulate key areas of the economy: transportation (Interstate Commerce Commission), communications (Federal Communications Commission), the securities markets (Securities and Exchange Commission), labor relations (National Labor Relations Board), and competitive trade practices (Federal Trade Commission). The regulations issued by these agencies are just as binding as statutes and, from a practical viewpoint, affect the lives of everyone. A violation of a regulation may be as serious as a violation of a statute.

In addition to writing rules and regulations, agencies issue orders, licenses, and advisory opinions and conduct hearings. These functions are called quasi-judicial because the administrative agencies act like courts. If you take a course in administrative law, you will learn the procedures through which the government officials exercise their power, and the checks the other branches of government have on the administrative branch.

We are concerned here not so much with procedure as with what the agencies do, an aspect of the law that is often ignored in law school. In this chapter, we will try to give you a brief look at administrative materials. We will examine the materials of federal agencies, their rules that implement legislation, and their power to adjudicate disputes concerning parties they regulate. The president's lawmaking actions will also be noted. State materials will be discussed briefly at the end of the chapter.

The *Federal Register* in Print Format

The U.S. Government Printing Office issues two publications that provide you with federal administrative regulations: the daily *Federal Register* and the

Figure 5.1 The *Federal Register*

annual *Code of Federal Regulations.* You need to understand both publications as well as the relationship between the two. In our examination of these publications, we will discuss both the print versions and the on-line versions.

Federal regulations are published *chronologically* in the *Federal Register (Fed. Reg.)* on a daily basis (Figure 5.1). In addition to publishing rules and regulations, the *Federal Register* publishes presidential documents; that is, presidential proclamations and executive orders. The *Federal Register* also publishes proposed rules. People are given the opportunity to comment on these proposed regulations before they are either adopted or rejected by federal agencies. The largest section of the *Federal Register* is the notice section, which contains information about agencies including orders, opinions, agency changes, and notices of meetings. The *Federal Register* may fill as many as 50,000 pages a year. It will look boring and confusing at first, but if you practice law in a heavily regulated area, you will come to realize its utility.

Since the *Federal Register* (published since 1936) consumes an enormous amount of shelf space, you will be able to find it with ease in your library. Its size and fineness of print are reminiscent of a big city telephone directory. Because of its size and its newsprint paper, many libraries have the historical volumes of the *Federal Register* on microfiche.

The *Code of Federal Regulations* in Print Format

The same regulations that appear in the *Federal Register* are arranged by *subject* in the *Code of Federal Regulations* or C.F.R. (Figure 5.2). The C.F.R. includes only regulations that are currently in force. The entire C.F.R. is recompiled annually with any new amendments added. Regulations that have been withdrawn are deleted. If a proposed regulation is never adopted, it will not appear in the C.F.R.—it will only appear as a proposed regulation in the *Federal Register.*

The C.F.R. is organized by titles, each of which represents a broad topic. Therefore, when you need to find all the federal regulations on electronic banking, you will look in the C.F.R. because it is arranged by subject. You will find that electronic banking is included in Title 12, which is dedicated to banking regulations. Using the *Federal Register* to find all of the regulations on a particular subject would be extremely difficult and time-consuming because the *Federal Register* is arranged chronologically. Therefore, you would have to search through approximately fifty-five years of the publication, page by page.

Figure 5.2 The *Code of Federal Regulations*

Within each title of the C.F.R., regulations are divided into chapters, each of which is devoted to the regulations of a particular agency. The chapters are further divided into parts, consisting of a body of regulations on a particular topic or agency function. Parts are divided into sections, the basic unit of the C.F.R., and if further breakdown is necessary, paragraphs are used (Figure 5.3).

Prefacing each part of the C.F.R. are notes provided by the agency that outline the statutory (legislative) authority under which the regulations are issued. Remember that regulations are adopted to implement specific pieces of legislation. The *authority note* is useful when you want to trace the regulation

Figure 5.3 The Organization of the C.F.R.

Agency

Federal Reserve System   **Part 205**

(g) *Reciprocal arrangements.* Finally, while a depository institution may enter into an arrangement with an unaffiliated third party wherein the third party agrees to stand ready to purchase time deposits held by the depository institution's customers, the Board will regard a reciprocal arrangement with another depository institution for purchase of each other's time deposits as a circumvention of the early withdrawal penalty rule and the purposes it is designed to serve.

[52 FR 47697, Dec. 16, 1987]

§ 204.132   Treatment of Loan Strip Participations.

(a) Effective March 31, 1988, the glossary section of the instructions for the Report of Condition and Income (FFIEC 031-034; OMB No. 7100-0036; available from a depository institution's primary federal regulator) ("Call Report") was amended to clarify that certain short-term loan participation arrangements (sometimes known or styled as "loan strips" or "strip participations") are regarded as borrowings rather than sales for Call Report purposes in certain circumstances. Through this interpretation, the Board is clarifying that such

Part

transactions should be treated as deposits for purposes of Regulation D.

Section

(b) These transactions involve the sale (or placement) of a short-term loan by a depository institution that has been made under a long-term commitment of the depository institution to advance funds. For example, a 90-day loan made under a five-year revolving line of credit may be sold to or placed with a third party by the depository institution originating the loan. The depository institution originating the loan is obligated to renew the 90-day note itself (by advancing funds to its customer at the end of the 90-day period) in the event the original participant does not wish to renew the credit. Since, under these arrangements, the depository institution is obligated to make another loan at the end of 90 days (absent any event of default on the part of the borrower), the depository institution selling the loan or participation in effect must buy

Authority Note

back the loan or participation at the maturity of the 90-day loan sold to or

funded by the purchaser at the option of the purchaser. Accordingly, these transactions bear the essential characteristics of a repurchase agreement and, therefore, are reportable and reservable under Regulation D.

(c) Because many of these transactions give rise to deposit liabilities in the form of promissory notes, acknowledgments of advance or similar obligations (written or oral) as described in § 204.2(a)(1)(vii) of Regulation D, the exemptions from the definition of "deposit" incorporated in that section may apply to the liability incurred by a depository institution when it offers or originates a loan strip facility. Thus, for example, loan strips sold to domestic offices of other depository institutions are exempt from Regulation D under § 204.2(a)(1)(vii)(A)(*1*) because they are obligations issued or undertaken and held for the account of a U.S. office of another depository institution. Similarly, some of these transactions result in Eurocurrency liabilities and are reportable and reservable as such.

[53 FR 24931, July 1, 1988]

PART 205—ELECTRONIC FUND TRANSFERS

Sec.
205.1   Authority, purpose, and scope.
205.2   Definitions and rules of construction.
205.3   Exemptions.
205.4   Special requirements.
205.5   Issuance of access devices.
205.6   Liability of consumer for unauthorized transfers.
205.7   Initial disclosure of terms and conditions.
205.8   Change in terms; error resolution notice.
205.9   Documentation of transfers.
205.10   Preauthorized transfers.
205.11   Procedures for resolving errors.
205.12   Relation to State law.
205.13   Administrative enforcement.
205.14   Services offered by financial institutions not holding consumer's account.

APPENDIX A—MODEL DISCLOSURE CLAUSES

SUPPLEMENTS I AND II—OFFICIAL STAFF INTERPRETATIONS

AUTHORITY: Pub. L. 95-630, 92 Stat. 3730 (15 U.S.C. 1693b).

107

back to its statutory authority. A *source note*, which lists the volume, page, and date of the *Federal Register* in which the regulation was published, follows the authority note (Figure 5.4). These two notes comprise the "administrative history" of the regulation.

Figure 5.4   Authority and Source Note in the C.F.R.

Authority Note

Source Note

§ 205.1   **12 CFR Ch. II (1-1-90 Edition)**

§ 205.1 Authority, purpose, and scope.

(a) *Authority.* This regulation, issued by the Board of Governors of the Federal Reserve System, implements title IX (Electronic Fund Transfer Act) of the Consumer Credit Protection Act, as amended (15 U.S.C. 1601 *et seq.*).

(b) *Purpose and scope.* In November 1978, the Congress enacted the Electronic Fund Transfer Act. The Congress found that the use of electronic systems to transfer funds provides the potential for substantial benefits to consumers, but that the unique characteristics of these systems make the application of existing consumer protection laws unclear, leaving the rights and liabilities of users of electronic fund transfer systems undefined. The Act establishes the basic rights, liabilities, and responsibilities of consumers who use electronic money transfer services and of financial institutions that offer these services. This regulation is intended to carry out the purposes of the Act, including, primarily, the protection of individual consumers engaging in electronic transfers. Except as otherwise provided, this regulation applies to all persons who are financial institutions as defined in § 205.2(i).

(Information collection requirements contained in this regulation have been approved by the Office of Management and Budget under the provisions of 44 U.S.C. 3501 *et seq.* and have been assigned OMB number 7100-0200)

[44 FR 18480, Mar. 28, 1979, as amended at 49 FR 40797, Oct. 18, 1984]

§ 205.2 Definitions and rules of construction.

For the purposes of this regulation, the following definitions apply, unless the context indicates otherwise:

(a)(1) "Access device" means a card, code, or other means of access to a consumer's account, or any combination thereof, that may be used by the consumer for the purpose of initiating electronic fund transfers.

(2) An access device becomes an "accepted access device" when the consumer to whom the access device was issued:

(i) Requests and receives, or signs, or uses, or authorizes another to use, the access device for the purpose of transferring money between accounts or obtaining money, property, labor or services;

(ii) Requests validation of an access device issued on an unsolicited basis; or

(iii) Receives an access device issued in renewal of, or in substitution for, an accepted access device, whether such access device is issued by the initial financial institution or a successor.

(b) "Account" means a demand deposit (checking), savings, or other consumer asset account (other than an occasional or incidental credit balance in a credit plan) held either directly or indirectly by a financial institution and established primarily for personal, family, or household purposes.

(c) "Act" means the Electronic Fund Transfer Act (Title IX of the Consumer Credit Protection Act, 15 U.S.C. 1601 et seq.).

(d) "Business day" means any day on which the offices of the consumer's financial institution are open to the public for carrying on substantially all business functions.

(e) "Consumer" means a natural person.

(f) "Credit" means the right granted by a financial institution to a consumer to defer payment of debt, incur debt and defer its payment, or purchase property or services and defer payment therefor.

(g) "Electronic fund transfer" means any transfer of funds, other than a transaction originated by check, draft, or similar paper instrument, that is initiated through an electronic terminal, telephone, or computer or magnetic tape for the purpose of ordering, instructing, or authorizing a financial institution to debit or credit an account. The term includes, but is not limited to, point-of-sale transfers, automated teller machine transfers, direct deposits or withdrawals of funds, and transfers initiated by telephone. It includes all transfers resulting from debit card transactions, including those that do not involve an electronic terminal at the time of the transaction. The term does not include payments made by check, draft, or similar paper instrument at an electronic terminal.

108

The C.F.R. is published once a year on a staggered basis; that is, all of the volumes are not issued at one time. Instead, the titles are issued at four different times of the year:

- Title 1 through Title 16—as of January 1
- Title 17 through Title 27—as of April 1
- Title 28 through Title 41—as of July 1
- Title 42 through Title 50—as of October 1

Because of these staggered dates, you must be careful to check the softbound cover of each title to determine the date of revision.

Fortunately, the U.S. Government Printing Office uses distinct colors for the covers of the C.F.R.—for example, 1990 was blue, 1991 red, and 1992 green. These boldly colored covers make it easy for you to see whether you have the correct year.

Finding Regulations in the Print Format of the Federal Register and the C.F.R.

Obviously, the easiest way to find a regulation is to get the citation to the *Federal Register* or the C.F.R. from a secondary source, such as a law review article. If you do not already have the *Federal Register* or the C.F.R. citation, you can either use the print indexes or access WESTLAW. The *Federal Register* has its own index. Each daily index contains a table of contents arranged by agency. There are also monthly and quarterly indexes and an annual index. These indexes are set up primarily by agency rather than by subject (Figure 5.5).

The C.F.R. publishes a single volume called *Index and Finding Aids,* which is revised once a year. However, this index suffers from several shortcomings—the main one being that it is not really a subject index at all! It is basically an agency index with a few subject terms interspersed (Figure 5.6).

To see how the index works, consider the following situation: Assume that your client, Jim, bought a new car from a dealer. The first time Jim washed his car, some of the paint rubbed off. Upon closer inspection, Jim discovered that the car had been in a wreck and had been painted to conceal the damage. Armed with a signed statement that the car was free from defect, Jim stormed into the dealer's office. The dealer claimed that she did not know that the car had been damaged. Furthermore, the dealer told Jim that since he did not receive a written warranty, he was out of luck.

Will a federal agency be able to help with this problem? To find out, you would look in the *Index and Finding Aids* under "Warranties." If you were aware that the Federal Trade Commission was involved with warranties, you could look under that agency. Looking under "Warranties" in the *Index and*

Figure 5.5   The *Federal Register* Index

NIH

NOTICES

Auto theft and comprehensive insurance premiums, Federal regulation; public review and comment on report, 30786

Fuel economy program, automotive; annual report to Congress, 11484

Fuel economy standards; exemption petitions, etc.:
Officine Alfieri Maserati, S.p.A., 22879, 25767

Grants and cooperative agreements; availability, etc.:
National occupant protection and impaired driving prevention programs, 7622
School bus safety projects; assistance to States, 32554
School bus safety; State matching of planning and administration costs, 40975

Highway safety analysis; police traffic accident reports; critical automated data reporting elements; list, 18220, 27327

Highway safety program; breath alcohol testing devices:
Evidential devices; model specifications and conforming products list, 6865, 32343

Highway traffic safety improvement; priority plan 1990-1992; availability, 47824

Meetings:
International Harmonization of Safety Standards, 13690
Motor Vehicle Safety Research Advisory Committee, 1764, 34639, 43060
National Driver Register Advisory Committee, 15096, 38186

Rulemaking, research, and enforcement programs, 9818, 25920, 40977, 41782

Motor vehicle defect proceedings; petitions, etc.:
Center for Auto Safety, 10570
Ditlow, Clarence M., III, 21140
Faircloth, Harvey G., et al., 6865
Fujimori, Warren W.T., 47600
Institute for Injury Reduction, Public Citizen, et al., 42144
Jarvis, Brian, 17348
Rand, M. Kristen, 42301
Roupinian, Paul, 21140
Skreba, Leonard T., 30072
Stewart, Gloria Jean, 20674
Sweeney, Harry M., 20382
Toyota Motor Co., 17349

Motor vehicle safety standards:
Nonconforming vehicles—
Final determinations, 32988
Importation eligibility; tentative determinations, 17518, 47418
Rear seat lap/shoulder belt retrofit kits, 35241

Motor vehicle safety standards; exemption petitions, etc.:
Automobiles Peugeot, 20382
Bridgestone (U.S.A.) Inc., 3297, 12617
Budd Co., 8632
Cadillac Plastic & Chemical Co., 11497, 28340
Cantab Motors, 11714, 21141
Consulier Industries, Inc., 5712, 12982
Cooper Tire & Rubber Co., 47823
Ferrari S.p.A., 3785
General Motors Corp., 21297, 34639, 40977
Goodyear Tire & Rubber Co., 2915
Hella, Inc., 37601
Marmon Motor Co., 7404
Mazda Motor Corp., 7404

Mazda Motor Corp. of Japan, 28341
Mazda Research & Development of North America, Inc., 26528, 49365
Officine Alfieri Maserati S.p.A., 78, 7405
Supreme Corp., Inc., 38186
Takata-Gerico Corp., 28341
Uniroyal Goodrich Tire Co., 40506

Motor vehicle theft prevention standard; exemption petitions, etc.:
American Honda Motor Co., Inc., 4746, 22004, 46126
General Motors Corp., 17854

New car assessment program:
Crash test results and analysis; deformable moving barrier, 40505

Passenger motor vehicle theft data, 7406, 18794, 41149

National Institute for Occupational Safety and Health

See Centers for Disease Control

National Institute of Corrections

NOTICES

Grants and cooperative agreements; availability, etc.:
Program plan/academy training schedule (1991 FY), 32980

Meetings:
Advisory Board, 5086, 24672, 39747

National Institute of Justice

NOTICES

Body armor users workshop, 17681

Drug program evaluations; special initiative, 7387

Grants and cooperative agreements; availability, etc.:
Boot camps for juvenile offenders; constructive intervention and early support, 28718, 32980
Discretionary programs (1990 FY), 10146
Technology assessment program information center, 31908

National Institute of Standards and Technology

RULES

Manufacturing technology transfer; regional centers establishment transfer, 38274

Organization, functions, and authority delegations:
National Institute of Standards and Technology, 38314

PROPOSED RULES

Manufacturing technology transfer; centers establishment transfer, 18124

NOTICES

Grants and cooperative agreements; availability, etc.:
Advanced structural ceramics, 20620
Fire research program, 29877
Manufacturing technology transfer; regional centers, 38280
Precision measurement program, 48665
Standard reference data program, 47789

Information processing standards, Federal:
COBOL, 1243, 2733
Computer output microform formats and reduction ratios, 7516, 9824
Database language SQL, 3627
Electronic data interchange (EDI), 28274, 29146

Family of input/output interface standards, 10272

Government Open Systems Interconnection Profile (GOSIP), 27666, 32451

Graphical kernel system (GKS), 10273, 12444

Interface between data terminal equipment (DTE) and data circuit-terminating equipment (DOE) for operation with packet-switched data networks, or between two DTEs by dedicated circuit, 10276

POSIX; portable operating system interface for computer environments, 11424, 12778, 23959

POSIX shell and utility application interface for computer operating system environments, 23959

Programming language C, 19768

Programming language MUMPS, 10278

Laboratory Accreditation Program, National Voluntary:
Airborne asbestos analysis, 38734
Directory of accredited laboratories; supplement, 32452

Meetings:
Advanced Technology Visiting Committee, 5644, 7019, 23455, 27667, 33948, 47504
Broadband Integrated Services Digital Network (B-ISDN) users and implementors workshop, 5046
Computer courseware standards, architectural proposals; discussion, 20620
Computer System Security and Privacy Advisory Board, 5045, 32452, 46093
Eighth North American ISDN Users' Forum, 5046
FORTRAN programming language standard test suit; workshop, 6676
Intergrated Services Digital Network (ISDN) users and implementors workshop, 27668
International Laboratory Accreditation Conference, 33741
International standards activities, U.S. participation, 12252
Malcolm Baldrige National Quality Award's Board of Overseers, 49558
Malcolm Baldrige National Quality Award's Panel of Judges, 6035, 23456, 28080, 33948, 49325
OSI Implementors workshop, 2256
Weights and Measures National Conference, 1245, 27294

National Fire Codes:
Fire safety standards, 3991, 32679
Technical committee reports, 3991, 32678

Senior Executive Service:
General and Limited Performance Review Boards; membership, 29878

National Institutes of Health

NOTICES

Committees; establishment, renewal, termination, etc.:
AIDS and Related Research Study Sections et al., 2705
American Stop Smoking Intervention Study (ASSIST) Committee, 40945
Biological and Clinical Aging Review Committee et al., 15021
Genome Research Review Committee, 26265
Human Genome Research National Advisory Council, 17309

Agency ────

Finding Aids leads you to the Magnuson-Moss Warranty Act, which then refers you to 16 C.F.R. 700 (Figure 5.7).

Fortunately for Jim, under 700.3(a) is a footnote that states that "a 'written warranty' is also created by a written affirmation of fact or a written promise that the product is defect free . . . ." It appears that he is not out of luck.

Figure 5.6   The C.F.R. Index

Subject

Agency

Agency

Agency

CFR Index	Farmers Home Administration

CFR Index

Medicaid services, requirements and
   limits, 42 CFR 441
Prisoners, 28 CFR 551
Public Health Service, general policies, 42
   CFR 50

Family Support Administration
See Child Support Enforcement Office
   Community Services Office
   Family Assistance Office
   Refugee Resettlement Office

FAR (Federal Acquisition Regulation)
See Government procurement

Farm Credit Administration
Classified information, 12 CFR 605
Employee responsibilities and conduct, 12
   CFR 601
Farm Credit Administration Board
   meetings, 12 CFR 604
Farm credit system
   Accounting and reporting requirements,
      12 CFR 621
   Administrative definitions, 12 CFR 619
   Coordination of activities and functions,
      12 CFR 616
   Disclosure to shareholders, 12 CFR 620
   Eligibility and scope of financing, 12
      CFR 613
   Examinations and investigations, 12
      CFR 617
   Funding and fiscal affairs, 12 CFR 615
   General provisions, 12 CFR 618
   Loan policies and operations, 12 CFR
      614
   Organization, 12 CFR 611
   Personnel administration, 12 CFR 612
   Regulatory accounting practices, 12
      CFR 624
Nondiscrimination on basis of handicap in
   federally conducted programs, 12
   CFR 606
Organization and functions, 12 CFR 600
Practice and procedure rules, 12 CFR 622
Practice before Farm Credit
   Administration, 12 CFR 623
Privacy Act regulations, 12 CFR 603
Releasing information, 12 CFR 602

Farm Credit System Assistance Board
Disclosure of records, Freedom of
   Information Act and Privacy Act, 12
   CFR 1300

Farmers Home Administration

Farmers
See Agriculture

Farmers Home Administration
Agricultural loan mediation program, 7
   CFR 1946
Availability of information, 7 CFR 2018
Borrower account servicing and
   collections, 7 CFR 1951
Claims, Federal statute of limitations, 7
   CFR 1927
County and/or area committees, election,
   employment, pay, and functions, 7
   CFR 2054
Credit reports, receiving and processing
   applications, 7 CFR 1910
Debt settlement, 7 CFR 1864
Debt settlement, 7 CFR 1956
Emergency livestock line of credit loan
   guarantees, 7 CFR 1845
Farm operating loans, 7 CFR 1941
Farmers, guaranteed loans, 7 CFR 1843
General provisions, 7 CFR 1900
Guaranteed loan programs, 7 CFR 1980
Guaranteed loans, general provisions, 7
   CFR 1841
Loans, timesaving and program
   improvement, 7 CFR 1890t
Loans and grants, program-related
   instructions, 7 CFR 1901
Management and supervision of loan and
   grant recipients, 7 CFR 1930
Organization, 7 CFR 2003
Personal property, servicing and
   liquidation of chattel security, 7 CFR
   1962
Property management, management and
   disposal, 7 CFR 1955
Real property, 7 CFR 1965
Rural association loans and grants for
   community facilities, development,
   conservation, utilization, 7 CFR 1823
Rural development loans and grants
   Area planning and energy impacted
      area development assistance
      program, 7 CFR 1948
   Community facilities, resource
      conservation and watersheds, 7
      CFR 1942
   Construction and repair provisions, 7
      CFR 1924
   Emergency assistance, 7 CFR 1945

227

Figure 5.7   Using the C.F.R. Index

Look under Warranties

Find the Magnuson-Moss
Warranty Act

16 C.F.R. 700

Tobacco products and cigarette papers
    and tubes
  Exportation without payment of tax or
      with drawback of tax, 27 CFR 290
  Importation, 27 CFR 275
Wholesaling and warehousing industry in
    Puerto Rico, 29 CFR 683
Wine production and sales, 27 CFR 240
Warranties
Acquisition regulations
  Agriculture Department, 48 CFR 446
  Defense Department, 48 CFR 246
  Environmental Protection Agency, 48
      CFR 1546
  General Services Administration, 48
      CFR 546
  National Aeronautics and Space
      Administration, 48 CFR 1846
  State Department, 48 CFR 646
  Transportation Department, 48 CFR
      1246
  United States Information Agency,
      quality assurance, 48 CFR 1946
Advertising of warranties and guarantees,
    guides, 16 CFR 239
Federal Acquisition Regulation, quality
    assurance, 48 CFR 46
Flammable Fabrics Act
  Flammability standards, clothing
      textiles, 16 CFR 1610
  General rules and regulations, 16 CFR
      1608
Fur Products Labeling Act, rules and
    regulations, 16 CFR 301
Magnuson-Moss Warranty Act
  Informal dispute settlement procedures,
      16 CFR 703
  Interpretations, 16 CFR 700
  Pre-sale availability of written warranty
      terms, 16 CFR 702
  Written consumer product warranty
      terms and conditions, disclosure, 16
      CFR 701
Manufactured home consumer manual
    requirements, 24 CFR 3283
Motor vehicles and motor vehicle
    engines, air pollution control, 40
    CFR 85
Textile Fiber Products Identification Act,
    rules and regulations, 16 CFR 303
Wool Products Labeling Act of 1939,
    rules and regulations, 16 CFR 300

Washington, D. C.
See District of Columbia

Waste treatment and disposal
See also Hazardous waste
          Recycling
          Sewage disposal
Air pollution control, performance
    standards for incinerators, 40 CFR 60
Alcohol fuels, biomass energy and
    municipal waste projects, loan
    guarantees for energy projects, 10
    CFR 799
Army Department, environmental
    protection and enhancement, 32 CFR
    650
Grants, State and local assistance, 40
    CFR 35
Mines Bureau grant programs, procedures
    for solid waste disposal grants, 30
    CFR 651
National Environmental Policy Act,
    Council on Environmental Quality
    requirements procedures
    implementation, 40 CFR 6
Panama Canal, sanitary requirements,
    vessel wastes, garbage, ballast, 35
    CFR 125
Rural development loans, community
    facilities, resource conservation and
    watersheds, 7 CFR 1942
Solid wastes
  Citizen suits, prior notice, 40 CFR 254
  Criteria for classification of solid waste
      disposal facilities and practices, 40
      CFR 257
  Identification of regions and agencies
      for solid waste management, 40
      CFR 255
  Land disposal guidelines, 40 CFR 241
  Medical waste, standards for tracking
      and management, 40 CFR 259
  National pollutant discharge elimination
      system, criteria and standards, 40
      CFR 125
  Residential, commercial, and
      institutional solid wastes, source
      separation for materials recovery
      guidelines, 40 CFR 246
  Residential, commercial, and
      institutional solid wastes, storage
      and collection guidelines, 40 CFR
      243

753

Commercial indexes are also available that are vastly superior to those of the C.F.R. and the *Federal Register*. Congressional Information Service has published an *Index to the Code of Federal Regulations* since 1981 and a *Federal Register Index* since 1984, and R. R. Bowker's *Code of Federal Regulations Index* has been published since 1988. With these publications, you can locate regulations by subject, agency, industry, geographic area, or authorizing legislation.

You may recall that in our discussion of the federal annotated codes in Chapter 4, we noted that both U.S.C.A. and U.S.C.S. list citations to the C.F.R. in the annotations after each section. Actually, if you are already working with a federal law, the easiest way to locate the regulations that will implement the law is to use one of the annotated codes. For example, the federal laws on warranties can be located in 15 U.S.C.A. 2301. This section of the U.S.C.A. refers you to the governing regulations in 16 C.F.R. 700.1 (Figure 5.8).

If you are not using the U.S.C.A., you can check the C.F.R. *Index and Finding Aids* for its useful Parallel Table of Authorities and Rules. This table allows you to locate the C.F.R. citation if you already have the U.S.C. citation (Figure 5.9).

Finding Regulations on WESTLAW

Fortunately, the full text of the *Federal Register* and the C.F.R. are on WESTLAW and other on-line services. On WESTLAW, the *Federal Register* is in the **fr** database, and the C.F.R. is in the **cfr** database.

The *Federal Register* (**fr**) database on WESTLAW dates from August 1980. The full text of the *Federal Register* is on-line within five days of the day issued. You would use the **fr** database when you are looking for a current document, one issued during the current year that has not yet appeared in the C.F.R. In an area such as asbestos regulation under the Clean Air Act, which changes on a weekly basis, you would want to search the daily **fr** database since the **cfr** database would be a year out of date. Type

> asbestos /p "clean air act" & da(1993)

and you will retrieve many documents in the 1993 *Federal Register*. You may also format a search in the **fr** database using WIN.

You would also use the **fr** database to search for material that is not included in the C.F.R. including proposed regulations (those never adopted by an agency) and agency notices. For example, suppose you want to locate the Department of Transportation's proposed rule of June 13, 1986, dealing with "replacement lighting equipment." Because this proposed rule was never adopted, it will only appear in the *Federal Register*. Figure 5.10 shows the result of the following search in the **fr** database:

> replac! /p light! & da(june 13, 1986)

Figure 5.8 Finding Citations to the C.F.R. in the U.S.C.A.

15 § 2225a

the publication in the Federal Register of the master list referred to in section 2224(b) of this title.

(Pub.L. 101–391, § 6, Sept. 25, 1990, 104 Stat. 751.)

Historical and Statutory Notes

Codification. Section was enacted as part of the "Hotel and Motel Fire Safety Act of 1990", and not as part of the "Federal Fire Prevention and Control Act of 1974", which enacted this chapter.

Effective Date

Section effective on the first day of the first fiscal year that begins after the expiration of the 425–day period that begins on the date of the publication in the Federal Register of the master list referred to in section 2224(b) of this title, pursuant to subsec. (d) of this section.

Legislative History. For legislative history and purpose of Pub.L. 101–391, see 1990 U.S.Code Cong. and Adm.News, p. 1173.

§ 2226. Dissemination of fire prevention and control information

The Director, acting through the Administrator, is authorized to take steps to encourage the States to promote the use of automatic sprinkler systems and automatic smoke detection systems, and to disseminate to the maximum extent possible information on the life safety value and use of such systems. Such steps may include, but need not be limited to, providing copies of the guidelines described in section 2225 of this title and of the master list compiled under section 2224(b) of this title to Federal agencies, State and local governments, and fire services throughout the United States, and making copies of the master list compiled under section 2224(b) of this title available upon request to interested private organizations and individuals.

(Pub.L. 93–498, § 30, as added Pub.L. 101–391, § 3(a), Sept. 25, 1990, 104 Stat. 748.)

Historical and Statutory Notes

Legislative History. For legislative history and purpose of Pub.L. 101–391, see 1990 U.S.Code Cong. and Adm.News, p. 1173.

CHAPTER 50—CONSUMER PRODUCT WARRANTIES

Law Review Commentaries

Concept of warranty duration: A tangled web. Max E. Klinger, 89 Dick.L.Rev. 935 (1985).

Effect of warranty disclaimers on revocation of acceptance under the Uniform Commercial Code.

Manning Gilbert Warren III and Michelle Rowe, 37 Ala.L.Rev. 307 (1986).

New Mexico's "Lemon Law": Consumer protection or consumer frustration? Joseph Goldberg, 16 New Mexico L.Rev. 251 (1986).

§ 2301. Definitions

Federal Practice and Procedure

Jurisdictional amount in controversy, see Wright, Miller & Cooper: Jurisdiction § 3701 et seq.

Code of Federal Regulations

Interpretations, see 16 CFR 700.1.

C.F.R. Citation

Law Review Commentaries

A comparative analysis of three lemon laws. Anne V. Swanson, 75 Ill.B.J. 436 (1987).

An informal resolution model of consumer product warranty law. Jean Braucher, Wis.L. Rev. 1405 (1985).

Consumer leases under Uniform Commercial Code Article 2A. Fred H. Miller, 39 Ala.L.Rev. 957 (1988).

Examining restraints on freedom to contract as an approach to purchaser dissatisfaction in the computer industry. 74 Cal.L.Rev. 2101 (1986).

Illinois lemon car buyer's options in a breach of warranty action. Lisa K. Jorgenson, 20 John Marshall L.Rev. 483 (1987).

Implied warranty and the Used Car Rule. 46 La.L.Rev. 1239 (1986).

Is revision due for Article 2? Fairfax Leary, Jr. and David Frisch, 31 Vill.L.Rev. 399 (1986).

Legislative responses to plight of new car purchasers. Richard L. Coffinberger and Linda B. Samuels, 18 UCC L.J. 168 (1985).

Product quality laws and the economics of federalism. David A. Rice (1985) 65 Boston U.L. Rev. 1.

Figure 5.9   The C.F.R. Parallel Table of Authorities and Rules

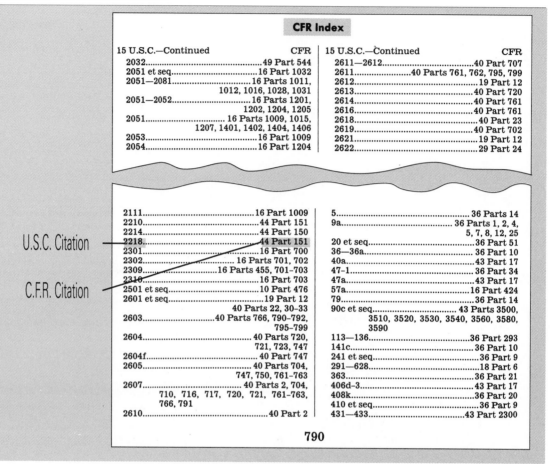

U.S.C. Citation

C.F.R. Citation

Figure 5.10   Finding a Proposed Regulation on WESTLAW

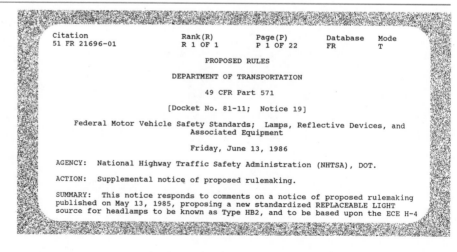

On WESTLAW, the current year of the C.F.R. has the database identifier **cfr.** To illustrate how you can search by either a U.S.C. citation or term, let us return to our warranty problem involving the car that was painted to conceal the damage. Type the following Terms and Connectors query:

```
15 +5 2301 & writ! /s warrant!
```

(As with the Federal Register database, the **cfr** database can also be searched with WIN Natural Language.) This query retrieves thirteen documents. Type l to view a list of document citations. Scanning the list, you can read the applicable regulation "700.3 Written warranty" by typing **3** (Figure 5.11).

Occasionally, you may need regulations that were in effect during an earlier year. The **cfr** databases are retrospective to 1984. If you want to find out how the regulation was stated in 1987, you would search the database **cfr87.** For example, the rule requiring labels in wool products to carry certain information on the reverse side was revised in 1988. To see how the rule read in

Figure 5.11 Searching by Using a U.S.C.A. Citation or Term

(a) List of Document Citations

```
CITATIONS LIST (Page 1)                 Search Result Documents: 13
Database: CFR

   1.  16 C.F.R. s 239.1   CODE OF FEDERAL REGULATIONS    TITLE 16--COMMERCIAL
       PRACTICES    CHAPTER I--FEDERAL TRADE COMMISSION    PART 239--GUIDES FOR
       THE ADVERTISING OF WARRANTIES AND GUARANTEES    s 239.1 Purpose and scope
       of the guides.

   2.  16 C.F.R. s 700.1   CODE OF FEDERAL REGULATIONS    TITLE 16--COMMERCIAL
       PRACTICES    CHAPTER I--FEDERAL TRADE COMMISSION    PART
       700--INTERPRETATIONS OF MAGNUSON-MOSS WARRANTY ACT    s 700.1 Products
       covered.

   3.  16 C.F.R. s 700.3   CODE OF FEDERAL REGULATIONS    TITLE 16--COMMERCIAL
       PRACTICES    CHAPTER I--FEDERAL TRADE COMMISSION    PART
       700--INTERPRETATIONS OF MAGNUSON-MOSS WARRANTY ACT    s 700.3 Written
       warranty.

   4.  16 C.F.R. s 700.4   CODE OF FEDERAL REGULATIONS    TITLE 16--COMMERCIAL
       PRACTICES    CHAPTER I--FEDERAL TRADE COMMISSION    PART
       700--INTERPRETATIONS OF MAGNUSON-MOSS WARRANTY ACT    s 700.4 Parties
       "actually making" a written warranty.
```

(b) Text of Third Document Ranked

```
Citation                Rank(R)          Page(P)          Database    Mode
16 CFR s 700.3          R 3 OF 13        P 1 OF 4         CFR         T

                        TITLE 16--COMMERCIAL PRACTICES
                           Federal Trade Commission
        Subchapter G--Rules, Regulations, Statements and Interpretations Under the
                           Magnuson-Moss Warranty Act
            Part 700--Interpretations of Magnuson-Moss Warranty Act

     s 700.3 WRITTEN WARRANTY.

      (a) The Act imposes specific duties and liabilities on suppliers who offer
     WRITTEN WARRANTIES on consumer products.  Certain representations, such as
     energy efficiency ratings for electrical appliances, care labeling of wearing
     apparel, and other product information disclosures may be express warranties
     under the Uniform Commercial Code. However, these disclosures alone are not
     WRITTEN WARRANTIES under this Act. Section 101(6) provides that a WRITTEN
     affirmation of fact or a WRITTEN promise of a specified level of performance
     must relate to a specified period of time in order to be considered a "WRITTEN
     WARRANTY." [FN1] A product information disclosure without a specified time
     period to which the disclosure relates is therefore not a WRITTEN WARRANTY.  In
     addition, section 111(d) exempts from the Act (except section 102(c)) any
     WRITTEN WARRANTY the making or content of which is required by federal law.
```

1987, you would access the **cfr87** database and type

`reverse alternat! /s side /s label & wool`

This search retrieves 16 C.F.R. 300.10 (Figure 5.12).

If you have a citation for the *Federal Register* or the C.F.R., you can retrieve it in a snap with Find. For example, to retrieve 54 FR 33737, type **fi 54 fr 33737**.

Because federal administrative law frequently deals with very specific things, on-line, full-text searching can work wonders. If you have a client who is interested in importing Bactrian camels, a word search in the **cfr** database could be the easiest way to find the applicable regulations—try it.

Figure 5.12   Searching for a Regulation in a Particular Year

```
Citation                    Rank(R)         Page(P)         Database    Mode
16 CFR s 300.10             R 1 OF 3        P 1 OF 3        CFR87       T

                        TITLE 16--COMMERCIAL PRACTICES
                            Federal Trade Commission
              Subchapter C--Regulations Under Specific Acts of Congress
                Part 300--Rules and Regulations Under the WOOL Act
                                    Labeling

    s 300.10 Arrangement of label information.

      (a) All items or parts of the information required to be shown and displayed
    in the label of the product, shall be set forth consecutively and separately on
    the outer surface of the label, in immediate conjunction with each other, and
    in type or lettering plainly legible and conspicuous, and all parts of the
    required fiber content information shall appear in type or lettering of equal
    size and conspicuousness;  such as for example:
    Distributed by:
    John Q. Doe Co., Inc.,
    New York, N.Y.
    Made of
    60% WOOL
    40% RECYCLED WOOL
```

Updating the C.F.R. with the *List of Sections Affected* and the *Federal Register*

Since the volumes of the C.F.R. are issued annually, you must always update your regulation by checking for new revisions and deletions in the Federal Register. Remember that regulations are revised constantly. You cannot rely on a regulation as it is printed in the C.F.R. or in the **cfr** database on WESTLAW without updating it.

You can easily update your WESTLAW C.F.R. search by using the **Update** service from a C.F.R. section. This will automatically bring you to any *Federal Register* entries affecting the C.F.R. section.

If you do not have access to WESTLAW to update your C.F.R. citation, you can still update your citation by using print sources (Figure 5.13). The following instructions may appear very cumbersome, but the process is quite mechanical and will work if you follow the instructions carefully:

1. Look up your section in the most recent C.F.R. paperback volume. Note the date of revision on the front cover.

Figure 5.13   Updating a C.F.R. Citation by Using Print Sources

20   **LSA—LIST OF CFR SECTIONS AFFECTED**

CHANGES JANUARY 2 THROUGH MARCH 30, 1990

TITLE 12 Chapter II—Con.   Page
220.18   (a) and (b) amended......... 11160
221   OTC margin stock list............ 2631
224   OTC margin stock list............ 2631
225   Authority citation revised... 6790
225.71—225.73   (Subpart H) Added; interim............................ 6790
229   Appendix F amended............ 11358
264b.3   (a) revised............................ 3576
    (a) amended.................................. 11360

Chapter III—Federal Deposit Insurance Corporation

312   Technical correction............... 1912
312.1   (c) revised;   (f) through added; interim.......................... 10412
312.4   Revised; interim.................. 10413
312.5   Added; interim.................... 10413
312.6   Revised; interim.................. 10413
312.7   Revised; interim.................. 10413
312.8   Added; interim.................... 10414
312.9   Added; interim.................... 10414
312.10   Added; interim.................. 10414
357   Added; interim....................... 11161

Chapter IV—Export-Import Bank of the United States

411   Added; interim............... 6737, 6747

Chapter V—Office of Thrift Supervision, Department of the Treasury

510.5   Added..................................... 7695
528   Revised..................................... 1388
545.75   (b)(3) revised; interim...... 11307
563.75   (i) removed.......................... 7300
563.80   (e)(2) revised...................... 7300
563.93   Revised; interim................ 11307
563.132   (c) and (d) removed;
    (e) redesignated as new (c)....... 4602
563d.2   Revised................................. 3041
567.13   Added..................................... 7478
571   Technical correction................. 696
571.19   (e) amended......................... 126

                     Page
611.1174   Regulation at 54 FR 1148 corrected.......................... 10042
612.2150   Regulation at 54 FR 50736 eff. 3-6-90...................... 7884
612.2160   Regulation at 54 FR 50736 eff. 3-6-90...................... 7884
614.4280   Regulation at 54 FR 50736 eff. 3-6-90...................... 7884
614.4320   Regulation at 54 FR 50736 eff. 3-6-90...................... 7884
614.4340   Regulation at 54 FR 50736 eff. 3-6-90...................... 7884
614.4345   Regulation at 54 FR 50736 eff. 3-6-90...................... 7884
614.4460   Regulation at 54 FR 50736 eff. 3-6-90...................... 7884
614.4511   Regulation at 54 FR 50736 eff. 3-6-90...................... 7884
614.5040   Regulation at 54 FR 50736 eff. 3-6-90...................... 7884
615.5104   Regulation at 54 FR 50736 eff. 3-6-90...................... 7884
615.5135   Regulation at 54 FR 50736 eff. 3-6-90...................... 7884
615.5143   Regulation at 54 FR 50736 eff. 3-6-90...................... 7884
615.5190   Regulation at 54 FR 50736 eff. 3-6-90...................... 7884
618.8060   Regulation at 54 FR 50736 eff. 3-6-90...................... 7884

Chapter VII—National Credit Union Administration

700   Authority citation revised... 1794
700.1   (h) and (i) removed;   (j) through (m) redesignated as (h) through (k).......................... 1794
701   Authority citation revised... 1794

Step 2: Changes in 12 C.F.R. 563 listed in LSA

2.   Consult the most recent monthly *List of C.F.R. Sections Affected (LSA)* pamphlet to see if your C.F.R. section is listed.   The LSA directs you to changes in the C.F.R. that were published in the *Federal Register*. Entries for rules are arranged numerically by C.F.R. title, chapter, part, section, and paragraph. If there has been a change, the LSA will refer you to the page numbers in the *Federal Register* where the action appears. There will also be a descriptive word or phrase indicating whether the change was an addition, revision, or removal. Make certain the coverage of the LSA pamphlet begins the day after the date of revision on the paperback C.F.R. volume, and note the month printed prominently on the front of the LSA.

Figure 5.13 Updating a C.F.R. Citation by Using Print Sources (continued)

ii **Federal Register** / Vol. 55, No. 83 / Monday, April 30, 1990 / Reader Aids

1011.....12369	**Proposed Rules:**	15223, 15320–15900, 17421,	146.....14966
1012.....12369	2.....12370	17422, 17595, 17931	162.....17596
1013.....12369	30.....12374, 13542	73.....13761, 17931	171.....17596
1030.....12369	40.....12374, 13542	75.....17423	178.....12342, 17596
1032.....12369	50.....12374, 13542	91.....13444, 15320–15900,	191.....17597
1033.....12369	55.....14288	17736	**Proposed Rules:**
1036.....12369	60.....12374, 13542	95.....13762	101.....17633
1040.....12369	61.....12374, 13542, 13797	97.....15244, 17424	141.....12385
1044.....12369	70.....12374, 13542	121.....13326–13332	
1046.....12369	72.....12374, 13542	125.....13332	**20 CFR**
1049.....12369	110.....12374, 13542	129.....13332	404.....17530
1050.....12369	150.....12374, 13542	135.....13444, 15320–15900	416.....14916
1064.....12369	708.....12668, 17453	382.....12336	626.....12992
1065.....12369	725.....15237	**Proposed Rules:**	636.....12992
1068.....12369		Ch. I.....12383, 13798,	638.....12992
1075.....12369	**11 CFR**	15240, 17987	675.....12992
1076.....12369	110.....13507	13.....15134	676.....12992
1079.....12369	**Proposed Rules:**	21.....12857	677.....12992
1093.....12369	106.....12499	23.....12857	678.....12992
1094.....12369	9003.....12499	25.....12316, 13886	679.....12992
1096.....12369	9007.....12499	29.....12316	680.....12992
1097.....12369	9033.....12499	39.....12503, 12859–12863,	684.....12992
1098.....12369	9035.....12499	13284, 13799, 13801, 14290,	685.....12992
1099.....12369	9038.....12499	14292, 14426, 14428, 15243,	688.....12992
1106.....12369		17453, 17631, 17860, 17987–	689.....12992
1108.....12369	**12 CFR**	17998	**Proposed Rules:**
1120.....12369	19.....13010	71.....12384, 13032, 13285–	416.....17999
1124.....12369	202.....12471, 14830	13287, 13802, 13803, 14293–	
1126.....12369	205.....12635	14295, 17632	**21 CFR**
1131.....12369	226.....13103, 17749	73.....13804	5.....14916
1132.....12369	500.....13507	75.....13287	74.....12171
1134.....12369	543.....13507	91.....12316	101.....17431
1135.....12369	544.....13507	93.....17584	173.....12171
1137.....12369	545.....13507	119.....14404	176.....13518
1138.....12369	546.....13507	121.....12316, 13886, 14404	178.....12171, 12344, 13521
1139.....12369, 12848	550.....13507	125.....12316, 14404	179.....14413
1485.....17618	552.....13507	127.....14404	300.....14968
1494.....17443	563.....13507	135.....12316, 13886, 14404,	430.....14239
1714.....12194, 12199	563b.....13507	17358	442.....14239
	563f.....13507	241.....14296	444.....14968
8 CFR	567.....13507	1266.....13912	452.....14090
103.....12627, 12628, 12815	574.....13507		455.....14378
210.....12629	584.....13507	**15 CFR**	510.....13901, 13902, 14830,
235.....14234	614.....12472	776.....13121	17951
242.....12627	615.....12473	779.....13121	514.....14831
287.....12627	620.....12472	799.....12635, 13121, 14089,	522.....13768, 13902
299.....12628	621.....12472	17530	544.....13902
499.....12628	1609.....14081	**Proposed Rules:**	558.....15099, 17598, 17951
Proposed Rules:	**Proposed Rules:**	295.....12504	610.....14037
103.....12666	21.....14424		640.....14037
	216.....12850	**16 CFR**	801.....17599
9 CFR	226.....13282	305.....13264	**Proposed Rules:**
1.....12630	701.....12852	1700.....13123–13127	101.....14429
71.....12631, 15320–15900	741.....12852	**Proposed Rules:**	872.....17455
75.....13504	747.....12855	1027.....13805	
78.....12163, 15320–15900	1611.....13543, 17715	1700.....13157	**23 CFR**
82.....12631			658.....17952
91.....12632	**13 CFR**	**17 CFR**	**Proposed Rules:**
92.....12632	121.....17419	1.....17932	655.....17634
Proposed Rules:	122.....17267	30.....14238	1327.....12509
3.....12202, 12667	**Proposed Rules:**	200.....17933	
78.....12848	120.....17280	230.....17933	**24 CFR**
101.....15233		241.....17949	882.....14243
113.....15233	**14 CFR**	**Proposed Rules:**	885.....14243
136.....15236	13.....15110	155.....13288	
201.....13796	14.....15110	156.....13545	**26 CFR**
318.....12203	21.....12328, 15214, 17589		1.....13521, 13769
381.....12203	23.....12328, 15214, 17589	**18 CFR**	301.....13289, 13521, 14244
	25.....13474	37.....14961	602.....14244
10 CFR	39.....12332, 12473–12477,	270.....17425	**Proposed Rules:**
11.....14288	12815–12817, 13259–13261,	272.....17425	1.....13808, 14429, 14437,
25.....14288	13755–13760, 14411, 14412,	284.....12167	17455, 17635, 17758
50.....12163	15217–15222, 17420, 17594,	381.....12169, 13899	31.....17758
72.....13883	17927–17930		301.....12386
95.....14288	71.....12336, 12482, 13263,	**19 CFR**	602.....14429, 14437, 17758
590.....14916	13264, 13761, 14234–14237,	141.....17596	
		142.....12342	

Step 3:
Check the CFR Parts
Affected Table

3. Consult the last issue of the month of the *Federal Register* for each complete month since the month on the cover of the LSA pamphlet. Check the CFR Parts Affected During [month] table near the back of the issue. This table cumulates through the month so you only need to check the last issue for each month.

Figure 5.13   Updating a C.F.R. Citation by Using Print Sources (continued)

Reader Aids

Federal Register

Vol. 55, No. 93

Monday, May 14, 1990

INFORMATION AND ASSISTANCE

Federal Register

Index, finding aids & general information	523–5227
Public inspection desk	523–5215
Corrections to published documents	523–5237
Document drafting information	523–5237
Machine readable documents	523–3447

Code of Federal Regulations

Index, finding aids & general information	523–5227
Printing schedules	523–3419

Laws

Public Laws Update Service (numbers, dates, etc.)	523–6641
Additional information	523–5230

Presidential Documents

Executive orders and proclamations	523–5230
Public Papers of the Presidents	523–5230
Weekly Compilation of Presidential Documents	523–5230

The United States Government Manual

General information	523–5230

Other Services

Data base and machine readable specifications	523–3408
Guide to Record Retention Requirements	523–3187
Legal staff	523–4534
Library	523–5240
Privacy Act Compilation	523–3187
Public Laws Update Service (PLUS)	523–6641
TDD for the deaf	523–5229

FEDERAL REGISTER PAGES AND DATES, MAY

18073–18302	1
18303–18584	2
18585–18716	3
18717–18850	4
18851–19046	7
19047–19232	8
19233–19616	9
19617–19716	10
19717–19870	11
19871–20110	14

CFR PARTS AFFECTED DURING MAY

At the end of each month, the Office of the Federal Register publishes separately a List of CFR Sections Affected (LSA), which lists parts and sections affected by documents published since the revision date of each title.

3 CFR

Proclamations:

6030 (See Proc. 6123)	18075
6122	18073
6123	18075
6124	18585
6125	18715
6126	18717
6127	19041
6128	19043
6129	19045
6130	19233
6131	19715
6132	20107
6133	20109

Executive Orders:

12675 (Amended by EO 12712)	18095
12712	18095
12713	18719
12714	19047
12715	19051

Administrative Orders:

Memorandums:

Apr. 26, 1990	18299

Presidential Determinations:

No. 90–17 of Apr. 25, 1990	18587
No. 90–18 of Apr. 25, 1990	18589

Order:

May 4, 1990	19235

5 CFR

1630	18851

7 CFR

2	18097
3	18591
13	18591
52	19001
210	18857
245	19237
301	19241
400	18097
704	19243
910	18858, 19717
920	19717
927	18097
979	19719, 19720
985	18859
993	19617
1012	18098
1139	18303
1478	19053
1980	19244

Proposed Rules:

220	18908, 20023
300	20023
301	18342

911	19740
929	19741
953	18909
1762	18606
1941	18607
1943	18607
1945	18607
948	19631
982	19632

8 CFR

286	18860

9 CFR

71	18099
78	19054
82	18099
85	19245
92	19245

Proposed Rules:

78	19268
94	18342
114	18345
308	19888
318	19888
320	19888
381	19888

10 CFR

590	18227

Proposed Rules:

Ch. I	19633
20	19890
30	19890
40	19890
50	18608
70	19890

12 CFR

207	18591
220	18591
221	18591
224	18591

Proposed Rules:

563g	18610
741	18613
1611	20023

13 CFR

302	18593
309	18594

Proposed Rules:

120	18614
124	18615
125	19633

14 CFR

13	18800
14	18800
15	18704
21	19050

Step 4: Check the CFR Parts Affected Table in the Most Recent *Federal Register*

4.   Consult the most recent issue of the *Federal Register* available and check the CFR Parts Affected During [month] table near the back. Note the date of the issue.

5. Finally, remember to check to see if the regulation is still valid. Check *Shepard's Code of Federal Regulation Citations* for cases that have interpreted the federal regulations.

Administrative Decisions

In addition to writing rules, agencies issue orders and opinions. Agencies report their opinions just as a court does. These reports are published by the U.S. Government Printing Office in either print format or microfiche.

An increasing number of agency decisions are available on-line on WEST-LAW. These decisions can be found in topical databases, such as the energy databases, which include decisions of the Federal Energy Regulatory Commission, the Nuclear Regulatory Commission, materials from two specialized publications, *Gower Federal Service* and the *Public Utilities Reports*, and applicable regulations from the *Federal Register* and the *Code of Federal Regulations,* among other materials.

In addition to the official reports and WESTLAW, administrative decisions can be located in various loose-leaf services. Loose-leaf services are so named because they are published in binders with removable pages. A loose-leaf service is constantly kept current with new pages. Loose-leaf services generally follow one of two formats. In the newsletter format, new pages are added at the end of each unit. *United States Law Week* (U.S.L.W.), which we discussed in Chapter 1, is an example of a newsletter format. The second type of loose-leaf services replaces pages that are out of date in addition to adding new information. The major publishers of loose-leaf services are The Bureau of National Affairs, Inc. (BNA), Commerce Clearing House, Inc. (CCH), and Prentice-Hall (P-H). Many loose-leaf reporters are now published on-line as well as in print format.

Presidential Documents

In discussing administrative materials, we cannot overlook the administrative actions of the president, who may direct agency action by issuing executive orders. The president may also issue proclamations that are either ceremonial in nature, such as the observance of National Library Week, or of a more substantive nature, often concerning trade matters. Both types of actions have the effect of law.

The daily *Federal Register* prints presidential documents including proclamations and executive orders as well as other documents that the president orders to be published, such as determinations, letters, memoranda, and reorganization plans. All executive orders and proclamations published in the *Federal Register* are compiled annually in Title 3 of the *Code of Federal Regulations* and in West's *United States Code Congressional and Administrative*

News. Proclamations and executive orders are available on WESTLAW in the Presidential Documents (**pres**) database (Figure 5.14).

State Administrative Law Materials

Administrative powers comparable to those of federal agencies are vested in state agencies, based upon the power of the states to regulate their internal commerce. Typical state agencies include state public service commissions and labor relations boards.

Figure 5.14   Retrieving Presidential Documents on WESTLAW

```
Citation            Rank(R)          Page(P)         Database        Mode
E.O. 12854          R 1 OF 101       P 1 OF 3        PRES            Term
58 FR 36587, 1993 WL 242363 (Pres.)

                              Executive Order 12854

                                 July 4, 1993

Implementation of the Cuban Democracy Act

 By the authority vested in me as President by the Constitution and the laws of
the United States of America, including the Trading with the Enemy Act, as
amended (50 U.S.C. App. 1-6, 7-39, 41-44), the Cuban Democracy Act of 1992
(Public Law 102-484, sections 1701-1712, October 23, 1992, 106 Stat. 2575)
(the "Act"), and section 301 of title 3, United States Code,
 I, WILLIAM J. CLINTON, President of the United States of America, hereby
order:
 Section 1. Implementation of the Act. All agencies are hereby directed to take
all appropriate measures within their authority, including the promulgation of
rules and regulations, to carry out the provisions of the Act.
 Sec. 2. Functions of the Department of State. The Secretary of State shall be
responsible for implementing sections 1704, 1707, and 1708 of the Act.
```

Many states have administrative codes similar in format to the *Code of Federal Regulations*. Many states also have registers similar to the *Federal Register*. But state administrative materials are frequently more difficult to find and less up-to-date if you do find them than are federal materials. Often an agency itself may be your best source for its own regulations and administrative decisions. Don't be afraid to make a phone call. You might well get things directly from an administrative agency that are not published in any organized manner.

State administrative law is voluminous; it is growing daily and prodigiously. More and more of it is now being added to WESTLAW. Several administrative codes, especially for the largest states, are now on WESTLAW. The **ag** database contains the opinions of the attorneys general of many states. Likewise, the **pur** database has the decisions of various public utilities regulatory commissions. Additional administrative law materials are included in various topical areas, such as taxation, corporations, or workers' compensation. On-line access to it all will make life easier for everyone.

Conclusion

Administrative law has intimidated people for years. Since law school courses generally avoid it, many new associates are surprised by administrative regulations and decisions. Nevertheless, the *Federal Register* can be your pal—well, sort of—and the C.F.R., with its annual volumes and links to the *Federal Register* through the *List of Sections Affected,* is quite a decent tool. This may be an area, though, where the WESTLAW service *is* the best answer. It is updated for you, and you can search by unique terms. Try it for administrative law.

6 BACKGROUND LEGAL SOURCES

Rather than beginning your research with one of the primary sources of the law, you may find it more productive—and less painful—to begin with various background materials. Just as you used secondary sources, such as encyclopedias and periodicals, for your college research papers, you can use legal background materials to become acquainted with a particular legal topic. An added advantage is that secondary materials, generally speaking, have good indexes. Consequently, the information is not only easy to understand, it is easy to get at as well.

Background materials are called secondary authority. These sources include annotations, legal periodicals, legal encyclopedias, treatises, restatements, dictionaries, and formbooks. All of these background materials include numerous citations to primary sources and narrative discussions of the principles of law; thus, they are tools for finding the primary authorities as well as commentaries on them.

Though they give excellent introductions to specific topics and related issues, secondary sources are not the law. These materials are not binding on the courts. Therefore, you should never limit your research to secondary materials; you must always follow through by reading the primary sources.

American Law Reports

We could have discussed the *American Law Reports* (ALR®) in the chapter on "Finding Cases" rather than in this chapter because the ALR is used both as a means of finding cases and as a secondary source, meaning that it contains commentary material. A fountain of information, the ALR is often an ideal starting place for your research (Figure 6.1).

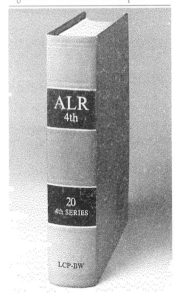

Figure 6.1   *American Law Reports*

The ALR, which is published by Lawyers Cooperative, is known for its thoroughly researched annotations written by an editorial staff who leave no citation uncovered. An ALR annotation is a legal essay on a very specific point of law. It traces the development of that point of law and presents its judicial treatment in all jurisdictions. As a law student, you will be surprised at how narrow the annotation topics tend to be. However, when you practice law, you will be grateful for the very narrow, well-defined topics since your research will revolve around very specific issues.

The ALR does not attempt to cover every legal topic, so it is possible that your topic will not appear. Generally, the topics covered in the ALR are of interest to attorneys of all jurisdictions, not just to those in the one in which the case was decided.

The ALR includes several series, as shown in Table 6.1. In general, if you are dealing with a federal problem, you will use *ALRFed.*; if your issue is one arising primarily under state statutes or in state cases, you will use the third, fourth, or fifth series. Annotations following the same format as those in the ALR also appear in the *United States Supreme Court Reports, Lawyers' Edition.*

To illustrate the features of the ALR, let's examine the following problem. Assume that your client is a hospital administrator who is concerned about his hospital's responsibility for administering blood transfusions.

To answer this question by using the ALR, you can access the ALR either by using the multivolume *ALR Index* or on-line through the LEXIS service. The *ALR Index* provides subject access to all of the ALR series (except the first). On LEXIS, you can access the full text of ALR, or you can find references to ALR annotations by using the LEXIS citator service known as Auto-Cite.

The *ALR Index* lists the entry "Liability of hospital, physician, or other individual medical practitioner for injury or death resulting from blood transfusion," which appears to be on target. Turning to the annotation in Volume 20 of the *ALR4th,* you find that the text of one important representative case *(Fisher v. Sibley Memorial Hospital)* precedes the annotation. This case acts as the theme for the annotation. Following the case are an outline of topics covered in the annotation, a word index of topics for the annotation, and a table of jurisdictions represented so you can turn to cases of a specific state. The

Table 6.1   ALR Series

Series	Years	Coverage
ALR1st	1919–1948	State and federal issues
ALR2d	1948–1965	State and federal issues
ALR3d	1965–1980	State issues and federal issues until 1969
ALR4th	1980–1991	State issues only
ALR5th	1992–date	State issues only
ALRFed.	1969–date	Federal issues only

most useful part of the annotation is the case and statute analysis, where the weight of authority is noted along with the direction of emerging trends. Here the holdings of hundreds of cases are summarized (Figure 6.2).

Figure 6.2   Abstracts of Cases in an Annotation

| 20 ALR4th | BLOOD TRANSFUSIONS
20 ALR4th 136 | § 3[a] |

The fact that the consequences of improper transfusion techniques may not appear until a much later date raises obvious questions as to the time when the statute of limitations begins to run. Thus, counsel for the patient should be aware that in choosing among the various remedies available for recovery, he should consider whether questions of limitations would be avoided thereby.[16]

Counsel on either side may find the hospital's records a valuable source of evidence. In states adopting the Uniform Business Records as Evidence

II. Liability of hospitals or their employees

§ 3. Transfusing wrong or incompatible type of blood

[a] Application of view that transaction constitutes a service not giving rise to liability without fault

The courts have generally ruled that a supplier of a product may not be held liable without fault for injuries caused by the product, if the transaction involved the supplying of

---

15. The foregoing list of nonvalid reasons are utilized by some hospitals for the guidance of the staff. See 11 Am Jur Proof of Facts 331, Transfusions, Supplement.

16. See, for example, Smith v McComb Infirmary Asso. (1967, **Miss**) 196 So 2d 91, a statutory wrongful death action based upon negligence of a hospital in mistyping the blood of a mother, wherein the court held that the plaintiff's declaration was cast under the wrongful death statute and that the statute of limitations began to run from the date of the infant's death in December, 1964, and not from the time of the alleged negligent act in 1958, and that therefore the trial judge had erred in sustaining the plea of limitation, and the judgment was reversed and the cause remanded. The trial judge had

based his opinion on the theory that the declaration of plaintiff was one charging malpractice and that the statute of limitations had run according to a rule that a cause of action for malpractice accrues and the statute begins to run on the date of the wrongful act or omission which constitutes the malpractice, and not from the time of the discovery thereof.

17. For example, the admissibility of hospital records tending to prove an incompatible blood transfusion was recognized in Joseph v W. H. Groves Latter Day Saints Hospital (1957) 7 **Utah** 2d 39, 318 P2d 330.

See, generally, 40 Am Jur 2d, Hospitals and Asylums § 43.

As to the admissibility of computerized hospital records, see § 8 of the annotation at 7 ALR4th 8.

143

ALR annotations have always included helpful references to treatment of the issue in other Lawyers Cooperative publications (Figure 6.3), but recently—as a supplement to *ALR4th* and as part of the annotations of *ALR5th*—those references have been enhanced with citations to West digest topic and key numbers, as well as sample electronic search queries (Figure 6.4).

Updating Your Research in the ALR

Since the annotations in the first and second series of the ALR were written before 1965, many of them have been rewritten and superseded by later ones. The most important step in using ALR, then, is to consult the Annotation History Table, located in Volume 6 of the *ALR Index* (Figure 6.5). This table will tell you whether or not an annotation has been supplemented or superseded by a later annotation. It would be a terrible waste of your energy to read an outdated annotation. Always check the Annotation History Table before you read the annotation.

Figure 6.3   An ALR Annotation

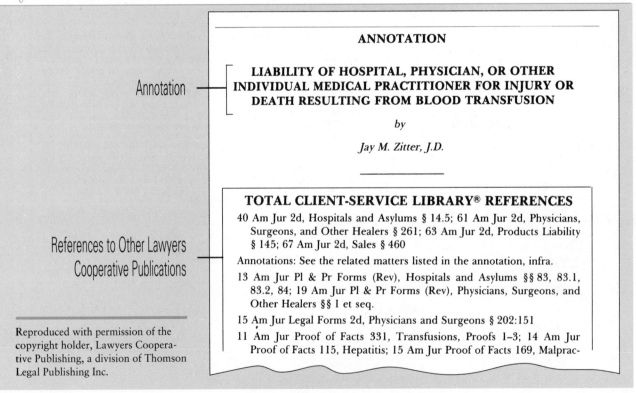

Annotation

References to Other Lawyers
Cooperative Publications

ANNOTATION

LIABILITY OF HOSPITAL, PHYSICIAN, OR OTHER INDIVIDUAL MEDICAL PRACTITIONER FOR INJURY OR DEATH RESULTING FROM BLOOD TRANSFUSION

by

Jay M. Zitter, J.D.

TOTAL CLIENT-SERVICE LIBRARY® REFERENCES

40 Am Jur 2d, Hospitals and Asylums § 14.5; 61 Am Jur 2d, Physicians, Surgeons, and Other Healers § 261; 63 Am Jur 2d, Products Liability § 145; 67 Am Jur 2d, Sales § 460

Annotations: See the related matters listed in the annotation, infra.

13 Am Jur Pl & Pr Forms (Rev), Hospitals and Asylums §§ 83, 83.1, 83.2, 84; 19 Am Jur Pl & Pr Forms (Rev), Physicians, Surgeons, and Other Healers §§ 1 et seq.

15 Am Jur Legal Forms 2d, Physicians and Surgeons § 202:151

11 Am Jur Proof of Facts 331, Transfusions, Proofs 1–3; 14 Am Jur Proof of Facts 115, Hepatitis; 15 Am Jur Proof of Facts 169, Malprac-

Figure 6.4   Sample Electronic Search Query and West Topic and Key Numbers in *ALR5th*

STRICT LIABILITY—USED PRODUCTS   9 ALR5th

9 ALR5th 1

Federal Statutes

15 USCS §§ 2051 et seq., 3901 et seq.

Digests and Indexes

ALR Digests, Products Liability § 1.5

ALR Index, Absolute Liability; Products Liability; Sale and Transfer of Property; Used or Secondhand Property

Auto-Cite®

Cases and annotations referred to herein can be further researched through the Auto-Cite® computer-assisted research service. Use Auto-Cite to check citations for form, parallel references, prior and later history, and annotation references.

RESEARCH SOURCES

The following are the research sources that were found to be helpful in compiling this annotation:

Texts

2 Lee and Lindahl, Modern Tort Law Liability and Litigation § 27.60

6 Speiser, Krause and Gans, The American Law of Torts § 18:25

Encyclopedias

63 Am Jur 2d, Products Liability §§ 572, 573

72 CJS Products Liability §§ 40, 43

Law Reviews

Sales of Defective Used Products: Should Strict Liability Apply?, 52 So Cal L Rev 805 (1979)

Protecting the Buyer of Used Products: Is Strict Liability For Commercial Sellers Desirable?, 33 Stan L Rev 535 (1981)

Electronic Search Query

(seller or dealer) w/10 (used or secondhand or second hand) w/10 (strict! or absolut! w/3 liable or liability)

West Digest Key Numbers

Automobiles 16

Aviation 13

Explosives 9

Judgment 181(33)

Products Liability 4, 5, 8, 16, 23,

25, 35, 39, 46, 47, 48, 49, 50, 51, 52, 53, 54, 55, 56, 57, 58, 60, 61, 62, 83.5, 85, 86

Torts 14.1

Weapons 18(1)

Obviously, the annotations in the ALR would lose their appeal if the citations to cases became outdated. Fortunately, you can update the cases that are cited in the text of the annotations by various means, depending on the series. For the third, fourth, fifth, and federal series, use the cumulative pocket parts inserted in the back of each volume (Figure 6.6). To update the cases in the second series, use the *ALR2d Later Case Service,* a separate supplemental set of books. For updates to the first series, check the set of books entitled *ALR1st Blue Book of Supplemental Decisions.* For the latest cases, use Insta-Cite—do not stop with the *ALR* system for updating.

Legal Periodicals

Articles that appear in legal periodicals provide an in-depth treatment of a topic with numerous references to primary and secondary authorities. Other articles, particularly those that appear in bar association periodicals, commercial journals, newsletters, and legal newspapers, include the most current topics not covered in other secondary sources. Usually, new developments in the law are discussed first in legal periodicals.

Figure 6.5 The Annotation History Table

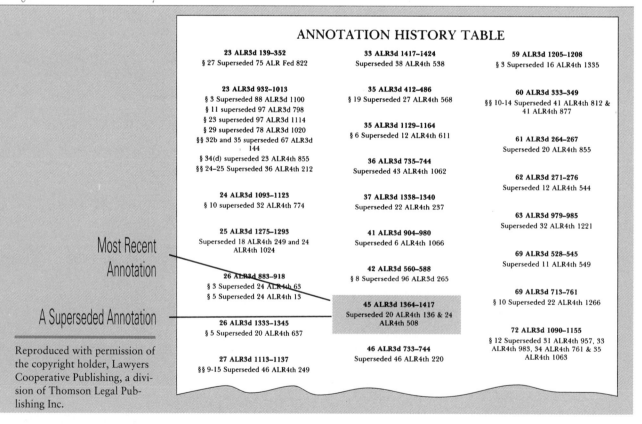

ANNOTATION HISTORY TABLE

Most Recent Annotation

A Superseded Annotation

23 ALR3d 139–352
§ 27 Superseded 75 ALR Fed 822

23 ALR3d 932–1013
§ 3 Superseded 88 ALR3d 1100
§ 11 superseded 97 ALR3d 798
§ 23 superseded 97 ALR3d 1114
§ 29 superseded 78 ALR3d 1020
§§ 32b and 35 superseded 67 ALR3d 144
§ 34(d) superseded 23 ALR4th 855
§§ 24–25 Superseded 36 ALR4th 212

24 ALR3d 1093–1123
§ 10 superseded 32 ALR4th 774

25 ALR3d 1275–1293
Superseded 18 ALR4th 249 and 24 ALR4th 1024

26 ALR3d 883–918
§ 3 Superseded 24 ALR4th 63
§ 5 Superseded 24 ALR4th 13

26 ALR3d 1333–1345
§ 5 Superseded 20 ALR4th 637

27 ALR3d 1113–1137
§§ 9–15 Superseded 46 ALR4th 249

33 ALR3d 1417–1424
Superseded 38 ALR4th 538

35 ALR3d 412–486
§ 19 Superseded 27 ALR4th 568

35 ALR3d 1129–1164
§ 6 Superseded 12 ALR4th 611

36 ALR3d 735–744
Superseded 43 ALR4th 1062

37 ALR3d 1338–1340
Superseded 22 ALR4th 237

41 ALR3d 904–980
Superseded 6 ALR4th 1066

42 ALR3d 560–588
§ 8 Superseded 96 ALR3d 265

45 ALR3d 1364–1417
Superseded 20 ALR4th 136 & 24 ALR4th 508

46 ALR3d 733–744
Superseded 46 ALR4th 220

59 ALR3d 1205–1208
§ 3 Superseded 16 ALR4th 1335

60 ALR3d 333–349
§§ 10-14 Superseded 41 ALR4th 812 & 41 ALR4th 877

61 ALR3d 264–267
Superseded 20 ALR4th 855

62 ALR3d 271–276
Superseded 12 ALR4th 544

63 ALR3d 979–985
Superseded 32 ALR4th 1221

69 ALR3d 528–545
Superseded 11 ALR4th 549

69 ALR3d 713–761
§ 10 Superseded 22 ALR4th 1266

72 ALR3d 1090–1155
§ 12 Superseded 31 ALR4th 957, 33 ALR4th 983, 34 ALR4th 761 & 35 ALR4th 1063

Figure 6.6   A Pocket Part for the ALR

An Update to the Annotation in the Pocket Part

SUPPLEMENT   20 ALR4th 136–184

For latest cases, call the toll free number appearing on the cover of this supplement.

whether, and the extent to which, a claimant qualifies for an award of reparations," was that police reports were to be considered as proof of truth of facts contained therein, and fact that such reports might contain conclusions, or that some statements might be first, second or third level hearsay, did not make any part of police report incompetent evidence; thus, award of panel of commissioners to claimant of full amount of work lost was contrary to manifest weight of evidence, and erroneously entered, where panel failed to consider police report. Re Grow (1983) 7 **Ohio** Misc 2d 26, 7 Ohio BR 175, 454 NE2d 618.

§ 19. [New] Appeal

See Re Application of Eader (1982) 70 **Ohio** Misc 17, 24 Ohio Ops 3d 83, 434 NE2d 757, § 15.

20 ALR4th 122–128

When statute of limitations commences to run on right of partnership accounting. 44 ALR4th 678.

Auto-Cite®: Cases and annotations referred to herein can be further researched through the Auto-Cite® computer-assisted research service. Use Auto-Cite to check citations for form, parallel references, prior and later history, and annotation references.

20 ALR4th 136–184

New sections and subsections added:

§ 11.5. Transfusing blood containing other injurious substances

§ 1. Introduction
[b] Related matters
Liability of blood supplier or donor for in-

to herein can be further researched through the Auto-Cite® computer-assisted research service. Use Auto-Cite to check citations for form, parallel references, prior and later history, and annotation references.

§ 3. Transfusing wrong or incompatible type of blood

[b] Cases determined in circumstances presented—liability held established or supportable

In action against medical lab alleging negligence in typing plaintiff's blood incorrectly with result that RH incompatability occurred between plaintiff and her unborn child, summary judgment for defendant was precluded where fact question arose as to whether incorrect typing could have been result of defendant's failure to either possess or use degree of care ordinarily possessed by laboratories which perform blood typing; action would be joined to action against physicians based on same injury, and limitations in action commenced running, not when faulty test was performed, but from time injury resulted to plaintiff. Guthrie v Bio-Medical Laboratories, Inc. (1983, **Ala**) 442 So 2d 92.

See Walker v Humana Medical Corp. (1982, **Ala** App) 415 So 2d 1107, later app (Ala App) 423 So 2d 891, § 7[a].

§ 5. —Cases determined in circumstances presented

[a] Liability held established or supportable

Hospital which purchased from blood bank blood contaminated with non-A/non-B hepatitis, which plaintiff contracted after she was given five units of packed red blood cells, was strictly liable for defect in blood. Shortess v Touro Infirmary (1988, **La**) 520 So 2d 389, on remand (La App 4th Cir) 535 So2d 446.

In action by patient who developed chronic hepatitis following blood transfusions, hospi-

You may also find an article that proposes legal reforms. One famous article that falls into this category is a piece by Gerald Gunther entitled "The Supreme Court, 1971 Term—Foreword: In Search of Evolving Doctrine on a Changing Court: A Model for a Newer Equal Protection," which appeared in the *Harvard Law Review* in 1972 (Figure 6.7). The information in this article would be very useful in supporting a point of view not held by the courts. Using a legal periodical article is often the best way to begin your research, particularly in a developing area of the law.

Figure 6.7 A Law Review Article Proposing Legal Reforms

HARVARD LAW REVIEW

CONTENTS

iii

Copyright © Volume 86, November 1972, Harvard Law Review

Law school law reviews, a very special type of legal periodical, include lengthy essays written by scholars or practitioners. Every law school has at least one law review (Figure 6.8). The authors discuss, in meticulous detail, aspects of the law perhaps not covered in other sources. The extensive footnotes (literally hundreds to thousands) are a great aid in finding primary sources. In addition to the lengthy articles, law reviews generally include a "Notes and Comments" section, which contains short articles written by the law review staff.

You can locate periodical articles very easily either on-line through WESTLAW or other on-line services, on laser disc, or in print format. In print, you can use the *Index to Legal Periodicals*, published by the H. W. Wilson Company, which dates back to 1908, or the *Current Law Index*, published by Information Access Company, which dates back to 1980.

Law schools have access through WESTLAW to the *Current Index to Legal Periodicals* database (**cilp**), which is produced by the University of Washington Law Library and indexes the most recent information from three hundred legal periodicals; and the *Legal Resource Index* database (**lri**). The **lri** database includes all the material covered in the *Current Law Index,* plus legal newspapers and law-related articles from the popular press. These indexes are extremely convenient to use on-line.

Using the indexes on-line is preferable to searching through the printed volumes since all of the indexes cumulate in one place and you can print your results. You can search these periodical indexes on WESTLAW the same way you would search any other database. For example, to retrieve recent articles discussing insider trading, access either **lri** or **cilp** and type

```
inside* /s trad*** & da(aft 1990)
```

Figure 6.9 shows the results of your search.

Figure 6.8   Some Representative Law Reviews

Figure 6.9 *Legal Resources Index On-Line*

```
CITATIONS LIST (Page 1)              Search Result Documents: 131
Database: LRI

   1.  TITLE:  Focus on insider trading; SEC examines relationship between
       issuers and    analysts. (Securities Law).   AUTHOR: Levine, Theodore
       A.; Callcott, W. Hardy.   YEAR:   Publication Date: December 7, 1992.
       1992 WL 431448 (LRI), 12/7/92 N.Y. L.J. 7, col. 2

   2.  TITLE:  Policies to halt abuses should be adopted. (Securities Law).
       AUTHOR:  Greenberg, Joel L.   YEAR:   Publication Date: December 7,
       1992.   1992 WL 431449 (LRI), 12/7/92 N.Y. L.J. 7, col. 2

   3.  TITLE:  New U.K. laws on insider trading.   AUTHOR: Moore, Lois.
       YEAR:   Publication Date:  December 3, 1992.   1992 WL 431429 (LRI),
       12/3/92 N.Y. L.J. 5, col. 1

   4.  TITLE:  Lawyer settles inside trading case with SEC. (Henry A. Singer of
       Morrison Cohen Singer & Weinstein).   YEAR:   Publication Date:
       November 9, 1992.   1992 WL 374358 (LRI), 11/9/92 Nat'l L.J. 6, col. 1

   5.  TITLE:  Insider dealing: the future. (insider trading) (United Kingdom).
       AUTHOR:  Woodcock, Tony.   YEAR:   Publication Date: November 6, 1992.
       1992 WL 432711 (LRI), 136 Solic. J. 1108
                     COPR. (C) WEST 1993 NO CLAIM TO ORIG. U.S. GOVT. WORKS
```

Using the indexes on-line is the most efficient way to research a current issue. If, however, you are dealing with an issue that is more retrospective in scope, such as the topic "dower," you must use the print *Index to Legal Periodicals* since that index dates back to the early 1900s, with predecessors indexing to the early nineteenth century.

You can also locate the *full text* of articles on WESTLAW. The Texts and Periodicals database **tp-all** on WESTLAW contains articles from law reviews, texts, and bar journals. You will be able to access every word in the text and footnotes. **Tp-all** may be searched using either WIN or Terms and Connectors.

Parts of articles that deal with subtopics of the main article can be searched on-line, too. These subtopics would not normally be found in the standard indexes. For example, if you are interested in articles on test anxiety, access the **tp-all** database and enter this WIN search:

test (exam) anxiety

By searching in the **tp-all** database, you retrieve an article entitled "Law School Academic Support Programs" that appeared in 40 Hastings L.J. 771 (1989); you would not retrieve this article in the standard indexes under the subject "test anxiety."

If you are looking for a specific article and you already know its citation, access the appropriate database and search in the citation field. For example, if the cite is 74 ABA J. 55, access the ABA Journal database (**abaj**) and type this Terms and Connectors query:

ci(74 +5 55)

Encyclopedias

The two national encyclopedias, *Corpus Juris Secundum*® (C.J.S.) and *American Jurisprudence 2d* (Am. Jur.2d), provide an elementary, objective statement of the law and cite literally hundreds of thousands of state and federal cases. Encyclopedias tend to concentrate on case law and ignore statutory materials. C.J.S. and Am. Jur.2d. are similar to general encyclopedias in that both sets contain alphabetically arranged summaries of legal topics and a multivolume index that provides easy access to the material.

In its introductory "Explanation," C.J.S., a West publication, defines its mission as ". . . a complete restatement of the entire American law as developed by all reported cases" (Figure 6.10). Due to this publishing philosophy, each page in C.J.S. contains about six lines of text and almost three-quarters of a page of citations to cases and materials. The citations to cases are arranged alphabetically by state. With such an arrangement, you can quickly find citations from your jurisdiction.

The editors of C.J.S. have undertaken a planned program of replacing volumes in subject areas that have seen substantial changes and developments, such as the area of criminal law. The new volumes state West's philosophy as ". . . a contemporary statement of American law as derived from reported cases and legislation." As a result in the change in West's approach, the number of cases cited has been reduced in the recompilation volumes.

Because it supplies West topic and key numbers, C.J.S. is perhaps most useful as a springboard into the West research system. Finding the topic and key numbers in C.J.S. circumvents the need to search through the Descriptive-Word Index when using the digests.

A five-volume *General Index* offers descriptive word entry into C.J.S. An alphabetical list of over 430 subjects, called "List of Titles," is located at the front of each volume. In using C.J.S., look up the most appropriate terms for your topic in the index. For example, if you were interested in an explanation of "nolo contendere," after a check in the C.J.S. *Index* you would turn to Criminal Law § 398 (Figure 6.11).

American Jurisprudence Second (Am. Jur.2d), published by Lawyers Cooperative, is more selective and contains fewer footnote references, which cite only leading decisions. A *Desk Book* provides useful reference information, such as the U.S. Constitution, the organization of the federal court system, and various tables. Am. Jur.2d includes a ring-bound volume *New Topic Service,* which includes current topics, such as "Alternative Dispute Resolution."

The complaint most law students have with the legal encyclopedias is that some of the volumes are rather musty. The encyclopedias do not always keep pace with the law as it grows and changes. Although both sets are kept up-to-date by pocket parts and replacement volumes, the sets are most useful for general information on traditional topics.

Figure 6.10   *Corpus Juris Secundum*

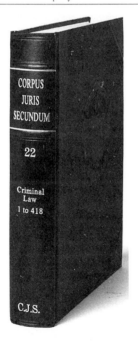

Figure 6.11   An Entry in *Corpus Juris Secundum*

22 C. J. S.   CRIMINAL LAW   § 398

ment or information is insufficient, from the standpoint of failing either to confer jurisdiction or to set forth facts sufficient to constitute a public offense, the plea of guilty confesses nothing,[62] and, accordingly, does not preclude accused from attacking the indictment or information on such grounds.[63] In fact, where the plea of guilty is to a void charge or one which fails to state facts sufficient to constitute a crime, the conviction is jurisdictionally defective and a nullity, and is not validated by the plea.[64]

A guilty plea does not waive a claim that the information or indictment, judged on its face, is constitutionally deficient in violation of the double jeopardy clause.[65]

Defects or irregularities in prior proceedings.

By pleading guilty to the charge contained in an indictment or information accused waives any technical defects or irregularities in prior proceedings[66] except such as go to jurisdiction.[67]

Involuntary plea.

Where a plea of guilty is so coerced that it is deprived of validity to support the conviction the coercion likewise deprives it of validity as a waiver of the right of accused to assail the conviction.[68]

Venue.

Since accused's plea of guilty is an admission of the material facts in the indictment or information, including the facts concerning the situs of the crime, the plea operates to waive any right to be tried in the county where the acts were actually committed, and the judgment cannot be collaterally attacked on that ground.[69]

Trial of accomplices.

Certainly, one who has pleaded guilty cannot question the procedure followed at the trial of his accomplices.[70]

2.   **Plea of Nolo Contendere**

§ 398. In General

The so-called plea of "nolo contendere," also called "no contest," is not, strictly speaking, a plea, but a formal declara-

tion by the accused that he will not contest the charge against him.

State Legal Encyclopedias

Many states have an encyclopedia that organizes and discusses the points of law applicable in that particular jurisdiction. State encyclopedias are extremely practical, timely, and a great way to find state cases, statutes, and formbooks. West publishes several state encyclopedias. They follow the pattern and style of C.J.S. in providing topic and key numbers, which makes it easy to access information in the state digests.

Legal Dictionaries

Undoubtedly, you have already had a need to consult a legal dictionary. Since the legal field has its own jargon, the need for a law dictionary is constant. Several legal dictionaries are available in your library. The two most prominent are *Black's Law Dictionary*, published by West, and *Ballentine's*, published by Lawyers Cooperative.

Legal dictionaries may give case citations as well as defining terms. A citation may lead you to a good case as a starting point to understanding the meaning of the term. Additionally, these dictionaries include a very handy table of abbreviations for just about any citation you need to interpret. You will also find that legal dictionaries are an aid in using the on-line services, since they supply alternative words for you to add as synonyms in your queries.

Black's Law Dictionary, 6th ed., is also available on WESTLAW. If you are reading a case or statute, you can type **di,** followed by your term, to learn its definition. To check the spelling of a term before using it as a search term in a query, type **di** followed by a portion of the term followed by an exclamation point (!). For example, type **es!** if you want to check the spelling of escheat (Figure 6.12).

Figure 6.12   Checking Spelling on WESTLAW in *Black's Law Dictionary*

(a) List of Words Retrieved

```
BLACK'S LAW DICTIONARY   6TH EDITION

  1. Escalation clause.
  2. Escalator clause.
  3. Escambio
  4. Escambium
  5. Escape.
  6. Escape clause.
  7. Escape period.
  8. Escape warrant.
  9. Escapio quietus
 10. Escapium
 11. Eschaeta derivatur a verbo gallico eschoir, quod est accidere, quia accidit
     domino ex eventu et ex insperato
 12. Eschaetae vulgo dicuntur quae decidentibus iis quae de rege tenent, cum non
     existit ratione sanguinis haeres, ad fiscum relabuntur
 13. Escheat
 14. Escheator

To see a definition, enter the number of the desired term.
To continue through the list of terms . . . . . . . Press ENTER .
To leave the Dictionary system. . . . . . . . . . Enter GOBACK or GB
COPR. (C) WEST 1993 NO CLAIM TO ORIG. U.S. GOVT. WORKS
```

(b) Definition of Escheat

```
BLACK'S LAW DICTIONARY   6TH EDITION                            P  1 OF  1

  Escheat

    A reversion of property to the state in consequence of a want of any
  individual competent to inherit.
    Escheat at feudal law was the right of the lord of a fee to re-enter upon
  the same when it became vacant by the extinction of the blood of the tenant.
  This extinction might either be per defectum sanguinis or else per delictum
  tenentis, where the course of descent was broken by the corruption of the
  blood of the tenant.  As a fee might be holden either of the crown or from
  some inferior lord, the escheat was not always to the crown.  The word
  ''escheat'', in this country, merely indicates the preferable right of the
  state to an estate left vacant, and without there being any one in existence
  able to make claim thereto.




  COPR. (C) WEST 1993 NO CLAIM TO ORIG. U.S. GOVT. WORKS
```

West also publishes *Words and Phrases*®, an expanded multivolume dictionary. This set can be used to locate cases that have defined a particular term. Hundreds of thousands of definitions are alphabetically arranged, couched in the language of the court. For example, numerous courts have defined the term "enjoyment" (Figure 6.13).

Figure 6.13   Definitions in *Words and Phrases*

A Court's Definition

ENJOYED WITHOUT LIMITATIONS

In a deed conveying a lot of land and "a free right of way for an alleyway 12 feet wide, extending from the rear end of said lot across another lot owned by said K. to the alley running to L. street," the word "free" qualifies and relates to "right of way" and is descriptive of the right of way, the thing granted, and not of the use to be made of the right of way. According to Webst.Dict., the word "free," when used in relation to a thing to be enjoyed or possessed, means "thrown open, or made accessible to all; to be enjoyed without limitations; unrestricted; not obstructed, engrossed, or appropriated; open." Applying that definition, the word "free," as used in the deed, indicates the condition and character of the right of way, which is the thing granted, and the thing to be enjoyed and possessed and, as thus interpreted, it means an unobstructed right of way as far as any future act of the owner of the servient lot is concerned.   Flaherty v. Fleming, 52 S.E. 857, 859, 58 W.Va. 669, 3 L.R.A., N.S., 461.

ENJOYMENT

Cross References

Accumulate; Accumulation
Adverse Enjoyment
Exclusive Enjoyment
Full Benefit and Enjoyment
Natural Use and Enjoyment
Necessary to the Enjoyment
Personal Enjoyment
Possession, Enjoyment or Right to Income from

The words "enjoyment" and "enjoy", as used in statutes relating to estate and gift taxes, are not terms of art, but connote substantial present economic benefit rather than technical vesting of title or estates. C. I. R. v. Holmes' Estate, Tex., 66 S.Ct. 257, 260, 326 U.S. 480, 90 L.Ed. 228.

Where trustees, including settlor had power to accomplish a complete diversion of trust income and an invasion of corpus,

ENJOYMENT—Cont'd

settlor had power to alter the "enjoyment" of trust property, within Revenue Act. Jennings v. Smith, D.C.Conn., 63 F.Supp. 834. 838.

"Enjoyment", within statute levying tax on succession to property by deed, sale, assignment or gift without consideration substantially equivalent to full value of property, if intended to take effect in possession or enjoyment at or after grantor's, vendor's, assignor or donor's death, is synonymous with comfort, consolation, contentment, ease, happiness, pleasure and satisfaction.   In re Heine's Estate, Ohio Pb., 100 N.E.2d 545, 554.

The rule that income is not taxable until "realized" is founded on administrative convenience, and is only a rule of postponement of the tax to the final event of "enjoyment" of the income, usually the receipt of it by the taxpayer, and not a rule of exemption from taxation where enjoyment is consummated by some event other than taxpayer's personal receipt of money or property.   Helvering v. Horst, 61 S.Ct. 144, 147, 148, 311 U. S. 112, 85 L.Ed. 75, 131 A.L.R. 655.

The power to dispose of income is the equivalent of "ownership" and the exercise of that power to procure the payment of income to another is the "enjoyment", and hence the "realization" of the income by him who exercises it, so as to render the income subject to tax.   Helvering v. Horst, 61 S.Ct. 144, 147, 148, 311 U.S. 112, 85 L.Ed. 75, 131 A.L.R. 655.

Under Internal Revenue Acts defining "gross income" in broad language, the power to dispose of income is tantamount to "ownership" of it, and exercise of that power in procuring payment to an assignee or nominee is the equivalent of the "enjoyment" of the income on part of him who exercises the right.   Duran v. Commissioner of Internal Revenue, C.C.A.10, 123 F.2d 324, 326.

A use of economic gain, the right to receive income, to procure a satisfaction which can be obtained only by the expenditure of money or property, would seem to be the "en-

293

In a literal sense, both WESTLAW and LEXIS are gigantic dictionaries. The databases contain every word of every opinion. Most words appear far too often to make the full-text dictionary feasible, but if you have a unique term, you can give it a try.

Treatises and Hornbooks

Treatises, simply stated, are books that describe an area of law. A treatise may consist of a single volume or multiple volumes. In your law school library, you will find thousands of treatises. In your course work, you probably are acquainted with hornbooks, a type of treatise (Figure 6.14).

Hornbooks explain the rudiments of a legal topic. The term "hornbook law" is often used to refer to points of law that are well settled by the courts. Hornbooks can be an excellent introduction to a topic in the traditional areas of law and can provide you with citations to key cases. Several publishers produce hornbooks. The two largest are West and Foundation Press. The West hornbooks may provide keys to search strategies in WESTLAW.

West also publishes a series called *nutshells*. These are paperback volumes, each of which is devoted to a single legal subject. Nutshells present the topic in a simplified format; hence, they are an excellent introduction to a subject.

You can locate a treatise by checking your library's catalog. In most law libraries, the hornbooks and most popular treatises, or those titles recommended for a course, will be on reserve—ask for help.

Figure 6.14   Hornbooks and Nutshells

 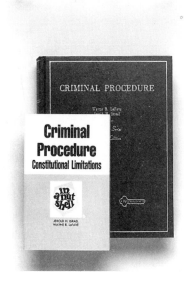

Restatements

You have probably also been introduced to restatements in your class work. Restatements are written by scholars under the auspices of the American Law Institute. The purpose of the restatements is to state what the law "is" on a particular subject. Pertinent excerpts from restatements are usually included in casebooks or reprinted as supplements to your casebooks; for example, Section 402A from the *Restatement of Torts* will be included in your torts casebook.

Restatements cover only ten fields of law, which include several first-year courses, such as Contracts, Torts, and Property. Each section begins with a boldface statement of principles, followed by comments intended to explain the statement. Since the series has a great deal of prestige among judges and scholars, you may want to present an issue using the "restatement view."

Formbooks and Practice Manuals

At some point, you may need works that deal with legal procedure. Although some works are written for the practicing attorney, they can be very useful in your procedure and litigation courses. For federal law, you may look to Wright and Miller's *Federal Practice and Procedure*® published by West or *West's Federal Forms*.

Conclusion

This chapter has introduced background legal sources, including annotations, legal periodicals, legal encyclopedias, dictionaries, treatises, restatements, and formbooks. You may feel more comfortable with these sources than with primary sources at this point in your law school career because they are the same types of materials that you used in your undergraduate or graduate days. Even though they are considered "secondary," you will more than likely use them first.

THE RESEARCH PROCESS

This book has tried to present you with an introduction to the full array of information that is available in the law library. We have talked about books and about computer databases. This material will not become meaningful or really useful to you, however, until you actually work through it. The great Zen koan of legal research is that you can't understand the materials without using them, and you can't use them very well without understanding them. Fortunately in the coming months, you will probably be assigned a series of research problems and undoubtedly will be subjected to an agonizing moot court experience, both of which will force you to plunge into the lake of legal research. This may be one of the few times when throwing the nonswimmer into the water and watching what happens is a historical inevitability. This book has attempted to provide you with a series of ideas, explanations, and overviews that should make the shock of the water a little less traumatic.

To succeed, you must look at legal research materials functionally, understanding how they fit together and why they look the way they do. If you only understand one way of using the books, you will be lost when something goes awry. If you understand why the books work the way they do, however, you will be able to improvise when caught in a corner.

This final chapter presents a few ideas on research methodology, i.e., how to go about attacking a research problem. We can't offer you a simple solution, but we would like to present you with a working model. Feel free to modify it as you wish; you may have to do so if you are to be successful. The point is that *some* model or plan is necessary. You have to have some overall concept of what you are doing, or you will simply drown in the mass of cases, statutes, administrative rules and regulations, and secondary sources that are available. Therefore we propose the following four-step model.

Step 1: Deciding Where to Start

A large portion of your first year of law school will be devoted to wading through facts and law, developing skills in how to attack a situation and how to distinguish what is important from what is not. This is a necessary first step

in any research process as well. We urge that you carry this procedure one step further. Once you have extracted the necessary issues, ask yourself what the "ideal" answer would be. In other words, *what* are you looking for? You would be surprised how many people plunge into the research process without really knowing where they want to end up. This is dangerous because many bears are lurking in the forest of the library. You have to know up front what you expect to find when you get in there. Do you want a statute? A case? An administrative rule or regulation? A clear explanation of a new area? Some guidance on how to update certain citations? There are probably a thousand different types of answers that you can pursue.

Only if you understand what your ideal answer is can you set out in search of it. It may turn out that your initial guess was incorrect, that once you get deeper into the problem, your ideal answer turns out to be not so ideal after all. But unless you have a goal in mind when your research begins, you will never reach a successful end.

Step 2: Thinking about How to Proceed

One thing that we hope this book has made you realize is that a whole host of research systems are available out there. West Publishing Company has an intricate self-referencing system of materials. Based on the National Reporter System, it flows into the American Digest System and the WESTLAW databases and filters into the family of annotated codes and other West products. As we have pointed out, there is a coherent philosophy behind the West system. The same can be said of other publishers. Indeed, many law firms now have their own internal information systems, consisting of briefs and memoranda that have been written on various matters.

The successful researcher must understand how to exploit these various systems. Part of that means understanding where to enter them. As you begin your research, once you know what your ideal answer is, you must decide which research process and which research system make sense for you. Oftentimes understanding this second step can save you enormous amounts of time. If what you really need is background information, you are far better off using an encyclopedia like *Corpus Juris Secundum* or *American Jurisprudence 2d* than you are starting out reading cases. If you need background on a particular case, you should probably begin by reading the hornbook explanation of that case rather than plunging into the dense verbiage of the case itself.

The point is that you should follow one of our first rules of research—find someone who has done the work for you. Use the collective wisdom of legal publishers, legal scholars, and your own colleagues and professors as much as you possibly can. At the same time, you must never lose sight of the distinction between a primary source (i.e., the law itself) and a secondary source (i.e., an interpretation of the law). Nevertheless, if you understand where to enter the research systems, you can save yourself grief, time, and money.

Step 3: Legal Research and Economics

Economics and the law is a very hot topic in substantive law school courses these days. In fact, we think it has a great deal to do with legal research. Once you are in practice, you will find that questions come with price tags attached. A partner may assign you a question where you will be allowed to do only $500 worth of research. It is just as bad to do $5,000 worth of research on a $50 problem as it is to do $50 worth of research on a $5,000 problem.

Law students often have difficulty understanding this concept, partly because of their experiences in law school. Law professors assume that law students have an infinite amount of time. A professor can ask you to rewrite, reresearch, and totally redo without giving any thought to how much available time you actually have. Once you are in practice, the rules of the game will change. You will be up against a very hard edge of billable hours in a private firm, an overwhelming caseload in a public interest practice, or a stack of files from a government agency, and you will have to complete the assignment before the deadline. To do so, you will have to allocate and budget your research time correctly. Start doing this now. Be an economist when it comes to your research. Plan how much time you can allocate to each part of the research process. Set goals for yourself. This will make the whole process easier.

If you have defined your question as we recommended in step 1 and picked the quick entry places as we suggested in step 2, then you can devise a time budget in step 3. Doing so will allow you to be an efficient, effective researcher and will lead to far better research results. There is no sadder sight than a student surrounded by piles of case reporters and statutory volumes working away late into the night in the law library. The student may have no concept of what to do with the problem or how much time should be spent on it.

The truly creative act is not locating materials, but reading and synthesizing them. That is why legal writing is such an important part of your first year. Remember, though, that you can't start on the truly creative part until you have assembled your materials. Factoring in time as a realistic constraint is part of that process.

Step 4: Knowing When to Stop

One of the things law schools often fail to teach is how to judge when you should stop your research process. Once again, this is due to the idea that student time is infinitely elastic. In law school, you are asked to go back to the beginning and reinvent every wheel, to build each new research edifice from brick number one. In other words, you are expected to look at every case ever decided in the history of humankind when writing your brief. In the real world, including the world in which you must live during your first year, you will have to make judgments as to when you can successfully stop your

research process. Devising stop rules is one of the current items in legal research training. We suggest the following stop rules for your consideration:

1. *Economic analysis or diminishing returns model.* This model suggests that when you are investing more in your research than you are getting in research returns, you should stop. The classic example of diminishing returns is the student in the library at 10:30 p.m. on Friday night, continuing to read cases that seem to be less and less useful. Because of the built-in paranoia that goes with being a law student, students feel that if they stop the very next case they would have read will turn out to be the perfect case, the one that defines the problem in clear, sharp prose. The wily, experienced researcher has a feel for when less is coming back than is being put in. This is a very tough rule to follow, however. To adhere to it, you must have confidence in your research abilities and must understand the relationship between what the materials can tell you and the time you can expend. This is a hard-body rule, one that is difficult for first-year students. But if you want to be an efficient researcher, you should consider using it.

2. *The loop rule.* This is the simplest rule for a first-year student to apply. When you start to see the same materials over and over again—the same cases, the same statutes, the same administrative agency rulings or regulations, the same types of citations in *Shepard's*—you should realize that you are probably done. This kind of loop can be dangerous, however, unless you are using the products of more than one publisher. Any publisher will have an internal cross-referencing system. We have already urged you to use the dynamics of the system in your research, but you should also use other research tools. However, once you recognize that you understand the cases, statutes, and rulings in your area, and you have updated everything, you will know that you are in control of the relevant literature. When you reach the point in your research where you know—or can guess—what you are going to see next, you have probably caught yourself in a loop. Remember there is almost never a "perfect" case, and once you have read enough to know what others think is out there, you have probably done enough.

3. *The Zen rule.* This is an aspirational rule, one for you to look forward to in the future. When you are in practice and have been working in one area for a long time, you will simply "know" when you are done. After a while you will become so familiar with the statutory and administrative architecture of your area—the common law implications of what is going on and the rule of the law makers and law interpreters in your particular specialty—that you will be the expert resource. This is why we urge you to use a human being in your research. Law school is often a very competitive experience, but it does not have to be. Instead of concentrating on competition, learn to exploit the utility and helpfulness of other humans. Ask a professor or another student for help. In practice, ask a senior partner, a more experienced associate, a colleague, or someone who works in the same department or division. A human being can enable you to avoid many research bottlenecks by telling you which research materials are universally accepted in your area and helping you find the answer that you need. At this point,

you will be in the Zen stopping stage. You will have found a person who is a research resource, and eventually you will become one yourself. You will be transformed from the caterpillar of the new researcher to the butterfly of the information expert. You will still have to struggle to keep up with the newest developments in your area, but you will be a major player in the research game.

No amount of methodology can substitute for simple common sense. And common sense is what legal research is really all about. It is easy to get lost in the first-year experience, easy to be baffled by all the books on the shelves. But think back to the research skills that you mastered in high school and college and to all the intelligence and hard work that got you here, and you will find that legal research is not so bad. Think about the wealth of information that is available, see how the parts of the systems fit together, and you will ride the wave rather than being crushed by it. Enjoy.

Appendix How to Search on WESTLAW

WESTLAW offers two methods of searching for documents addressing your issue: WIN (WESTLAW Is Natural) and Terms and Connectors. Natural language searching (WIN) is available for searching case law, statutes, law reviews and journals, texts and periodicals, regulations, administrative decisions and other miscellaneous databases. The Terms and Connectors search method may be used to search all databases on WESTLAW. West topic and key numbers may also be used to retrieve cases using either the WIN natural language and the Terms and Connectors search methods.

This appendix will explain how to formulate a search request with WIN and with Terms and Connectors, how to perform a topic and key number search, and how to tailor search requests with field restrictions.

WIN Natural Language Search Method

The natural language search method (WIN) is extremely easy and, for most of your on-line legal research, will yield excellent results, even for the most advanced "Terms and Connectors searcher." This search method allows you to type in a description of your legal issue or fact pattern in standard English, for example:

Is an insurance agent an agent of the insurer or insured?

or

Find cases on admissibility of DNA evidence.

There is no need to translate your legal issue into a query first, as with the Terms and Connectors method. When you enter your description, WIN completes the following steps:

1. WIN processes the description, removing common words such as *is* and *for*.
2. WIN identifies legal phrases and puts them in quotation marks.

3. WIN's stemming program generates variations of terms in your description, such as *defame, defamed,* and *defaming* for *defamation.*

4. The legal phrases and the remaining terms—which are considered the concepts in your description—are each given a weight:

   ■ The more often a concept appears in the database, the less weight it is given.

   ■ The more often a concept appears in the document, the greater weight it is given.

5. WIN retrieves the twenty documents that are most likely to match your description. These documents are ranked according to the probability that they match your description, from most likely to least likely.

Performing a Natural Language Search

Enter a description of your issue in plain English. Press Enter. You will retrieve twenty documents, ranked in order of statistical relevance, with the most relevant document displayed first.

If you wish to retrieve more than twenty documents, return to the WESTLAW Options Directory (type **opt**) to select a document retrieval number between 1 and 100. The number selected will become the set default unless you change it again.

Browsing Your WIN Search Results

Reviewing search results is essentially the same whether you have used the WIN search method, the Terms and Connectors method, or the topic and key number method. You may choose to browse in term (**t**) or page (**p**) mode, advance by rank (**r**), or locate a particular word or words in your search result (**loc**). With the WIN search method, you have the advantage of an additional browsing mode: best. By typing **best** or **b,** you will be taken to the statistically most relevant portion of each document.

Adding Alternative Terms to Your WIN Search

You may use the WESTLAW Thesaurus for assistance in adding alternative terms or concepts to your search, or you may add your own alternatives.

To access the Thesaurus to add similar concepts to your issue description, type **thes.** This will display the concepts from your search that have thesaurus entries (Figure A.1). Type the retrieval number preceding the concept to be expanded. Then, select alternatives by typing the number assigned to the alternatives (Figure A.2).

To add your own concepts, simply type **q** to recall your query, and add alternative terms in parentheses, separating each alternative term by spaces, behind the related concept.

Adding Restrictions to Your WIN Search

You may limit your WIN search to a certain date or range of dates, court, judge, or attorney by specifying certain restrictions either before or after you run your search. To add restrictions, type **res.** Enter the appropriate information, using the Terms and Connectors method, into each area that you want to restrict, using the Tab key to move to each entry field (Figure A.3).

Figure A.1   Using the WESTLAW Thesaurus to Obtain Alternative Concepts

```
2                                    WESTLAW THESAURUS

Your description is:
MUST A THERAPIST DISCLOSE A PATIENT'S THREATS

The concepts in your description that have related concepts are:

  1   THERAPIST
  2   DISCLOSE
  3   PATIENT'S
  4   THREATS




If you wish to:
  View related concepts for a concept listed above, type the concept NUMBER
     and press ENTER
  Return to the description screen, press ENTER
```

Figure A.2   A List of Related Concepts

```
7, 8                                 WESTLAW THESAURUS

Related concepts for  DISCLOSE  are:

  1   APPRISE        13   DISSEMINATE   24   REVEAL   ,
  2   BRIEF          14   POPULARIZE    25   UNMASK
  3   COMMUNICATE    15   PROMOTE       26   UNVEIL
  4   IMPART         16   PROMULGATE
  5   INFORM         17   PROPAGATE
  6   NOTIFY         18   PUBLISH
  7   REPORT         19   SPREAD
  8   REVEAL              -----
      -----          20   DIVULGE
  9   ANNOUNCE       21   EXPOSE
 10   BROADCAST      22   LEAK
 11   CIRCULATE           -----
 12   COMMUNICATE    23   EXPOSE


If you wish to:
  Add related concepts to your description, type one or more concept NUMBERS
     (e.g. 2,3) and press ENTER
  Return to the Thesaurus concept list, press ENTER
```

Figure A.3   Adding Restrictions to a WIN Search

```
                              RESTRICTIONS
Enter search restrictions in the fields below:

 Decided Date:  DA ( AFTER 7-1-93                                        )

   Added Date:  AD (                                                     )

       Court:   CO (                                                     )

       Judge:   JU (                                                     )

    Attorney:   AT (                                                     )

NOTE: You must specify dates in a valid  WESTLAW format.
      You can specify one or more of the courts that are valid in this database.
      Press TAB to move the cursor.



If you wish to:
  Change the restrictions, modify them as desired and press  ENTER
  Return to the edit description screen, press ENTER
```

Terms and Connectors Search Method

The Terms and Connectors search method is preferable when you know specific facts or details about a case or cases, such as the name of a party, judge, or product, or if you want *every* document containing that information (rather than the twenty most statistically relevant). The Terms and Connectors search method requires you to enter a query, using connectors, root expanders, and, if appropriate, field restrictions. WESTLAW then retrieves a set of documents, in reverse chronological order, that contain your search terms in the relationship specified in your query and that also satisfy any field restrictions in your query.

Formulating a Terms and Connectors Query

To use the Terms and Connectors search method, you must translate your issue into a query WESTLAW can understand. Follow these steps to translate your issue or request into a query:

- *Terms:* Choose the search terms significant to your issue. Enter your terms in the singular, nonpossessive form. If you select the singular form of a term, WESTLAW automatically retrieves regular and irregular plurals. If you enter the nonpossessive form of a word, both the possessive and the nonpossessive forms will be retrieved.

  If your term is an acronym, format it with periods and without spaces to retrieve all variations of the acronym:

The Term	Retrieves
e.p.a.	e.p.a.
	e. p. a.
	e p a
	epa

To retrieve various forms of a compound word, use its hyphenated form.

The Term	Retrieves
good-will	good-will
	good will
	goodwill

Consider synonyms or antonyms as alternative search terms. You may wish to consult the WESTLAW Thesaurus (**thes**) for assistance.

Your Term	Alternatives
attorney	lawyer counsel
constitutional	unconstitutional

Consider using a root expander (!) or universal character (*) to retrieve variations of word forms. The root expander is a symbol placed at the end of a root term to retrieve words with variant endings:

The Term	Retrieves
know!	know
	known
	knowing
	knowingly
	knowingful
	knowable
	knows
	knowledge
	knowledgeable
	But not knew

The universal character (*) can be used to represent one variable character anywhere in a term except at the beginning. Think of the universal character as a blank Scrabble® piece. When you place the asterisk within a term, it requires that a character appear in that position:

fea*t retrieves feast but not feat

When you place an asterisk or asterisks at the end of the term, you specify the maximum length of the term:

jur** retrieves jury and juror but not jurisdiction

■ *Connectors:* Decide which connector(s) would most effectively link your search terms. Connectors are symbols you place between search terms to specify the relationship between those terms in your retrieved documents.

1. Use the **OR** connector to search for alternative terms. Simply leave a space or type **or** between a term and its alternatives. The query

attorney lawyer counsel

retrieves any documents containing at least one of these terms.

2. Use the **AND** connector to retrieve documents containing both search terms anywhere in the document. Simply type **and** or **&** between terms. The query

narcotic & warrant

requires both words to appear somewhere in the document

3. Grammatical connectors allow you to search for terms in a grammatical relationship, without specifying an exact numerical relationship. To retrieve documents with your terms in the same paragraph, use the paragraph connector (**/p**), the most widely used and most versatile connector on WESTLAW:

hearsay /p utterance

Documents with your terms in the same sentence can be retrieved with a sentence connector (**/s**):

design*** /s defect!

You can use a **+s** connector to specify the order in which the search terms should appear in a sentence. The **+s** requires that the term to the left of the connector precede the term to the right within the same sentence:

capital +s gain

4. Numerical connectors (**/n** or **+n**) require search terms to appear within a specified number of terms of each other, from 1 to 255:

attorney /5 fee

bill william +3 clinton

The **+n** connector is especially helpful when you are restricting your search to the citation field or searching for documents referring to a particular citation:

20 +5 1080

5. WESTLAW also has an exclusionary connector available. With the **BUT NOT** connector (**%**), you can exclude documents that contain certain terms:

tax taxation % income /3 tax taxation

This search would not retrieve any documents containing the words *income* and *tax* or *taxation* within three words of each other.

6. To search for a phrase on WESTLAW, place the phrase in quotation marks. For example, to search for *summary judgment,* type

"summary judgment"

Phrase searching should be used only when you are certain the phrase will not appear in other ways. For example, you would not want to use the phrase "blood alcohol" in your query because some cases might say "the amount of alcohol in the blood" instead. A more successful query in that case would be

blood /3 alcohol

Restricting Your Terms and Connectors Search by Field

Almost all WESTLAW documents consist of several parts called fields, which reflect logical divisions of a document. As discussed in Chapter 2, you can restrict your Terms and Connectors search to a particular field, such as title, synopsis, or digest, rather than searching the entire document. Searching with an appropriate field restrictions saves searching and browsing time and makes your Terms and Connectors search more efficient.

The fields available vary by database. Type **f** while in your selected database to view the field restrictions available in that database.

To restrict a search to a particular field, type the field name (or its abbreviation, which is usually the first two letters of the field name) immediately followed by the search terms enclosed in parentheses. For example, either

title(texaco)   or   ti(texaco)

will retrieve cases in which *Texaco* appears in the title. For additional case law fields, see Table A.1.

- *Date restrictions:* To restrict your Terms and Connectors search to a certain date or range of dates, type a valid date restriction in parentheses following the word **date** or the abbreviation **da.** All of the following are acceptable forms:

da(1993)
da(aft 1989)
da(aft 1985 & bef 1990)
da(> 1989)
da(3-93)
da(bef aug. 11, 1982)

You may not run the date restriction alone as your search. You must add the date restriction to a Terms and Connectors search. Use the **&** connector:

hypno! /s testi! & da(1993)

Table A.1 Case Law Fields

Field	Identifier	Contents	Query
Judge	**ju**	Judge authoring lead opinion; e.g., Justice Brennan	**ju(brennan)**
Attorney	**at**	Names, cities, and firms of attorneys representing parties or participating in appeal	**at(liman)**
Digest	**di**	Combination of headnote and topic fields	**di(standing /p air /p quality pollut!)**
Synopsis	**sy**	Brief description of the facts and holding of the case; includes court syllabi.	**sy(commerce /2 clause /p hodel)**
Topic	**to**	West digest topic name(constitutional law), number (92), hierarchy information, key line text, and former classification, if any.	**to(constitutional /2 law) or to(92)**
Headnote	**he**	West-prepared summary of a single point of law. Also contains statute and rule citations.	**he(304)**
Opinions	**op**	Text of majority, concurring, and dissenting opinions and names of authoring judges.	**op(attorney lawyer /s negligen***)**

- *Court Restrictions:* Several databases on WESTLAW contain opinions from more than one type of court or jurisdiction. To restrict your search to cases from a particular court within a state or from a particular state within a circuit, you can add a court restriction to your query. To restrict a Terms and Connectors search to a particular court, type **co** followed by words describing the court in parentheses. Attach this term to the rest of your query with the & connector. The following query, run in the database containing all federal district court databases (**dct**), would retrieve only Texas and Florida federal district court cases on this issue:

  age /s discriminat! & co(tx fl)

- *Combining field searches:* To combine a field search with your query, use the & connector. For example, to retrieve antitrust cases with *Texaco* in the title field, use this query:

  anti-trust & ti(texaco)

  To search for the same terms in more than one field, separate the field abbreviations with a comma but no space, e.g., **sy,di(comatose & incompe-**

tent). Use the & connector to add a second field search or court or date restriction to your search:

```
sy,di(comatose & incompetent) & da(aft 1970)
```

Topic and Key Number Searching

You may search by topic and key number on WESTLAW to retrieve cases classified under a particular topic and key number in the West digest system. A topic and key number search may be performed using either WIN natural language or Terms and Connectors.

To format a topic and key number search, type the topic number, the letter **k,** and the key number classified under that specific topic. For example, after accessing the relevant database, type **92k90.3** to retrieve all cases in your database classified under topic 92 (Constitutional Law) and key number 90.3 (Advertising; Signs and Billboards).

You can also combine a topic and key number search with a Terms and Connectors search to customize your results even more. Connect your topic and key number and word search with a paragraph connector (**/p**) to retrieve cases containing your word(s) and the topic and key number in the same headnote screen:

```
92k90.3 /p zoning
```

Figure A.4 shows the results of your search.

Where can you find the West digest topic and key numbers?

1. *Headnotes in West's case reporters:* As you learned in Chapter 2, each issue of law in a West reporter case is summarized in a headnote. Each issue is

Figure A.4 Results from Combining a Topic and Key Number Search with a Terms and Connectors Search

```
541 A.2d 692          R 1 OF 4        P 9 OF 30        NJ-CS        P
(Cite as: 110 N.J. 384,  541 A.2d 692)
Bell v. Stafford Tp.
► [7]
► 92        CONSTITUTIONAL LAW
► 92V        Personal, Civil and Political Rights
► 92k90        Freedom of Speech and of the Press

► 92k90.3  k. Advertising;  signs and billboards.
N.J.,1988.
Township's ordinance prohibiting billboards within any zoning district of
township would be declared facially unconstitutional;  it appeared that
curtailment affected by ordinance would apply to commercial forms of expression
as well as noncommercial speech, there had been no adequate showing that
ordinance left open alternative means of communication, and township had not
presented evidence demonstrating its ordinance furthered particular,
substantial government interest and was sufficiently narrow to further only
that interest without unnecessarily restricting freedom of expression.
                COPR. (C) WEST 1993 NO CLAIM TO ORIG. U.S. GOVT. WORKS
```

then assigned to a digest topic and a key number. If you find a relevant topic and key number while reviewing the headnotes, jot down the *name* of the topic and the key *number*. Then find the number assigned to your *topic* in the *WESTLAW Reference Manual* or in the Key Number service on WESTLAW (described in item 4 below).

2. *Headnotes on WESTLAW:* If you find a relevant case on WESTLAW review the headnotes and their assigned topic and key numbers. From the topic and key number classification hierarchy above the text of the headnote, choose the topic and key number at the most appropriate level of specificity. The most specific level is found at the last line of the hierarchy, e.g., 203k357(4) (Figure A.5).

3. *West's Digests:* As explained in Chapter 2, find relevant *key numbers* within topic categories in West's digests. Then find the numerical designation for the overall *topic* in the Key Number service on WESTLAW or in the *WESTLAW Reference Manual.*

4. *The Key Number Service on WESTLAW:* The outline of West's digest topics and all of their key numbers (is now available on WESTLAW. To access the Key Number service, type **key.**

To find the number assigned to a topic, page through the topic list or type **key** followed by the first few letters of the desired topic. You will arrive at the location of your selected topic in the topic list. Here, you will see the number assigned to your topic (Figure A.6).

To view the key numbers for your selected topic, **tab** to the highlighted marker next to your topic. Press **Enter** to view the broad subdivisions of your topic. Using the tab key, select the appropriate subdivision. Continue to selection process through successive levels of subdivision until you see the key numbers for your topic (Figure A.7).

Figure A.5   Topic and Key Numbers in Headnotes

```
 823 P.2d 22           R 1 OF 2          P 6 OF 88        AZ-CS         P
(Cite as: 170 Ariz. 155,   823 P.2d 22)
 State v. Greenway
▶ [4]
▶ 203    HOMICIDE
▶ 203XI     Sentence and Punishment
▶ 203k355      Death Penalty
▶ 203k357         Considerations Determining Propriety of Death Sentence

▶ 203k357(4)  k. Aggravation or mitigation in general.
 Ariz.,1991.
 Evidence supported finding of aggravating factors during capital murder
 sentencing hearing and trial, so as to justify death sentence, where two
 witnesses testified that defendant confessed to them, defendant attempted to
 sell victim's car stereo on morning after incident, and expert testimony
 indicated that one victim was shot in leg before fatal wounds were inflicted on
 either of two victims.  A.R.S. s 13-703.
                 COPR. (C) WEST 1993 NO CLAIM TO ORIG. U.S. GOVT. WORKS
```

Figure A.6   The Topic List in the Key Number Service

```
                  Copyright (c) 1993 West Publishing Company
                             KEY NUMBER SERVICE
 >                              Topic List
-------------------------------------------------------------------------------
> 313A PRODUCTS LIABILITY
> 314  PROHIBITION
> 315  PROPERTY
> 316  PROSTITUTION
> 316A PUBLIC CONTRACTS
> 317  PUBLIC LANDS
> 317A PUBLIC UTILITIES
> 318  QUIETING TITLE
> 319  QUO WARRANTO
> 319H RACKETEER INFLUENCED AND CORRUPT ORGANIZATIONS
> 320  RAILROADS
> 321  RAPE
> 322  REAL ACTIONS
> 323  RECEIVERS

If you wish to:
   View an item in more detail, SELECT its JUMP marker
   View the next or previous page, type P or P- and press ENTER
   View the list of Key Number commands, type CMDS and press ENTER
   Go back to the previously accessed service, type GB and press ENTER
```

Figure A.7   A Display of Key Numbers in the Key Number Service

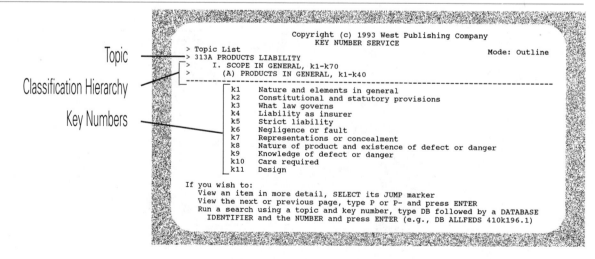

```
                        Copyright (c) 1993 West Publishing Company
                                   KEY NUMBER SERVICE
> Topic List                                              Mode: Outline
> 313A PRODUCTS LIABILITY
>     I.  SCOPE IN GENERAL, k1-k70
>         (A) PRODUCTS IN GENERAL, k1-k40
-------------------------------------------------------------------------------
         k1    Nature and elements in general
         k2    Constitutional and statutory provisions
         k3    What law governs
         k4    Liability as insurer
         k5    Strict liability
         k6    Negligence or fault
         k7    Representations or concealment
         k8    Nature of product and existence of defect or danger
         k9    Knowledge of defect or danger
         k10   Care required
         k11   Design

If you wish to:
   View an item in more detail, SELECT its JUMP marker
   View the next or previous page, type P or P- and press ENTER
   Run a search using a topic and key number, type DB followed by a DATABASE
      IDENTIFIER and the NUMBER and press ENTER (e.g., DB ALLFEDS 410k196.1)
```

Topic

Classification Hierarchy

Key Numbers

Common WESTLAW COMMANDS

Searching Commands

db xxx	Select a database, move to new database
sdb xxx	Run same search in *new* database
s	New search in *same* database
q	Retrieve query for editing
nat	Change your search method to WIN natural language
tc	Change your search method to Terms and Connectors
thes	Display related concepts for revising a WIN search
res	Display screen for date, added date, court, attorney, or judge restrictions

Browsing Commands

t	Term mode browsing
p	Page mode browsing
b	Best mode browsing; advance to statistically most relevant portion of your documents (only available with WIN search method)
r	Display the next ranked document
list	Retrieve a citation list of retrieved documents
loc	Locate selected terms within your retrieved documents
f	Display a list of fields available for a database

Citator Commands

ic, sh, sp, qc	Access Insta-Cite, Shepard's, Shepard's PreView or Quick*Cite*

INDEX

A

abaj database, 124
Acronyms (WESTLAW), 139
Administrative codes, 96–100. *See also Code of Federal Regulations*
Administrative decisions, 85, 112
Administrative law, 96–114
  administrative decisions, 85, 112
  Federal Register and *Codes of Federal Regulations* in print, 96–104
  presidential documents, 112–13
  regulations on WESTLAW, 104–8
  state materials, 113–14
  updating, 108–12
Administrative registers, 6, 96–97. *See also Federal Register*
Advance (pamphlets to *United States Code Services*), 75
Advance sheets, 5, 11, 12, 57, 58, 65
  Table of Cases Reported, 15, 16, 41
ag database, 113
allfeds database, 66
allstates database, 66
Alternative terms (WESTLAW), 137, 140
American Digest System, 34, 39, 132
American Jurisprudence 2d (Am. Jur. 2d), 125, 132
American Law Institute, 130
American Law Reports (ALR), 115–18
  updating, 118–20, 121
AND (&) connector, 45, 141, 142, 143, 144
Annos service, 90
Annotated codes, 5, 78–85, 132

B

Annotation History Table (ALR), 118, 120
Attorneys (names of, in cases), 28, 30
  searching for, on WESTLAW, 48, 143
Authority note *(Code of Federal Regulations)*, 97, 99
Auto-Cite, 116

Ballentine's (legal dictionary), 126
Bankruptcy Reporter, 13
Best mode, 49
Bills (legislative), 71–73
Black's Law Dictionary, 9, 126, 127
Blackstone, Sir William, 3
Bluebook. See A Uniform System of Citation
Boole, George, 4
Boolean logic, 4
Briggs, James, 5
Browsing commands (WESTLAW), 147
BUT NOT connector (WESTLAW), 141

C

Caption field, 89, 90
Case citations. *See* Citations
Cases/case law, 9–30, 31–51
  browsing on WESTLAW, 49–50
  citations, 17–20
    parallel, 20–22
  court reporters, 9–12

finding, 31–51
  in digests, 35–41
  on WESTLAW, 41–49
  parts of a case, 23–30
  special courts, 13, 15
  state courts, 15–17, 18
  Supreme Court and lower federal courts, 12–13, 14
  unpublished, 10, 18, 46
  updating research, 52–70. *See also* Citators
Certiorari, writ of, 12
cfr database, 104, 107, 108
Chronological arrangement (of sources), 5, 6
cilp database, 123
Citations, 25
  in advance sheets and bound reporters, 11
  deciphering, 9, 17–20
  finding a case by, on WESTLAW, 42
  Insta-Cite, 20
  parallel, 20–22
  Shepard's, 20, 52–63
  Supreme Court, 12
  unofficial and official reporters in, 12
Citator commands (WESTLAW), 147
Citators
  Insta-Cite, 20, 66–70
  Quick*Cite,* 66, 67
  Shepard's Citations, 52–63
  WESTLAW and, 63–65
Code(s), 5, 6, 76–95. *See also* specific codes
  administrative, 6, 96–100

West's Commitment to the Environment
In 1906, West Publishing Company began recycling materials left over from the production of books. This began a tradition of efficient and responsible use of resources. Today, up to 95 percent of our legal books and 70 percent of our college texts are printed on recycled, acid-free stock. West also recycles nearly 22 million pounds of scrap paper annually—the equivalent of 181,717 trees. Since the 1960s, West has devised ways to capture and recycle waste inks, solvents, oils, and vapors created in the printing process. We also recycle plastics of all kinds, wood, glass, corrugated cardboard, and batteries, and have eliminated the use of styrofoam book packaging. We at West are proud of the longevity and the scope of our commitment to our environment.